Fodor's 17th Edition

P9-CJZ-325

Hong Kong

The complete guide, thoroughly up-to-date

Packed with details that will make your trip

The must-see sights, off and on the beaten path

What to see, what to skip

Mix-and-match vacation itineraries

City strolls, countryside adventures

Smart lodging and dining options

Essential local do's and taboos

Transportation tips, distances, and directions

Key contacts, savvy travel tips

When to go, what to pack

Clear, accurate, easy-to-use maps

Background essays on food and culture

Fodor's Travel Publications • New York, Toronto, London, Sydney, Auckland
www.fodors.com

Fodor's Hong Kong

EDITOR: Melissa Klurman

Editorial Contributors: Denise Cheung, Eva Chui, Tobias Parker, Lara Wozniak

Editorial Production: Tom Holton

Maps: David Lindroth, *cartographer*; Rebecca Baer, Robert Blake, *map editors*

Design: Fabrizio La Rocca, *creative director*; Guido Caroti, *art director*; Jolie Novak, *senior picture editor*; Melanie Marin, *photo editor*

Cover Design: Pentagram

Production/Manufacturing: Colleen Ziemba

Cover Photograph: Walter Bibikow/©Folio, Inc.

Copyright

17th Edition

ISBN 0–676–90197–2

ISSN 1070–6887

"Impacts and Images" is an extract from *Hong Kong* by Jan Morris. Copyright © 1997 by Jan Morris. Reprinted by kind permission of Random House, Inc., and A. P. Watt Limited on behalf of Jan Morris.

Special Sales

Fodor's Travel Publications are available at special discounts for bulk purchases for sales promotions or premiums. Special editions, including personalized covers, excerpts of existing guides, and corporate imprints, can be created in large quantities for special needs. For more information contact your local bookseller or write to Special Markets, Fodor's Travel Publications, 280 Park Ave., New York, NY 10017. Inquiries from Canada should be directed to your local Canadian bookseller or sent to Random House of Canada, Ltd., Marketing Department, 2775 Matheson Blvd. E, Mississauga, Ontario L4W 4P7. Inquiries from the United Kingdom should be sent to Fodor's Travel Publications, 20 Vauxhall Bridge Road, London, England SW1V 2SA.

PRINTED IN THE UNITED STATES OF AMERICA

10 9 8 7 6 5 4 3 2 1

Important Tip

Although all prices, opening times, and other details in this book are based on information supplied to us at press time, changes occur all the time in the travel world, and Fodor's cannot accept responsibility for facts that become outdated or for inadvertent errors or omissions. So **always confirm information when it matters,** especially if you're making a detour to visit a specific place.

CONTENTS

On the Road with Fodor's   v

Don't Forget to Write *v*

Smart Travel Tips A to Z   x

1   Destination: Hong Kong   1

From China to China *2*
What's Where *7*
Pleasures and Pastimes *8*
Great Itineraries *8*
Fodor's Choice *10*
Festivals and Seasonal Events *13*

2   Exploring Hong Kong   15

Hong Kong Island *19*
CLOSE-UP: *Feng Shui at Work 21*
Kowloon *41*
The New Territories *46*
CLOSE-UP: *Religions and Traditions 50*
The Outer Islands *54*

3   Dining   60

Hong Kong Island *62*
CLOSE-UP: *A Chinese Sampler 63*
Kowloon *79*
CLOSE-UP: *The Dim Sum Experience 82*
Outer Islands *86*

4   Lodging   88

Hong Kong Island *90*
Kowloon *98*
The New Territories and the Outer Islands *108*

5   Nightlife and the Arts   111

Nightlife *112*
CLOSE-UP: *Lan Kwai Fong 113*
The Arts *119*
CLOSE-UP: *Martial Arts Goes Hollywood 122*

6   Sports and Outdoor Activities   124

Participant Sports *125*
CLOSE-UP: *Smooth Moves 127*
Spectator Sports *132*
Beaches *133*

7   Shopping   136

Major Shopping Areas *138*
Shopping Centers and Malls *145*
Department Stores *146*

Markets and Bazaars *148*
Specialty Shopping *149*
CLOSE-UP: *A Shopper's Paradise 150*

8   Side Trip to Macau   166

Exploring *169*
Dining *183*
Lodging *187*
Nightlife *191*
Outdoor Activities and Sports *193*
Shopping *195*
Macau A to Z *198*

9   Side Trips to South China   202

Exploring *205*
South China A to Z *213*

10   Portraits of Hong Kong   216

"Impacts and Images," by Jan Morris *217*
"Food and Drink in Hong Kong and Macau," by Barry Girling *220*
"Doing Business in Hong Kong," by Tim Healy *224*
Books and Videos *227*

Index   228

Maps

Hong Kong *vi–vii*
World Time Zones *viii–ix*
Hong Kong Island *17*
Hong Kong Mass Transit Rail-
  way *18*
Central and Western Districts
  22–23
Wanchai, Causeway Bay, Happy
  Valley, and North Point *32–33*
South Side *39*
Kowloon *43*
The New Territories and Outer
  Islands *48–49*

Dining *64–65*
Kowloon Dining *80*
Lodging *92–93*
Kowloon Lodging *99*
Shopping Centers, Department
  Stores, and Markets *140–141*
Kowloon Shopping *143*
Macau *171*
Taipa and Coloane Islands *181*
The Pearl River Delta *206*

ON THE ROAD WITH FODOR'S

THE MORE YOU KNOW before you go, the better your trip will be. Hong Kong's most fascinating small museum or its most innovative fish house could be just around the corner from your hotel, but if you don't know it's there, it might as well be on the other side of the globe. That's where this book comes in. It's a great step toward making sure your next trip lives up to your expectations. As you plan, check out the Web as well. Guidebooks have been helping smart travelers find the special places for years; the Web is one more tool. Whatever reference you consult, be savvy about what you read, and always consider the source. Images and language can be massaged to make places appear better than they are. And one traveler's quaint is another's grimy. Here at Fodor's, and at our on-line arm, Fodors.com, our focus is on providing you with information that's not only useful but accurate and on target. Every day Fodor's editors put enormous effort into getting things right, beginning with the search for the right contributors-people who have objective judgment, broad travel experience, and the writing ability to put their insights into words. There's no substitute for advice from a like-minded friend who has just come back from where you're going, but our writers, having seen all corners of Hong Kong, are the next best thing. They're the kind of people you'd poll for tips yourself if you knew them.

Hong Kong native **Denise Cheung** has combined a career in journalism with a taste for travel that has taken her far and wide. Particularly enamored of Hong Kong's booming restaurant scene, she has written for a number of publications, including the *South China Morning Post* and *HK* magazine about food and lifestyle. She has also worked in the hospitality industry and is familiar with the travel business.

Born in Hong Kong and raised in Australia, **Eva Chui** returned to her birthplace in 1995. For two years she reported on the city's arts and popular-culture scenes as the entertainment editor for *HK* magazine, a weekly finger on Hong Kong's pulse. Moving to broadcast media, she then spent three years as a producer for Channel V, Asia's No.1 music-TV station. Currently, she divides her time between writing and working in the television and film industries in Hong Kong.

Tobias Parker, who updated the Lodging chapter for this edition, arrived in Hong Kong in 1996 shortly before his government's departure. After renouncing the world of print publishing, where he was an editor and journalist for a number of books and magazines, he joined the on-line industry. As content manager for the Hong Kong Tourist Board's Web site, he built up their on-line presence and developed the successful weekly *Hong Kong This Week*.

Lara Wozniak, a Hong Kong resident for many years, is a U.S. lawyer and an assistant editor for the *Far Eastern Economic Review,* a daily English-language newspaper in Hong Kong. She also regularly contributes to American, Canadian, and British newspapers and magazines. She wrote the Nepal chapter for the *Fodor's Nepal, Tibet, and Bhutan, 1st edition,* and updated the Smart Travel Tips, Outdoor Activities and Sports, Shopping, and Side Trip to South China chapters for this edition.

We'd also like to thank the Hong Kong Tourist Board and Macau Government Tourist Office for their help in preparing this edition.

Don't Forget to Write

Your experiences—positive and negative—matter to us. If we have missed or misstated something, we want to hear about it. We follow up on all suggestions. Contact the Hong Kong editor at editors@fodors.com or c/o Fodor's, 280 Park Avenue, New York, New York 10017. And have a fabulous trip!

Karen Cure
Editorial Director

Hong Kong

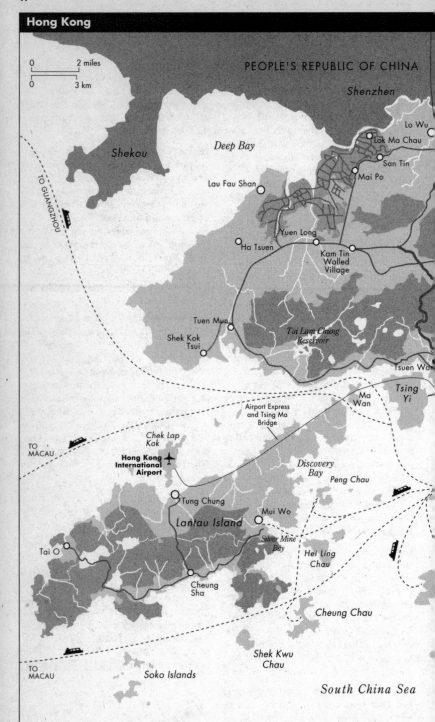

PEOPLE'S REPUBLIC OF CHINA

Shenzhen

Shekou

Deep Bay

Lo Wu

Lok Ma Chau

San Tin

Mai Po

Lau Fau Shan

Yuen Long

Ha Tsuen

Kam Tin
Walled
Village

Tuen Mun

Tai Lam Chung
Reservoir

Shek Kok
Tsui

Tsuen Wan

Tsing
Yi

Ma
Wan

TO GUANGZHOU

Airport Express
and Tsing Ma
Bridge

Chek Lap
Kok

Discovery
Bay

Peng Chau

TO
MACAU

Hong Kong
International
Airport

Tung Chung

Lantau Island

Mui Wo

Silver Mine
Bay

Hei Ling
Chau

Tai O

Cheung
Sha

Cheung Chau

TO
MACAU

Shek Kwu
Chau

Soko Islands

South China Sea

0   2 miles
0   3 km

N

Crooked Island

Sheung
Shui

Fanling

Wu Kau
Tang

Plover Cove
Reservoir

Grass
Island

Taipo

Tolo Channel

Kam Shan

Pan
Chung

Tolo Harbour

NEW TERRITORIES

Chek
Keng

Shatin

Sai Kung

Ho Chung

High Island

Sung Dynasty Village

Port Shelter

KOWLOON

Kowloon
Bay

Basalt
Island

Victoria

Victoria
Harbour

Yau Tong

Junk Bay

Tai Wan
Tau

HONG KONG

Tei Tong
Tsui

Tung Lung
Chau

Shek O

Stanley

Lamma
Island

Stanley
Peninsula

Po Toi
Islands

KEY

Ferry Lines
Rail Lines

World Time Zones

MONDAY
SUNDAY

International Date Line

+12 +13

-9

-10

-11

-10

+11

+12

-11 -10 -7 -8 -6 -5 -4 -3 -4 -5 -4 -3 -3:30 25

-7

+11 +12 - -11 -10 -9 -8 -7 -6 -5 -4 -3 -2

Numbers below vertical bands relate each zone to Greenwich Mean Time (0 hrs.).
Local times frequently differ from these general indications,
as indicated by light-face numbers on map.

Algiers, **29**	Berlin, **34**	Delhi, **48**	Jerusalem, **42**
Anchorage, **3**	Bogotá, **19**	Denver, **8**	Johannesburg, **44**
Athens, **41**	Budapest, **37**	Dublin, **26**	Lima, **20**
Auckland, **1**	Buenos Aires, **24**	Edmonton, **7**	Lisbon, **28**
Baghdad, **46**	Caracas, **22**	Hong Kong, **56**	London
Bangkok, **50**	Chicago, **9**	Honolulu, **2**	(Greenwich), **27**
Beijing, **54**	Copenhagen, **33**	Istanbul, **40**	Los Angeles, **6**
	Dallas, **10**	Jakarta, **53**	Madrid, **38**
			Manila, **57**

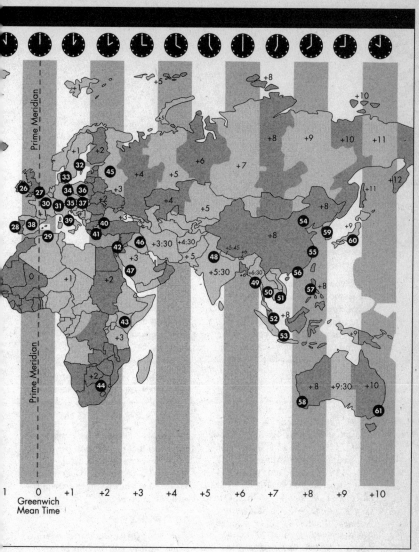

Mecca, **47**

Mexico City, **12**

Miami, **18**

Montréal, **15**

Moscow, **45**

Nairobi, **43**

New Orleans, **11**

New York City, **16**

Ottawa, **14**

Paris, **30**

Perth, **58**

Reykjavík, **25**

Rio de Janeiro, **23**

Rome, **39**

Saigon (Ho Chi Minh City), **51**

San Francisco, **5**

Santiago, **21**

Seoul, **59**

Shanghai, **55**

Singapore, **52**

Stockholm, **32**

Sydney, **61**

Tokyo, **60**

Toronto, **13**

Vancouver, **4**

Vienna, **35**

Warsaw, **36**

Washington, D.C., **17**

Yangon, **49**

Zürich, **31**

ESSENTIAL INFORMATION

AIR TRAVEL

BOOKING

Most people choose a flight based on price, but because of the time and distance involved in traveling to Hong Kong, there are other issues to consider. These include connections, departure times, and a carrier's frequent-flyer partners, which allow you to credit mileage earned on one airline to your account with another.

When you book **look for nonstop flights** and **remember that "direct" flights stop at least once.** Try to avoid connecting flights, which require a change of plane. For more booking tips and to check prices and make on-line flight reservations, log on to www.fodors.com.

CARRIERS

➤ TO HONG KONG: **Asiana** (☎ 800/227–4262). **Canadian** (☎ 800/426–7000). **Cathay Pacific Airways** (☎ 800/233–2742 in the U.S.; 800/268–6868 in Canada). **China Airlines** (☎ 800/227–5118). **Continental** (☎ 800/231–0856). **Korean Air** (☎ 800/438–5000). **Northwest** (☎ 800/447–4747). **Qantas** (☎ 800/227–4500). **Singapore Airlines** (☎ 800/742–3333). **United Airlines** (☎ 800/241–6522). **Virgin Atlantic** (☎ 800/862–8621).

➤ TO MACAU: **Asiana** (☎ 800/227–4262). **Korean Air** (☎ 800/438–5000). **Northwest** (☎ 800/447–4747).

➤ FROM THE U.K.: **British Airways** (☎ 0345/222111). **Cathay Pacific Airways** (☎ 020/7/747–8888). **Virgin Atlantic** (☎ 01293/747747).

CHECK-IN & BOARDING

Check in at least two hours before departing from Hong Kong International Airport at Chek Lap Kok. If you plan on taking the train to the airport, **check your luggage at the Airport Express Railway station** on Hong Kong Island. You must check in at least three hours in advance for this wonderfully efficient, time-saving service.

Assuming that not everyone with a ticket will show up, airlines routinely overbook planes. When everyone does, airlines ask for volunteers to give up their seats. In return, these volunteers usually get a certificate for a free flight and are rebooked on the next flight out. If there are not enough volunteers, the airline must choose who will be denied boarding. The first to get bumped are passengers who checked in late and those flying on discounted tickets, so **get to the gate and check in as early as possible,** especially during peak periods.

Always **bring a government-issued photo I.D. to the airport;** a passport is best. You may be asked to show it before you are allowed to check in.

Remember to **retain your Hong Kong entry slip** that the customs official gives you at passport control. You will need to return this paper when you present your passport for your return trip home.

CUTTING COSTS

The least expensive airfares to Hong Kong must usually be purchased in advance and are nonrefundable. It's smart to **call a number of airlines, and when you are quoted a good price, book it on the spot**—the same fare may not be available the next day. Always **check different routings** and look into using different airports. Travel agents, especially low-fare specialists (☞ Discounts & Deals, *below*), are helpful.

Consolidators are another good source. They buy tickets for scheduled international flights at reduced rates from the airlines, then sell them at prices that beat the best fare available directly from the airlines, usually without restrictions. Sometimes you can even get your money back if you need to return the ticket. Carefully read the fine print detailing penalties for changes and cancellations, and **confirm your consolidator reservation with the airline.**

➤ CONSOLIDATORS: **Cheap Tickets** (☎ 800/377–1000). **Discount Airline Ticket Service** (☎ 800/576–1600). **Unitravel** (☎ 800/325–2222). **Up & Away Travel** (☎ 212/889–2345). **World Travel Network** (☎ 800/409–6753).

ENJOYING THE FLIGHT

For more legroom, **request an emergency-aisle seat.** Don't sit in the row in front of the emergency aisle or in front of a bulkhead, where seats may not recline. If you have dietary concerns, **ask for special meals when booking.** These can be vegetarian, low-cholesterol, or kosher, for example. On long flights, try to maintain a normal routine, to help fight jet lag. At night, **get some sleep.** By day, **eat light meals, drink water** (not alcohol), and **move around the cabin** to stretch your legs. For additional jet-lag tips consult *Fodor's FYI: Travel Fit & Healthy* (available at bookstores everywhere).

Airlines flying into Hong Kong usually no longer permit in-flight smoking. Check with your carrier before booking the flight. Smoking is also not permitted within the airport (the fine is HK$1,000) or on the Airport Express Railway.

FLYING TIMES

Flying time to Hong Kong is around 16 hours and 30 minutes direct from Newark/New York, 13 hours direct from Los Angeles, or 12¼ hours direct from San Francisco. Macau is a 20-minute flight from Hong Kong.

Luckily for travelers, in the Spring of 2001, direct flights from the New York area to Hong Kong were initiated by both Continental and United Airlines. **Book yourself on a nonstop flight** as it will save you several hours of layover time en route, and eliminate the possibility of a missed connection—unfortunately a more frequently occurring problem.

HOW TO COMPLAIN

If your baggage goes astray or your flight goes awry, complain right away. Most carriers require that you **file a claim immediately.**

➤ AIRLINE COMPLAINTS: U.S. Department of Transportation **Aviation Consumer Protection Division** (✉ C-75, Room 4107, Washington, DC 20590, ☎ 202/366–2220, WEB www.dot.gov/airconsumer). **Federal Aviation Administration Consumer Hotline** (☎ 800/322–7873).

RECONFIRMING

If you are flying on a mainland Chinese airline, you must reconfirm your ticket at least 24 hours before leaving Hong Kong or risk losing your seat. You can also call your travel agent to do this for you. Other airlines might not be as strict as the Chinese airlines operating out of Hong Kong. Check with your travel agent or contact your carrier when booking your flight.

AIRPORTS & TRANSFERS

The gateway to Hong Kong is the sleek and sophisticated Hong Kong International Airport at Chek Lap Kok. However, HKIA is never called by its official name; it's universally referred to as Chek Lap Kok. The new airport is mammoth: the passenger terminal is a mile long and could encompass those at Heathrow and JFK combined. It is also well marked and employs a helpful staff. Note that because the Arrival Hall is so vast passengers often have trouble finding those who come to meet them. (An unofficial meeting place is the McDonald's between the two arrival gates.) Remember to hold on to HK$50 for the airport tax, payable on departure from the country. It is only levied on those 12 years and older and is waived for all transit and transfer passengers who arrive and leave on the same day.

The nearby Macau International Airport gives you more flight options; from here you can simply connect with sea transport for the one-hour journey to Hong Kong.

➤ AIRPORT INFORMATION: **Hong Kong International Airport** (☎ 852/2181–

0000). **Macau International Airport** (☎ 853/861–111).

TRANSFERS TO AND FROM HONG KONG INTERNATIONAL AIRPORT

The spectacular, high-speed, high-frequency **Airport Express Railway** whisks passengers between the airport and Kowloon in 19 minutes via Tsing Ma Bridge, and to and from Hong Kong Island (Central) in 23 minutes. This is the most convenient and economical way to get to and from the airport. There is plenty of luggage space, legroom, and comfortable seating with television screens on the backs of the passenger seats showing tourist information and the latest news. A newsworthy feature of Airport Express is the convenient in-town check-in, whereby you **check your luggage, get your boarding pass, and pay departure tax while still on Hong Kong Island.** To do this, you must purchase an Airport Express ticket and get to the train station three hours before your flight. Some people check in early in the day—the office is open 6 AM–1 AM—and board the train of their choice later on. The Airport Express station is connected to the MTR's Central station (albeit via a long, underground walkway with no luggage carts). One-way fare to or from Central is HK$70; from Kowloon, HK$60. Round-trip tickets valid for one month cost HK$120 for both destinations.

The Airport Express also runs a free shuttle bus between major hotels and its Hong Kong or Kowloon Stations. To board, you must show your ticket, boarding pass, or Airport Express ticket.

Airbus has eight routes covering just about every hotel and hostel in Hong Kong, Kowloon, and the New Territories. Prices range from HK$20 to HK$45 for the one-hour trip.

A 24-hour **Airport Shuttle** bus departs major hotels every 30 minutes and costs HK$120.

A number of regular public buses—including service by **Cityflyer, Kowloon Motor Bus,** and **Long Wing Bus Company**—serve the airport; though cheaper (HK$23 and under), these take longer than express options.

Taxis from the airport cost up to HK$400 for Hong Kong Island destinations and up to HK$320 for Kowloon destinations, plus HK$5 per piece of luggage.

DCH Limo Service is located at Kiosk 4 in the Arrival Hall. Depending on the zone and the type of car, limo rides from the airport range from HK$450 to HK$600. A pick-up service is available at the same rates, as is a car service at HK$300–HK$360 per hour, minimum two hours.

➤ TRANSFERS TO AND FROM HKIA: **Airbus** (☎ 2745–4466). **Airport Express Rail** (☎ 2881–8888). **Airport Shuttle** (☎ 2377–0733). **Cityflyer** (☎ 2873–0818). **DCH Limo Service** (☎ 2262–1888, FAX 2753–6768). **Kowloon Motor Bus** (☎ 2745–4466). **Long Wing Bus Company** (☎ 2786–6036).

DUTY-FREE SHOPPING

In Hong Kong, the only place you can buy duty-free liquor and tobacco is at the Chek Lap Kok. Ten duty-free liquor and tobacco shops are located at the restricted boarding level, with two pre-order shops on the nonrestricted departures check-in level. The shops are open from 7 AM to 11:30 PM. Airport tax is not levied on transit and transfer passengers.

BOAT & FERRY TRAVEL

The century-old **Star Ferry** is a Hong Kong landmark. Double-bowed, green-and-white vessels connect Hong Kong Island with Kowloon in just eight minutes; the ride costs HK$2.20 upper deck, HK$1.70 lower deck. Ferries also run to and between Wanchai and Tsim Sha Tsui; both rides cost HK$5.

Two companies, **Hong Kong & Yau Ma Tei Ferry Company** and Discovery **Bay Transportation Services,** run various ferries from Central to the outlying islands of Lantau, Cheung Chau, Lamma, and Ping Chau. (Note: The high-speed ferries to Discovery Bay, which run 24 hours a day, are located on the Star Ferry Concourse.) Printed schedules are obtainable at the HKTB Information and Gift Centres at two locations: the Star Ferry Concourse, Kowloon, and The Center, 99 Queen's Road Central, Central; as well as through the HKTB

Visitor Hot Line. Return fares vary from HK$15 to HK$50.

For information about ferry service to Macau and locations in China, *see* Macau A to Z *in* Chapter 8 *and* South China A to Z *in* Chapter 9.

➤ BOAT & FERRY INFORMATION: **Discovery Bay Transportation Services** (☎ 2987–7351). **HKTB Visitor Hot Line** (☎ 2508–1234). **Hong Kong & Yau Ma Tei Ferry Company** (☎ 2525–1108). **Star Ferry** (☎ 2366–2576 or 2845–2324).

BUS TRAVEL

AROUND HONG KONG

Double-decker buses run from 6 AM to midnight, and cover most parts of Hong Kong. Bus drivers usually don't speak English, so you may have to ask other passengers for help or you must know exactly where you want to disembark.

When determining bus direction, buses ending with the letter L will eventually connect to the Kowloon-Canton Railway; buses ending with the letter M connect to an MTR station; and buses ending with the letter X are express buses.

As with other big cities, buses can be quite busy during rush hours, public holidays, and at weekends, so it's best to use them during nonpeak times.

Maxicabs and minicabs both seat 16 people. Maxicabs are cream color, with green roofs, and a route number and fixed price prominently displayed. Minibuses are also cream color but have red roofs. Minibuses display both fares and destinations (albeit in very small English letters), though these can change based on demand. Maxicabs and minibuses are both quick, though they cost slightly more than buses. Both can be waved down at any point.

For information, call the HKTB Visitor Hot Line or, for double-decker-bus route maps, stop in at the HKTB Information and Gift Centres at The Center, 99 Queen's Road Central in Central or at the Star Ferry Concourse in Kowloon.

➤ BUS INFORMATION: **HKTB Visitor Hot Line** (☎ 2508–1234).

PAYING

Double-decker bus fares range from HK$1.20 to HK$45; the fare is paid when entering the bus. Maxicab fares range from HK$1.50 to HK$18. Similarly, you pay as you board. Minibus fares range from HK$2 to HK$20, but you pay as you exit. For all three types of transportation you must pay exact change.

Long-staying visitors should consider purchasing an "Octopus" stored-value card (☞ Train Travel, *below*), which you can use on the city bus as well as the Mass Transit Railway, Kowloon-Canton Railway, Light Rail, and Airport Express.

SMOKING

Smoking is not permitted on public transportation.

BUSINESS & TRADE SERVICES
& CONTACTS

BUSINESS CENTERS

Hong Kong supports many business centers outside hotels, and some are considerably cheaper than hotel facilities. Others cost about the same but offer private desks (from HK$250 per hour for desk space to upward of HK$8,000 a month for a private office). Amenities include a private address and phone-answering and forwarding services. Many centers are affiliated with accountants and lawyers who can expedite company registration. Some will even process visas and wrap gifts for you.

Harbour International Business Centre provides typing, secretarial support, and office rentals. Reservations are not required.

The **American Chamber of Commerce** can arrange a Breakfast Briefing Program at your hotel for a fee based on group size. The chamber hosts luncheons and seminars, and the Young Professionals Committee holds cocktail parties at least once a month. Facilities include a library and China trade services.

Other business organizations of note are **AMS Management Service Ltd., Brauner's Business Centre, Business Executive Centre, Business Station,** and **Central Executive Business Centre.**

➤ BUSINESS CENTER INFORMATION:
American Chamber of Commerce
(✉ Bank of America Tower, Room
1904, 12 Harcourt Rd., Central,
Hong Kong Island, ☎ 2526–0165,
FAX 2810–1289). **AMS Management
Service Ltd.** (✉ Wilson House, 19–27
Wyndham St., 18th floor, Central,
☎ 2846–3100, FAX 2810–7002).
Brauner's Business Centre (✉ Kow-
loon Centre, 29–43 Ashley Rd.,
Room 903–5, 9th floor, Tsim Sha
Tsui, ☎ 2376–2855, FAX 2376–3360).
Business Executive Centre (✉ Kin-
wick Centre, 32 Hollywood Rd.,
23rd floor, Central, ☎ 2827–7322,
FAX 2827–4227). **Business Station**
(✉ Cosmos Bldg., 8–11 Lan Kwai
Fong, 6th floor, Central, ☎ 2523–
6810, FAX 2530–5071). **Central Ex-
ecutive Business Centre** (✉ Central
Bldg., 1 Pedder St., 11th floor, Cen-
tral, ☎ 2841–7888, FAX 2810–1868).
**Harbour International Business Cen-
tre** (✉ 2802 Admiralty Centre Tower
I, 18 Harcourt Rd., ☎ 2529–0356,
FAX 2861–3420).

CELLULAR PHONES

Hong Kong Telecom International
(HKTI) rents cellular phones from
offices throughout Hong Kong. The
24-hour office is at Hermes House,
though phones can only be rented
between 9 and 6; there's another
office on D'Aguilar Street.

➤ CELLULAR PHONES CONTACTS:
Hong Kong Telecom International
(HKTI; ✉ Hermes House, 10 Middle
Rd., Tsim Sha Tsui, ☎ 2888–7184
or 2888–7185; ✉ 1 D'Aguilar St.,
Central, ☎ 2810–0660).

CHAMBERS OF COMMERCE

**American Chamber of Commerce in
Hong Kong** (✉ Bank of America
Tower, 12 Harcourt Rd., Room 1904,
Central, Hong Kong Island, ☎ 2526–
0165, FAX 2810–1289).

Australian Chamber of Commerce
(✉ Lucky Bldg., 39 Wellington St.,
4th floor, Central, Hong Kong Island,
☎ 2522–5054, FAX 2877–0860.

British Chamber of Commerce
(✉ Tung Wai Commercial Bldg.,
109–111 Gloucester Rd., Room
1401–2, Wanchai, Hong Kong Island,
☎ 2824–2211, FAX 2824–1333).

Chinese Manufacturers' Association
(✉ CMA Bldg., 64–66 Connaught
Rd., 5th floor, Central, Hong Kong
Island, ☎ 2542–8600, FAX 2541–
4541).

Federation of H.K. Industries (✉ 407
Hankow Centre, 5–15 Hankow Rd.,
Kowloon, ☎ 2732–3188, FAX 2721–
3494.

**Hong Kong General Chamber of
Commerce** (✉ United Centre, 95
Queensway, 5th floor, Hong Kong
Island, ☎ 2529–9229, FAX 2527–
9843).

**Hong Kong Japanese Chamber of
Commerce and Industry** (✉ Hennessy
Centre, 500 Hennessy Rd., 38th floor,
Causeway Bay, Hong Kong Island,
☎ 2577–6129, FAX 2577–0525).

Hong Kong Productivity Council
(✉ HKPC Bldg., 78 Tat Chee Ave.,
Kowloon Tong, ☎ 2788–5678,
FAX 2788–5900).

**Indian Chamber of Commerce Hong
Kong** (✉ Hoseinee House, 69 Wynd-
ham St., 38th floor, Central, Hong
Kong Island, ☎ 2523–3877,
FAX 2845–0300).

Swedish Chamber of Commerce
(✉ Allied Capital Resource Bldg., 32–
38 Ice House St., 10th floor, Central,
Hong Kong Island, ☎ 2525–0349,
FAX 2537–1843).

CONVENTION CENTER

The Hong Kong Convention and
Exhibition Centre is a state-of-the-
art, 693,000-square-ft complex on
the Wanchai waterfront, capable
of handling 140,000 visitors a day.
There are five exhibition halls and
two main convention halls; the section jutting into the harbor hosted
the 1997 handover ceremony. The
largest complex in Asia, the center
houses two hotels, the 600-room
Grand Hyatt, and the 900-room
New World; an apartment block;
and a 54-story trade center/office
building.

➤ CONVENTION CENTER INFORMA-
TION: **Hong Kong Convention and
Exhibition Centre** (✉ 1 Expo Dr.,
Wanchai, Hong Kong Island,
☎ 2582–8888, FAX 2802–0000).

COPY SERVICES

All hotels and business centers have photocopy machines, as do many stores scattered throughout Hong Kong. For heavy-duty, oversize, and color copying, try Xerox.

➤ COPY SERVICE INFORMATION: **Xerox** (✉ Central: New Henry House, 10 Ice House St., 2nd floor, ☎ 2524–9799, FAX 2845–9271; ✉ Admiralty: United Centre, Unit 34, 95 Queensway, 2nd floor, ☎ 2527–6162, FAX 2529–5416; ✉ Wanchai: Shanghai Ind. Investment Bldg., 58 Hennessy Rd., ☎ 2528–0761, FAX 2865–0799; ✉ Tsim Sha Tsui: China Hong Kong City, 33 Canton Rd., Shop 3, 2nd floor, ☎ 2736–6011, FAX 2736–6278).

FAX SERVICES

The post office and Hong Kong Telecom International (HKTI) offer a joint service called "Postfax." Inquire at the General Post Office to see which post offices have the service. Postfax is available at HKTI's 24-hour office.

➤ FAX SERVICE INFORMATION: **General Post Office** (✉ 2 Connaught Rd., next to Star Ferry Terminal, Central, Hong Kong, ☎ 2921–2222). **HKTI** (✉ Hermes House, 10 Middle Rd., Tsim Sha Tsui, Kowloon, ☎ 2724–8322).

MESSENGERS

Most business centers offer delivery service, and you can sometimes arrange a delivery through your hotel concierge. There's a good chance that both, however, will contact DHL's local courier service. Major buildings and various MTR stations have numerous DHL Express centers the company will also pick up from your hotel. Price is based on weight and distance.

➤ MESSENGER INFORMATION: **DHL Express** (☎ 2765–8111)

OVERNIGHT MAIL

The post office has an overnight express service called Speedpost. Large international couriers in Hong Kong include DHL, Federal Express, and UPS.

➤ OVERNIGHT MAIL INFORMATION: **DHL** (☎ 2765–8111, FAX 2334–1228).

Federal Express (☎ 2730–3333, FAX 2730–6588). **UPS** (☎ 2735–3535, FAX 2738–5070).

TELEX

If your business center is closed and you want to avoid a hotel surcharge, HKTI has one 24-hour office to handle public telephone, fax, and telex.

➤ TELEX INFORMATION: **HKTI** (✉ Hermes House, 10 Middle Rd., Tsim Sha Tsui, Kowloon, ☎ 2724–8322).

TRADE INFORMATION

Hong Kong Trade Development Council (✉ Office Tower Convention Plaza, 1 Harbour Rd., 38th floor, Hong Kong Island, ☎ 2584–4333, FAX 2824–0249). **Industry Department** (✉ Ocean Centre, 5 Canton Rd., 14th floor, Kowloon, ☎ 2737–2573, FAX 2730–4633). **Trade Department** (✉ Trade Department Tower, 700 Nathan Rd., Kowloon, ☎ 2392–2922, FAX 2789–2435).

TRANSLATION SERVICES

CIAP Hong Kong (✉ 2A, Tower 10, Pak Pat Shan, Red Hill, Hong Kong, ☎ 2697–5114). **Polyglot Translations** (✉ 14B Time Centre, 53 Hollywood Rd., Central, ☎ 2851–7232). **Translation Business** (✉ 13D, Chinaweal Centre, 414–424 Jaffe Rd., Wanchai, ☎ 2893–5000).

BUSINESS HOURS

Nearly all businesses, even tourist-related ones, will shut down for major holidays such as Chinese Lunar New Year, Christmas, and New Year's.

BANKS & OFFICES

Banks are open weekdays 9–4:30 and Saturday 9–12:30. Cash machines are plentiful. Office hours are more or less the same as in the West—9 to 5 or 6. Some offices are open 9–noon on Saturday. Lunch hour is 1 PM–2 PM; don't be surprised if the office closes during lunch.

MUSEUMS & SIGHTS

Museums and sights are usually open six days a week from 9 to 5. Each site picks a different day, usually a Monday or Tuesday, for its day off. Call the destination before visiting.

PHARMACIES

Pharmacies are generally open from about 10 AM until about 9 PM. There are no 24-hour pharmacies.

SHOPS

Stores usually open around 10 AM and stay open until 9 or 9:30 PM, especially in tourist and residential areas. Here's an estimate of store hours by neighborhood: Central, 10–6; Causeway Bay and Wanchai, 10–9:30; Tsim Sha Tsui East, 10–7:30; Tsim Sha Tsui, Yau Ma Tei, and Mong Kok, 10–9.

CAMERAS & PHOTOGRAPHY

You are neither permitted to photograph customs and immigration procedures at border crossings nor allowed to photograph the police or military. At sites where photography is barred there are usually clearly marked NO PHOTOGRAPHY signs.

Although Hong Kong is picturesque, it can be quite cloudy, smoggy, or foggy, so be prepared for poor lighting at times.

Victoria Peak and Repulse Bay both offer visually stunning backdrops for photographs, but don't miss the unforgettable urban scenery of neon-lit streets at night or crowded market scenes by day.

The *Kodak Guide to Shooting Great Travel Pictures* (available at bookstores everywhere) is loaded with tips on getting the perfect shot.

EQUIPMENT PRECAUTIONS

Don't pack film and equipment in checked luggage, where it is much more susceptible to damage. X-ray machines used to view checked luggage are becoming much more powerful and therefore are much more likely to ruin your film. Always **keep film and tape out of the sun.** Carry an extra supply of batteries, and **be prepared to turn on your camera or camcorder** to prove to security personnel that the device is real. Always **ask for hand inspection of film,** which becomes clouded after repeated exposure to airport X-ray machines, and **keep videotapes away from metal detectors.**

FILM & DEVELOPING

Kodak and Fuji color film are easy to find in hotel shops, corner grocery stores, and camera shops throughout Hong Kong. Expect to pay about HK$28 for a 36-exposure roll of 200 film. For instamatic cameras, you will pay about HK$100 for a 10-picture pack of Polaroid Spectra Instant Film. One-hour developing is available at Kodak express stalls in malls, hotels, and street corners in Hong Kong. Expect to pay HK$48 to HK$80 for the speedy service.

CAR RENTAL

Avoid renting a car on Hong Kong Island or Kowloon. Driving conditions, traffic jams, and parking are bound to make life more difficult. Public transportation is excellent here, and taxis are inexpensive. If you do decide to rent a car, you may want to hire a driver as well; this can be arranged through your hotel. The fee is HK$800–HK$1,200 for the first four hours (depending on car model) and HK$200–HK$300 for each subsequent hour.

Rental rates begin at HK$702 per day and HK$2,900 per week for an economy car with air-conditioning, automatic transmission, and unlimited mileage.

➤ MAJOR AGENCIES: **Alamo** (☎ 800/522–9696; 020/8759–6200 in the U.K.). **Avis** (☎ 800/331–1084; 800/879–2847 in Canada; 02/9353–9000 in Australia; 09/525–1982 in New Zealand; 0870/606–0100 in the U.K.). **Budget** (☎ 800/527–0700; 0870/607–5000 in the U.K., through affiliate Europcar). **Dollar** (☎ 800/800–6000; 0124/622–0111 in the U.K., through affiliate Sixt Kenning; 02/9223–1444 in Australia). **Hertz** (☎ 800/654–3001; 800/263–0600 in Canada; 020/8897–2072 in the U.K.; 02/9669–2444 in Australia; 09/256–8690 in New Zealand). **National Car Rental** (☎ 800/227–7368; 020/8680–4800 in the U.K., where it is known as National Europe).

➤ LOCAL AGENCIES: **Ace Hire Car** (✉ 16 Min Fat St., Happy Valley, ☎ 2893–0541; turn left at Hong Kong Bank). **Fung Hing Hire Co.** (✉ 58 German St., ground floor, Happy Valley, ☎ 2572–0333) rents chauffeured cars only.

CUTTING COSTS

To get the best deal, **book through a travel agent who will shop around.** Payment must be made before you leave home.

INSURANCE

When driving a rented car you are generally responsible for any damage to or loss of the vehicle as well as for any property damage or personal injury that you may cause. Before you rent, see what coverage your personal auto-insurance policy and credit cards provide.

REQUIREMENTS & RESTRICTIONS

Your own driver's license is valid in Hong Kong, but an International Driver's Permit is always a good idea; it's available from the American and Canadian automobile associations and, in the United Kingdom, from the Automobile Association or Royal Automobile Club. These permits are universally recognized, so having one in your wallet may save you a problem with the local authorities.

SURCHARGES

Before you pick up a car in one city and leave it in another, **ask about drop-off charges or one-way service fees,** which can be substantial. Note, too, that some rental agencies charge extra if you return the car before the time specified in your contract. To avoid a hefty refueling fee, **fill the tank just before you turn in the car,** but be aware that gas stations near the rental outlet may overcharge.

CAR TRAVEL

The best advice we can give is **don't drive in Hong Kong.** In addition to the fact that gasoline and parking are so prohibitively expensive that the only cars you're likely to see on Hong Kong Island are chauffeured Rolls Royces driven by former race-car-driving Triad members, the local bus and truck drivers seem to think slamming on their breaks (and sending their passengers flying forward) is the only way to stop—making it an exceptionally difficult city to drive in. If you don't have to, don't drive here.

RULES OF THE ROAD

If you insist on driving here, remember in this former British colony, the road rules are drive on the left and signage is British symbols. Always remember to **look left before you cross the street.**

CHILDREN IN HONG KONG

If you are renting a car, don't forget to **arrange for a car seat** when you reserve.

For general advice about traveling with children, consult *Fodor's FYI: Travel with Your Baby* (available in bookstores everywhere).

FLYING

If your children are two or older, **ask about children's airfares.** As a general rule, infants under two not occupying a seat fly at greatly reduced fares or even for free. When booking, **confirm carry-on allowances** if you're traveling with infants. In general, for babies charged 10% of the adult fare you are allowed one carry-on bag and a collapsible stroller; if the flight is full, the stroller may have to be checked or you may be limited to less.

Experts agree that it's a good idea to use safety seats aloft for children weighing less than 40 pounds. Airlines set their own policies: U.S. carriers usually require that the child be ticketed, even if he or she is young enough to ride free, since the seats must be strapped into regular seats. Do **check your airline's policy about using safety seats during takeoff and landing.** And since safety seats are not allowed everywhere in the plane, get your seat assignments early.

When reserving, **request children's meals or a freestanding bassinet** if you need them. But note that bulkhead seats, where you must sit to use the bassinet, may lack an overhead bin or storage space on the floor.

FOOD

Some Western restaurants offer children's meals, but Cantonese restaurants do not, as the style of ordering is to select several small or "child size" dishes anyway. Children are often present at all but the most upscale restaurants.

LODGING

Most hotels in Hong Kong allow children under a certain age to stay in their parents' room at no extra charge, but others charge for them as extra adults; be sure to **find out the cutoff age for children's discounts.** Baby-sitting prices are around HK$15 an hour at almost all hotels.

PRECAUTIONS

The traffic flows by quickly, so be especially careful to warn children to look both ways. Otherwise Hong Kong is as safe as any major city in the world. Simply use common sense.

SIGHTS & ATTRACTIONS

Places that are especially appealing to children are indicated by a rubber-duckie icon (☕) in the margin.

SUPPLIES & EQUIPMENT

Baby supplies such as diapers range in price from HK$64 for a box of 30 medium-size Huggies to HK$76 (around US$12) for a box of 28 extra-large Pampers, and are widely available throughout the city. Similarly, a variety of brands of baby-powder milk, sold in 1 kilogram–size tin containers, are available for about HK$136 Heinz baby foods, Johnson & Johnson lotions and powders, and Gerber plastic nursers and silicone nipples are all readily found. You can shop in supermarkets, or at pharmaceutical/cosmetics chain stores such as **Watson's** (☎ 2186–8595) or **Fanda Perfume Co., Ltd.** (☎ 2526–6623), which are scattered throughout Hong Kong. Call for the nearest location.

TRANSPORTATION

Most public transportation services charge half price for children under 12.

COMPUTERS ON THE ROAD

Hong Kong is computer-friendly. If your spare battery or adapter fails you, no worries; you can buy a new one in Hong Kong. In general, for computer purchases make sure the product's voltage compatibility is that of your home country and verify that all parts, pieces, and an international warranty are packed with your purchase. Shop around, as prices may vary within a few months. Consider purchasing your product with a credit card, which might increase the price by 3% to 5%, but will make it easier if you need to return or claim a refund for your purchase from the manufacturer or store once you return home.

While using surge protection is a good computer habit, you'll have no worries plugging your computer directly into the socket at a Hong Kong hotel or business building. The electricity is stable.

CONCIERGES

Concierges, found in many hotels, can help you with theater tickets and dinner reservations: a good one with connections may be able to get you seats for a hot show or prime-time dinner reservations at the restaurant of the moment. You can also turn to your hotel's concierge for help with travel arrangements, sightseeing plans, services ranging from aromatherapy to zipper repair, and emergencies. Always, **always tip** a concierge who has been of assistance (☞ Tipping, *below*).

CONSUMER PROTECTION

Whenever shopping or buying travel services in Hong Kong, **pay with a major credit card,** if possible, so you can cancel payment or get reimbursed if there's a problem. Note, however, that this will often increase the price of your purchase by 3% to 5%. If you're doing business with a particular company for the first time, **contact your local Better Business Bureau and the attorney general's offices** in your state and (for U.S. businesses) the company's home state as well. Have any complaints been filed? Finally, if you're buying a package or tour, always **consider travel insurance** that includes default coverage (☞ Insurance, *below*).

➤ BBBs: **Council of Better Business Bureaus** (✉ 4200 Wilson Blvd., Suite 800, Arlington, VA 22203, ☎ 703/276–0100, FAX 703/525–8277, WEB www.bbb.org).

CRUISE TRAVEL

Cruise ships in Hong Kong tend to cater to a mix of passengers from Hong Kong, Singapore, Thailand, and Malaysia alongside Westerners. The large cruise lines are beginning to expand their range of itineraries; in the meantime, you can **book a cruise** with a local operator that specializes in a specific part of Southeast Asia.

➤ CRUISE LINES: **Star Cruise** (✉ Ocean Centre, 5 Canton Rd., No. 1, 15th floor, Tsim Sha Tsui, ☎ 2317–7711) runs cruises out of Hong Kong.

CUSTOMS & DUTIES

When shopping, **keep receipts** for all purchases. Upon reentering the country, **be ready to show customs officials what you've bought.** If you feel a duty is incorrect or object to the way your clearance was handled, note the inspector's badge number and ask to see a supervisor. If the problem isn't resolved, write to the appropriate authorities, beginning with the port director at your point of entry.

IN AUSTRALIA

Australian residents who are 18 or older may bring home A$400 worth of souvenirs and gifts (including jewelry), 250 cigarettes or 250 grams of tobacco, and 1,125 ml of alcohol (including wine, beer, and spirits). Residents under 18 may bring back A$200 worth of goods. Prohibited items include meat products. Seeds, plants, and fruits need to be declared upon arrival.

➤ INFORMATION: **Australian Customs Service** (Regional Director, ✉ Box 8, Sydney, NSW 2001, Australia, ☎ 02/9213–2000, FAX 02/9213–4000, WEB www.customs.gov.au).

IN CANADA

Canadian residents who have been out of Canada for at least seven days may bring home C$500 worth of goods duty-free. If you've been away fewer than seven days but more than 48 hours, the duty-free allowance drops to C$200; if your trip lasts 24–48 hours, the allowance is C$50. You may not pool allowances with family members. Goods claimed under the C$500 exemption may follow you by mail; those claimed under the lesser exemptions must accompany you. Alcohol and tobacco products may be included in the seven-day and 48-hour exemptions but not in the 24-hour exemption. If you meet the age requirements of the province or territory through which you reenter Canada, you may bring in, duty-free,

1.14 liters (40 imperial ounces) of wine or liquor *or* 24 12-ounce cans or bottles of beer or ale. If you are 16 or older you may bring in, duty-free, 200 cigarettes and 50 cigars. Check ahead of time with Revenue Canada or the Department of Agriculture for policies regarding meat products, seeds, plants, and fruits.

You may send an unlimited number of gifts worth up to C$60 each duty-free to Canada. Label the package UNSOLICITED GIFT—VALUE UNDER $60. Alcohol and tobacco are excluded.

➤ INFORMATION: **Revenue Canada** (✉ 2265 St. Laurent Blvd. S, Ottawa, Ontario K1G 4K3, Canada, ☎ 613/993–0534; 800/461–9999 in Canada, FAX 613/991–4126, WEB www.ccra-adrc.gc.ca).

IN HONG KONG

Except for the usual prohibitions against narcotics, explosives, firearms, and ammunition (all but narcotics must be declared upon arrival and handed over for safekeeping until departure), and modest limits on alcohol, tobacco products, and perfume, you can bring anything you want into Hong Kong, including an unlimited amount of money.

Nonresident visitors may bring in, duty-free, 200 cigarettes or 50 cigars or 250 grams of tobacco, and 1 liter of alcohol.

➤ INFORMATION: **Hong Kong Customs and Excise Department** (✉ 10/F, Canton Road Government Offices, 393 Canton Rd., Kowloon, ☎ 2815–7711, FAX 2542–3334, WEB www.info.gov.hk/customs).

IN NEW ZEALAND

Homeward-bound residents 17 or older may bring back NZ$700 worth of souvenirs and gifts. Your duty-free allowance also includes 4.5 liters of wine or beer; one 1,125-ml bottle of spirits; and either 200 cigarettes, 250 grams of tobacco, 50 cigars, or a combination of the three up to 250 grams. Prohibited items include meat products, seeds, plants, and fruits.

➤ INFORMATION: **New Zealand Customs** (Custom House, ✉ 50 Anzac Ave., Box 29, Auckland, New Zealand, ☎ 09/300–5399, FAX 09/359–6730, WEB www.customs.govt.nz).

IN THE U.K.

From countries outside the EU, including Hong Kong, you may bring home, duty-free, 200 cigarettes or 50 cigars; 1 liter of spirits or 2 liters of fortified or sparkling wine or liqueurs; 2 liters of still table wine; 60 ml of perfume; 250 ml of toilet water; plus £136 worth of other goods, including gifts and souvenirs. If returning from outside the EU, prohibited items include meat products, seeds, plants, and fruits.

➤ INFORMATION: **HM Customs and Excise** (✉ Dorset House, Stamford St., Bromley, Kent BR1 1XX, U.K., ☎ 020/7202–4227, WEB www.hmce.gov.uk).

IN THE U.S.

U.S. residents who have been out of the country for at least 48 hours (and who have not used the US$400 allowance or any part of it in the past 30 days) may bring home US$400 worth of foreign goods duty-free.

U.S. residents 21 and older may bring back 1 liter of alcohol duty-free. In addition, regardless of your age, you are allowed 200 cigarettes and 100 non-Cuban cigars. Antiques, which the U.S. Customs Service defines as objects more than 100 years old, enter duty-free, as do original works of art done entirely by hand, including paintings, drawings, and sculptures.

You may also mail or ship packages home duty-free: up to US$200 worth of goods for personal use, with a limit of one parcel per addressee per day (except alcohol or tobacco products or perfume worth more than US$5); label the package PERSONAL USE and attach a list of its contents and their retail value. Do not label the package UNSOLICITED GIFT or your duty-free exemption will drop to US$100. Mailed items do not affect your duty-free allowance on your return.

➤ INFORMATION: **U.S. Customs Service** (✉ 1300 Pennsylvania Ave. NW, Washington, DC 20229, WEB www.customs.gov; inquiries ☎ 202/354–1000; complaints c/o ✉ 1300 Pennsylvania Ave. NW, Room 5.4D, Washington, DC 20229; registration of equipment c/o ✉ Resource Management, ☎ 202/927–0540).

DINING

The restaurants we review are the cream of the crop in each price category. Prices are indicated as follows:

CATEGORY	COST*
$$$$	over HK$280
$$$	HK$180–HK$280
$$	HK$80–HK$180
$	under HK$80

*per person, not including 10% service charge

MEALS & SPECIALTIES

With more than 9,000 restaurants, Hong Kong has food to please every palate.

Hong Kong is famous for its Cantonese restaurants, since most residents trace their roots to Guangdong (Canton) Province. The Cantonese are noted for cooking foods you might not think edible. As the saying goes, if it has four legs and isn't a table, the Cantonese will steam, stir-fry, or boil it. Specialties include pigeon, shark's-fin soup, and abalone.

You shouldn't leave Hong Kong without trying the Cantonese specialty dim sum. These light snacks, served for lunch or breakfast in local teahouses as well as fine restaurants, are usually served in steaming bamboo baskets. Dim sum includes a variety of dumplings, buns, and pastries containing meat and vegetables.

Of course, you can also find restaurants serving specialties from throughout China. Peking foods use noodles and dumplings and are strongly spiced with coriander, peppers, and garlic. Shanghainese cuisine is typically seasoned with sugar, soy sauce, and wine. Late autumn is the best time to try a Shanghainese specialty, freshwater hairy crabs. Szechuan food includes some of the spiciest dishes in China (check the chili codes on the menus) but not all dishes are spicy.

Seafood is a year-round favorite in Hong Kong. Plentiful and delicious, live fish and shellfish are kept in tanks at many restaurants, so you can hand pick your dinner and be assured of freshness. Steamed garoupa (grouper) and poached shrimp with chili and soy sauce are two specialties.

MEALTIMES

Dim sum restaurants normally open about 7:30 AM and close about 2:30 PM. Some are shut between 10 and 11:30 AM. Dim sum restaurants often teem with people on the weekends, so expect to wait at the more popular places.

Western-style restaurants, such as Irish pubs and steak houses, are open from about 11 AM to 11 PM daily; dinner is busiest, around 7 PM.

Unless otherwise noted, the restaurants listed in this guide are open daily for lunch and dinner.

PAYING

Try not to be shocked when you get your bill. You'll be charged for everything, including tea, rice, and even those side dishes placed automatically on every table, which are often mistaken for complimentary snacks. Tips are expected (10% average gratuity) at most restaurants, even if the bill includes a service charge.

RESERVATIONS & DRESS

Reservations are always a good idea; we note only when they're essential, which is often the case at lunchtime (between 1 and 2) or at dinnertime (between 7 and 10) on weekends. Book as far ahead as you can, and reconfirm as soon as you arrive. We mention dress only when men are required to wear a jacket or a jacket and tie.

WINE, BEER, & SPIRITS

The drinking age in bars is 18, and is fairly strictly enforced. You can find most brands of imported alcohol and an excellent array of imported beers as well as the locally brewed San Miguel. Most nightlife spots offer happy-hour specials, sometimes starting as early as 3 PM and continuing until 10 PM.

DISABILITIES & ACCESSIBILITY

Hong Kong is not the easiest of cities for people in wheelchairs, and few ramps or other provisions for access are provided. Progress is being made, however; the airport, City Hall, the Academy for Performing Arts, and the Hong Kong Arts Centre have made efforts to assist people in wheelchairs. For more information, consult the *Hong Kong Access Guide for Disabled Visitors*, available from the Hong Kong Tourist Board (HKTB). The guide lists those rare places that have special facilities for people with disabilities, in addition to the best access to hotels, shopping centers, government offices, consulates, restaurants, and churches.

RESERVATIONS

When discussing accessibility with an operator or reservations agent, **ask hard questions.** Are there any stairs, inside *or* out? Are there grab bars next to the toilet *and* in the shower/tub? How wide is the doorway to the room? To the bathroom? For the most extensive facilities meeting the latest legal specifications, **opt for newer accommodations.**

TRANSPORTATION

The vast airport has moving walkways that transport arriving or departing passengers from the most remote gates in about 70 seconds. Ramps, lifts, and escalators are provided for unavoidable changes of level.

While taxis in Hong Kong do not adapt to special needs of passengers with physical disabilities, walking aids such as wheelchairs and crutches are carried free of charge.

The Kowloon Canton Railway (KCR), which operates along North East New Territories, has lifts at all stations except the Racecourse Station. The KCR Light Rail, which operates in the North West New Territories, has ramps from the street to the platform at all stations. The Mass Transit Railway (MTR), which services Hong Kong and Kowloon and also connects to Tung Chungk and the Chek Lap Kok airport, has ramps or lifts at 19 stations.

Ancillary facilities such as tactile guide paths, escalator audible devices, and light emitting diode (LED) display boards are available at most stations.

The lower deck on the ferries is more accessible than the upper deck for passengers using wheelchairs.

▶ COMPLAINTS: **Aviation Consumer Protection Division** (☞ Air Travel, *above*) for airline-related problems. **Civil Rights Office** (✉ U.S. Department of Transportation, Departmental Office of Civil Rights, S-30, 400 7th St. SW, Room 10215, Washington, DC 20590, ☎ 202/366–4648, FAX 202/366–9371, WEB www.dot.gov/ost/docr/index.htm) for problems with surface transportation. **Disability Rights Section** (✉ U.S. Department of Justice, Civil Rights Division, Box 66738, Washington, DC 20035-6738, ☎ 202/514–0301 or 800/514–0301; 202/514–0383 TTY; 800/514–0383 TTY, FAX 202/307–1198, WEB www.usdoj.gov/crt/ada/adahom1.htm) for general complaints. **MTR** (☎ 2881–8888) for inquiries.

TRAVEL AGENCIES

In the United States, the Americans with Disabilities Act requires that travel firms serve the needs of all travelers. Some agencies specialize in working with people with disabilities.

▶ TRAVELERS WITH MOBILITY PROBLEMS: **Access Adventures** (✉ 206 Chestnut Ridge Rd., Scottsville, NY 14624, ☎ 716/889–9096, dltravel@prodigy.net), run by a former physical-rehabilitation counselor. **CareVacations** (✉ 5-5110 50th Ave., Leduc, Alberta T9E 6V4, Canada, ☎ 780/986–6404 or 877/478–7827, FAX 780/986–8332, WEB www.carevacations.com), for group tours and cruise vacations. **Flying Wheels Travel** (✉ 143 W. Bridge St., Box 382, Owatonna, MN 55060, ☎ 507/451–5005 or 800/535–6790, FAX 507/451–1685, WEB www.flyingwheelstravel.com).

DISCOUNTS & DEALS

Be a smart shopper and **compare all your options** before making decisions. A plane ticket bought with a promotional coupon from travel clubs, coupon books, and direct-mail offers or on the Internet may not be cheaper than the least expensive fare from a discount ticket agency. And always keep in mind that what you get is just as important as what you save.

DISCOUNT RESERVATIONS

To save money, **look into discount reservations services** with toll-free numbers, which use their buying power to get a better price on hotels, airline tickets, even car rentals. When booking a room, always **call the hotel's local toll-free number** (if one is available) rather than the central reservations number—you'll often get a better price. Always ask about special packages or corporate rates.

When shopping for the best deal on hotels and car rentals, **look for guaranteed exchange rates,** which protect you against a falling dollar. With your rate locked in, you won't pay more, even if the price goes up in the local currency.

▶ HOTEL ROOMS: **Hotel Reservations Network** (☎ 800/964–6835, WEB www.hoteldiscount.com). **Players Express Vacations** (☎ 800/458–6161, WEB www.playersexpress.com). **Steigenberger Reservation Service** (☎ 800/223–5652, WEB www.srs-worldhotels.com). **Travel Interlink** (☎ 800/888–5898, WEB www.travelinterlink.com). **Turbotrip.com** (☎ 800/473–7829, WEB www.turbotrip.com). **VacationLand** (☎ 800/245–0050, WEB www.vacation-land.com).

PACKAGE DEALS

Don't confuse packages and guided tours. When you buy a package, you travel on your own, just as though you had planned the trip yourself. Fly/drive packages, which combine airfare and car rental, are often a good deal. In cities, ask the local visitors' bureau about hotel packages that include tickets to major museum exhibits or other special events.

ELECTRICITY

To use electric-powered equipment purchased in the United States or Canada, **bring a converter and adapter.** The electrical current in Hong Kong is 220 volts, 50 cycles alternating current (AC); in Macau it's also 220 volts, 50 cycles. Some outlets in Hong Kong take plugs with three round prongs, while others use plugs with two square prongs. There is no standard plug size in Macau; check with your hotel regarding its setup.

If your appliances are dual-voltage, you'll need only an adapter. Don't use 110-volt outlets marked FOR SHAVERS ONLY for high-wattage appliances such as blow-dryers. Most laptops operate equally well on 110 and 220 volts and so require only an adapter.

EMBASSIES

➤ AUSTRALIA: **Australian Consulate** (✉ Harbour Centre, 25 Harbour Rd., 24th floor, Wanchai, ☎ 2827–8881, FAX 2585–4459).

➤ CANADA: **Canadian Consulate** (✉ Tower 1, Exchange Sq., 8 Connaught Pl., 11th–14th floors, Hong Kong Island, ☎ 2810–4321, FAX 2810–8736).

➤ NEW ZEALAND: **Consulate General** (✉ Central Plaza, Central, Hong Kong, ☎ 2525–5044).

➤ UNITED KINGDOM: **British Trade Commission** (✉ Visa Section, 1 Supreme Court Rd., 3rd floor, Hong Kong Island, ☎ 2901–3111).

➤ UNITED STATES: **U.S. Consulate** (✉ 26 Garden Rd., Hong Kong Island, ☎ 2523–9011, FAX 2845–1598).

EMERGENCIES

Locals and police are usually quite helpful in an emergency situation. Most police officers speak some English or will contact someone who does. There are no 24-hour pharmacies; however, Fanda Perfume Co., Ltd. and Watson's both have pharmacy departments and numerous shops throughout the city; they are usually open until 9 PM.

➤ EMERGENCY SERVICES: **Police, fire, and ambulance** (☎ 999). **Hong Kong Police and Taxi Complaint Hotline** (☎ 2527–7177).

➤ HOSPITALS: **Prince of Wales Hospital** (✉ 30–32 Ngan Shing St., Shatin, New Territories, ☎ 2632–2211), **Princess Margaret Hospital** (✉ 2–10 Princess Margaret Hospital Rd., Laichikok, Kowloon, ☎ 2990–1111), **Queen Elizabeth Hospital** (✉ 30 Gascoigne Rd., Kowloon, ☎ 2958–8888), **Queen Mary Hospital** (✉ 102 Pok Fu Lam Rd., Hong Kong, ☎ 2855–3111), and **Tang Shiu Kin Hospital** (✉ 282 Queen's Rd. E, Hong Kong, ☎ 2291–2000).

➤ PHARMACIES: **Fanda Perfume Co., Ltd.** (☎ 2526–6623). **Watson's** (☎ 2915–9065).

ENGLISH-LANGUAGE MEDIA

English-language newspapers are available in Hong Kong. Two English television channels broadcast local English programs weekday mornings and evenings and all day on weekends and holidays. Satellite and Cable TV are also available.

BOOKS

Most bookstores throughout the city have English-language selections.

➤ BOOKSTORES: **Bookazines Ltd.** (✉ Pacific House, 20 Queen's Rd., Central, ☎ 2521–1649) has a wide selection of books and magazines.

NEWSPAPERS & MAGAZINES

English newspapers printed in Hong Kong include the *South China Morning Post, Hong Kong iMail,* the *Asian Wall Street Journal,* the *International Herald Tribune,* and *USA Today International.* The *HK* and the *BC Magazine* are free. The former is an alternative weekly tabloid, the latter a twice-a-month magazine; both provide comprehensive weekly listings.

The *Far Eastern Economic Review* is a Dow Jones publication, and leads the pack for serious, locally produced business publications. *Time* and *Newsweek* both print editions in Hong Kong, joined by the native *Asiaweek* which is part of the Time-Warner family.

RADIO & TELEVISION

There are 13 radio channels, with everything from Cantonese pop music to English news. Stations with English-speaking disc jockeys include: RTHK Radio 3 (AM 567 or 1584, FM 97.9 or 106.8), which airs news, finance, and current affairs; RTHK Radio 4 (FM 97.6 to 98.9), which plays Western and Chinese classical music; and RTHK Radio 6 (AM 675), which airs the BBC World Service relay. Metro Plus (AM 1044) has regional news, finance programs, and international music.

English-language television channels include ATV World and TVB Pearl. Satellite selections include Star and

AUSTV; on cable you can get BBC, CNN, ESPN, and HBO.

ETIQUETTE & BEHAVIOR

It won't hurt to **brush up on your use of chopsticks.** Silverware is common in Hong Kong, but it might be seen as a respectful gesture if you try your hand at chopsticks. Dining is a communal event. Everyone orders at least one dish, which are then placed in the center of the table and shared. Your meal will usually include rice or soup. It is considered proper to hold the bowl close to your lips and shovel the rice or soup into your mouth.

Smoking is common in Hong Kong, yet you should know that in July 1998 smoking was officially banned in all indoor public areas, including malls, banks, department stores, and supermarkets.

Hong Kong is extremely crowded; pushing, shoving, and gentle nudges are commonplace. As difficult as this may be to accept, it's not considered rude, it's unavoidable. Becoming angry or taking offense to an inadvertent push is considered rude.

However, while a gentle shove on the streets may be common, it is not typical of strangers to be excessively touchy-feely with one another. A gregarious hug and boisterous hello will be off-putting to Hong Kongers who don't know you. When you are first meeting local people, try to **be low-key and subdued,** even if its not in your nature.

BUSINESS ETIQUETTE

Hong Kongers have a keen sense of hierarchy in the office. Egalitarianism may be admired in the United States, but it's often insulting in Hong Kong. **Let the tea lady get the tea** and coffee—that's what she's there for. Your assistant or Chinese colleague is thought to have better things to do than make copies or deliver messages. Hong Kongers are very attached to business cards, presumably because they're tangible evidence of one's place in the hierarchy. **Have plenty of cards available** (printed, if possible, in English on one side and Chinese on the other). Exchange cards by proffering yours with both hands and a slight bow, and receiving one in the same way.

GAY & LESBIAN TRAVEL

Criminal sanctions on homosexual relations between consenting adults in Hong Kong were lifted in 1991. Currently, Hong Kong has an often not-spoken-about, but hopping gay nightlife. Interestingly, despite the fact that many local Hong Kongers tend to be intensely xenophobic among themselves (Hong Kongers look down on Shanghainese who look down on Beijingers, etc.), they don't take notice of homosexuals and don't discriminate against them.

Contacts, a magazine covering the local gay scene, is available for HK$35 at the **Fetish Fashion** boutique. Among popular nightspots are **Rice Bar, Petticoat Lane,** and **Propaganda**, the largest gay and lesbian bar in Hong Kong.

➤ LOCAL RESOURCES: **Fetish Fashion** (✉ 32 Cochrane St., mezzanine floor, Central, ☎ 2544–1155). **Petticoat Lane** (✉ 2 Tun Wo La., Midlevels, ☎ 2973–0642). **Propaganda** (✉ 1 Hollywood Rd., Central, ☎ 2868–1316). **Rice Bar** (✉ 33 Jervois St., Sheung Wan, ☎ 2851–4800).

➤ GAY- & LESBIAN-FRIENDLY TRAVEL AGENCIES: **Different Roads Travel** (✉ 8383 Wilshire Blvd., Suite 902, Beverly Hills, CA 90211, ☎ 323/651–5557 or 800/429–8747, FAX 323/651–3678, lgernert@tzell.com). **Kennedy Travel** (✉ 314 Jericho Turnpike, Floral Park, NY 11001, ☎ 516/352–4888 or 800/237–7433, FAX 516/354–8849, WEB www.kennedytravel.com). **Now Voyager** (✉ 4406 18th St., San Francisco, CA 94114, ☎ 415/626–1169 or 800/255–6951, FAX 415/626–8626, WEB www.nowvoyager.com). **Skylink Travel and Tour** (✉ 1006 Mendocino Ave., Santa Rosa, CA 95401, ☎ 707/546–9888 or 800/225–5759, FAX 707/546–9891, WEB www.skylinktravel.com), serving lesbian travelers.

HEALTH

FOOD & DRINK

The major health risk for travelers overseas is traveler's diarrhea, caused by eating contaminated fruit or vegetables or drinking contaminated water. **Watch what you eat:** stay away from ice, uncooked food, and unpasteurized milk and milk products. Note, too, that eating raw shellfish has been associated with recent hepatitis outbreaks in Hong Kong. **Drink only bottled water** or water that has been boiled for at least 20 minutes, even when you're brushing your teeth. Expect to pay HK$7 to HK$20 for a liter bottle of distilled water.

OVER-THE-COUNTER REMEDIES

Familiar over-the-counter medications such as aspirin, Tylenol, etc., are available in supermarkets such as Wellcome or even 7-Eleven shops, which are scattered throughout the city. The drugstore chains **Fanda Perfume Co., Ltd** (☎ 2526–6623) and **Watson's** (☎ 2915–9065) both have pharmacy departments and numerous shops throughout the city.

HOLIDAYS

Major holidays in Hong Kong include New Year's (the first weekday in January), Chinese New Year, Easter, Labour Day (May 1), National Day (October 1), and Christmas and Boxing Day (December 25 and 26). There are also numerous Chinese holidays throughout the year.

INSURANCE

The most useful travel-insurance plan is a comprehensive policy that includes coverage for trip cancellation and interruption, default, trip delay, and medical expenses (with a waiver for preexisting conditions).

Without insurance you will lose all or most of your money if you cancel your trip, regardless of the reason. Default insurance covers you if your tour operator, airline, or cruise line goes out of business. Trip-delay covers expenses that arise because of bad weather or mechanical delays. Study the fine print when comparing policies.

If you're traveling internationally, a key component of travel insurance is coverage for medical bills incurred if you get sick on the road. Such expenses are not generally covered by Medicare or private policies. U.K. residents can buy a travel-insurance policy valid for most vacations taken during the year in which it's purchased (but check preexisting-condition coverage). British and Australian citizens need extra medical coverage when traveling overseas.

Always **buy travel policies directly from the insurance company**; if you buy them from a cruise line, airline, or tour operator that goes out of business you probably will not be covered for the agency or operator's default, a major risk. Before making any purchase, **review your existing health and home-owner's policies** to find what they cover away from home.

➤ Travel Insurers: In the United States: **Access America** (✉ 6600 W. Broad St., Richmond, VA 23230, ☎ 804/285–3300 or 800/284–8300, FAX 804/673–1586, WEB www.previewtravel.com), **Travel Guard International** (✉ 1145 Clark St., Stevens Point, WI 54481, ☎ 715/345–0505 or 800/826–1300, FAX 800/955–8785, WEB www.noelgroup.com).

➤ Insurance Information: In Australia: **Insurance Council of Australia** (✉ Level 3, 56 Pitt St., Sydney, NSW 2000, ☎ 03/9614–1077, FAX 03/9614–7924). In Canada: **Voyager Insurance** (✉ 44 Peel Center Dr., Brampton, Ontario L6T 4M8, Canada, ☎ 905/791–8700; 800/668–4342 in Canada). In New Zealand: **Insurance Council of New Zealand** (✉ Box 474, Wellington, New Zealand, ☎ 04/472–5230, FAX 04/473–3011, WEB www.icnz.org.nz). In the United Kingdom: **Association of British Insurers** (✉ 51–55 Gresham St., London EC2V 7HQ, U.K., ☎ 020/7600–3333, FAX 020/7696–8999, WEB www.abi.org.uk).

LANGUAGE

Hong Kong's official languages are English and Chinese. The most commonly spoken Chinese dialect is Cantonese, but Mandarin—the official language of China, known in Hong Kong as Putonghua—is gaining in popularity. Macau's official languages are Portuguese and Chinese, but many people speak some English. Here, too, Mandarin is growing in popularity.

In hotels, major restaurants, stores, and tourist centers, almost everyone speaks English. This is not the case, however, with taxi drivers, bus drivers, and workers in small shops, cafés, and market stalls.

Language study courses are available, but most last at least one month. Contact the Chinese Language Centre at the Chinese University of Hong Kong (www.cuhk.edu.hk/lac) for more information.

LODGING

Hong Kong hotels operate on the European Plan, i.e., with no meals included. Rooms have private baths unless otherwise noted.

The lodgings we review are the cream of the crop in each price category. We always list the facilities available, but we don't specify whether they cost extra; so when pricing accommodations, always ask what's included and what's not.

CATEGORY	COST*
$$$$	over HK$2,500
$$$	HK$1,800–HK$2,500
$$	HK$1,100–HK$1,800
$	under HK$1,100

All prices are for a standard double room, excluding 10% service charge and 3% tax.

Bargain lodging has become increasingly rare in Hong Kong. If none of our moderately priced suggestions pan out, try the STB Hostel, that has dorm-style sleeping quarters, or the YMCA International House.

➤ BARGAIN LODGING INFORMATION: **STB Hostel** (⊠ HK Ltd., Great Eastern Mansion, 255–261 Reclamation St., 2nd floor, Mong Kok, Kowloon, ☎ 2710–9199, FAX 2385–0153). **YMCA International House** (⊠ 23 Waterloo Rd., Yau Ma Tei, Kowloon, ☎ 2771–9111, FAX 2771–5238).

APARTMENT RENTALS

If you want a home base that's roomy enough for a family and comes with cooking facilities, **consider a furnished rental.** These can save you money, especially if you're traveling with a group. Home-exchange directories sometimes list rentals as well as exchanges.

Hong Kong landlords usually require a minimum one-month stay for apartment rentals. Contact real-estate agencies to find out what is currently available.

➤ INTERNATIONAL AGENTS: **Hideaways International** (⊠ 767 Islington St., Portsmouth, NH 03801, ☎ 603/ 430–4433 or 800/843–4433, FAX 603/ 430–4444, WEB www.hideaways.com; membership US$129).

➤ LOCAL AGENTS: **Eaton House** (⊠ 380 Nathan Rd., Kowloon, ☎ 2710–1800, FAX 2388–6971) and **Hong Kong & Shanghai Hotels Ltd.** (⊠ 8/F St. Georges House, 2 Ice House St., Central, ☎ 2840–7788, FAX 2845–5526) both handle rentals area wide.

HOSTELS

No matter what your age, you can **save on lodging costs by staying at hostels.** The Hong Kong Youth Hostels Association is a full member of the International Youth Hostel Federation (Hostelling International). The main hostels, Bradbury Lodge and Ma Wui Hall are easily accessible by public transport. Both are less than HK$50 per night.

Membership in any HI national hostel association, open to travelers of all ages, allows you to stay in HI-affiliated hostels at member rates; one-year membership is about US$25 for adults (C$26.75 in Canada, £9.30 in the United Kingdom, A$30 in Australia, and NZ$30 in New Zealand); hostels run about US$10–$25 per night. Members have priority if the hostel is full; they're also eligible for discounts around the world, even on rail and bus travel in some countries.

➤ HOSTEL INFORMATION: **Bradbury Lodge** (⊠ 66 Ting Kok Rd., Tai Mei Tuk Tai Po, New Territories, ☎ 2662–5123). **Ma Wui Hall** (⊠ Top of Mt. Davis Path, Mt. Davis, Western District, Hong Kong, ☎ 2817–5715).

➤ ORGANIZATIONS: **Australian Youth Hostel Association** (⊠ 10 Mallett St., Camperdown, NSW 2050, Australia, ☎ 02/9565–1699, FAX 02/9565–1325, WEB www.yha.com.au). **Hostelling International—American Youth Hostels** (⊠ 733 15th St. NW, Suite 840, Washington, DC 20005, ☎ 202/783–6161, FAX 202/783–6171, WEB www.hiayh.org). **Hostelling International—Canada** (✉ 400–205 Catherine St., Ottawa, Ontario K2P 1C3, Canada, ☎ 613/237–7884, FAX 613/237–7868, WEB www.hostellingintl.ca). **Youth Hostel Association of England and Wales** (✉ Trevelyan House, 8 St. Stephen's Hill, St. Albans, Hertfordshire AL1 2DY, U.K., ☎ 0870/8708808, FAX 01727/844126, WEB www.yha.org.uk). **Youth Hostels Association of New Zealand** (✉ Box 436, Christchurch, New Zealand, ☎ 03/379–9970, FAX 03/365–4476, WEB www.yha.org.nz).

HOTELS

All hotels listed have private bath unless otherwise noted.

MAIL & SHIPPING

Hong Kong has an excellent reputation for its postal system. Airmail letters to any place in the world should take three to eight days.

➤ POST OFFICES: The **Kowloon Central Post Office** (✉ 10 Middle Rd., Tsim Tsa Shui) and the **General Post Office** (✉ 2 Connaught Rd., Central) are open 8 AM to 6 PM Monday through Saturday.

OVERNIGHT SERVICES

Overnight delivery services are available throughout the city. You will find drop-off boxes or offices in most subway stations, malls, and hotels. Fzor the office nearest you, call the company.

➤ MAJOR SERVICES: **DHL** (☎ 2765–8111), **Federal Express** (☎ 2730–3333), **United Parcel Service** (☎ 2735–3535).

POSTAL RATES

Letters sent from Hong Kong are thought of as going to one of two zones. Zone 1 includes China, Japan, Taiwan, South Korea, Southeast Asia, Indonesia, and Asia. Zone 2 is everywhere else. International airmail costs HK$2.10 for a letter or postcard weighing under 10 grams mailed to a Zone 1 address, and HK$2.60 for a letter sent to a Zone 2 address. For each additional 10 grams, you will be

charged HK$1.10 for Zone 1 and HK$1.20 for Zone 2.

RECEIVING MAIL

The **General Post Office** and **Kowloon Central Post Office** have poste restante counters.

Travelers with American Express cards or traveler's checks can receive mail at the **American Express** office (✉ 5 Queen's Rd., Central, ☎ 2811–6888). Have mail addressed c/o Client Mail Service at this address.

MONEY MATTERS

Prices throughout this guide are given for adults. Substantially reduced fees are almost always available for children, students, and senior citizens. For information on taxes, *see* Taxes, *below.*

ATMS

Reliable and safe, ATMs are widely available throughout Hong Kong. If your card was issued from a bank in an English-speaking country, the instructions on the ATM machine will appear in English.

CREDIT CARDS

Throughout this guide, the following abbreviations are used: **AE,** American Express; **DC,** Diners Club; **MC,** MasterCard; and **V,** Visa.

CURRENCY

Units of currency are the Hong Kong dollar ($) and the cent. Bills come in denominations of 1,000, 500, 100, 50, 20, and 10 dollars. Coins are 10, 5, 2, and 1 dollar and 50, 20, and 10 cents. At press time the Hong Kong dollar was fixed at approximately 7.8 dollars to the U.S. dollar, 6.52 to the Canadian dollar, and 12.5 to the pound sterling. The image of Queen Elizabeth II will not appear on new coins, but the old ones are still valid.

The official currency unit in Macau is the pataca, which is divided into 100 avos. Bank notes come in five denominations: 500, 100, 50, 10, and 5 patacas. Coins are 5 and 1 patacas and 50, 20, and 10 avos. The pataca is pegged to the Hong Kong dollar (within a few cents); at press time there were 8 patacas to the U.S. dollar. **Hong Kong currency circulates freely in Macau but not vice versa,** so remember to change your patacas before you return to Hong Kong.

CURRENCY EXCHANGE

There are no currency restrictions in Hong Kong. You can exchange currency at the airport, in hotels, in banks, and through private money changers scattered through the tourist areas. For the most favorable rates, **change money at banks.** You'll get better rates from a bank or money changer than from a hotel; just **beware of money changers who advertise "no selling commission"** without mentioning the "buying commission" you must pay when you exchange foreign currency or traveler's checks for Hong Kong dollars. Although ATM transaction fees may be higher abroad than at home, ATM rates are excellent because they are based on wholesale rates offered only by major banks. You won't do as well at exchange booths in airports or rail and bus stations, in hotels, in restaurants, or in stores. To avoid lines at airport exchange booths, **get a bit of local currency before you leave home.**

➤ EXCHANGE SERVICES: **International Currency Express** (☎ 888/278–6628 for orders, WEB www.foreignmoney. com). **Thomas Cook Currency Services** (☎ 800/287–7362 for telephone orders and retail locations, WEB www. us.thomascook.com).

TRAVELER'S CHECKS

Do you need traveler's checks? It depends on where you're headed. If you're going to rural areas and small towns, go with cash; traveler's checks are best used in cities. Lost or stolen checks can usually be replaced within 24 hours. To ensure a speedy refund, buy your own traveler's checks— don't let someone else pay for them: irregularities like this can cause delays. The person who bought the checks should make the call to request a refund.

PACKING

Dress in Hong Kong is generally informal. However, this is a city where suits are still *de rigueur* for meetings. From May through September, Hong Kong's high humidity warrants light clothing; but air-conditioning in hotels and restaurants can be arctic, so bring a sweater or shawl for evening use indoors. Don't forget your swimsuit and sunscreen; several hotels have pools, and you may want to spend some time on one of Hong Kong's many beaches. In October, November, March, and April, a jacket or sweater should suffice, but from December through February bring a raincoat or a light overcoat. At any time of year it's wise to **pack a folding umbrella.**

In your carry-on luggage, **pack an extra pair of eyeglasses or contact lenses and enough of any medication you take** to last the entire trip. You may also ask your doctor to write a spare prescription using the drug's generic name, since brand names may vary from country to country. In luggage to be checked, **never pack prescription drugs or valuables.** To avoid customs delays, carry medications in their original packaging. And don't forget to carry with you the addresses of offices that handle refunds of lost traveler's checks.

Check *Fodor's How to Pack* (available in bookstores everywhere) for more tips.

CHECKING LUGGAGE

Airlines flying *out* of Hong Kong are strictly enforcing carry-on rules, particularly among holders of economy tickets. Coach-class passengers are allowed only one bag, measuring not more than 9 x 14 x 22 inches and weighing not more than 44 pounds (20 kilograms), in addition to a handbag or briefcase. Business-class passengers get two bags, first-class passengers three.

If you are flying internationally, note that baggage allowances may be determined not by piece but by weight— generally 88 pounds (40 kilograms) in first class, 66 pounds (30 kilograms) in business class, and 44 pounds (20 kilograms) in economy.

Airline liability for baggage is limited to US$1,250 per person on flights within the United States. On international flights it amounts to US$9.07 per pound or US$20 per kilogram for checked baggage (roughly US$640 per 70-pound bag) and US$400 per passenger for unchecked baggage. You can buy additional coverage at check-in for about US$10 per US$1,000 of coverage, but it excludes a rather extensive list of items, shown on your airline ticket.

Before departure, **itemize your bags' contents** and their worth, and label the bags with your name, address, and phone number. (If you use your home address, cover it so potential thieves can't see it readily.) Inside each bag, **pack a copy of your itinerary.** At check-in, **make sure that each bag is correctly tagged** with the destination airport's three-letter code. If your bags arrive damaged or fail to arrive at all, file a written report with the airline before leaving the airport.

PASSPORTS & VISAS

When traveling internationally, **carry your passport** even if you don't need one (it's always the best form of I.D.) and **make two photocopies of the data page** (one for someone at home and another for you, carried separately from your passport). If you lose your passport, promptly call the nearest embassy or consulate and the local police.

ENTERING HONG KONG

Citizens of the United Kingdom need only a valid passport to enter Hong Kong for stays of up to six months. Australian, Canadian, New Zealand, and U.S. citizens need only a valid passport to enter Hong Kong for stays up to three months. It is best to have at least six months' validity on your passport before traveling to Asia.

PASSPORT OFFICES

The best time to apply for a passport or to renew is in fall and winter. Before any trip, check your passport's expiration date, and, if necessary, renew it as soon as possible.

➤ AUSTRALIAN CITIZENS: **Australian Passport Office** (☎ 131–232, WEB www.dfat.gov.au/passports).

➤ CANADIAN CITIZENS: **Passport Office** (☎ 819/994–3500; 800/567–6868 in Canada, WEB www.dfait-maeci.gc.ca/passport).

➤ NEW ZEALAND CITIZENS: **New Zealand Passport Office** (☎ 04/494–0700, WEB www.passports.govt.nz).

➤ U.K. CITIZENS: **London Passport Office** (☎ 0870/521–0410, WEB www.ukpa.gov.uk) for fees and documentation requirements and to request an emergency passport.

➤ U.S. CITIZENS: **National Passport Information Center** (☎ 900/225–5674; calls are 35¢ per minute for automated service, US$1.05 per minute for operator service; WEB www.travel.state.gov/npiinfo.html).

REST ROOMS

Public rest rooms are difficult to find in Hong Kong. Clean, Western-style rest rooms (as opposed to squatters, which are merely holes in the ground) are even more difficult to find. Although the situation is gradually improving, bring tissues or a toilet-paper roll. Using hotel and restaurant bathrooms is the best bet for a clean environment.

RICKSHAWS

Because rickshaws are a tourist attraction rather than a common mode of transportation, prices run high. Rates are supposed to be around HK$50 for a five-minute ride, but rickshaw operators are merciless. A posed snapshot can cost almost as much as a ride. When you hire a rickshaw or take an operator's picture, **bargain aggressively and agree on the price in advance.**

SAFETY

Hong Kong is a relatively safe city day or night. The Hong Kong Police who served under the British government continue to maintain law and order. Avoid carrying large amounts of cash or valuables. Pickpockets are an increasing problem in Hong Kong.

SENIOR-CITIZEN TRAVEL

To qualify for age-related discounts, **mention your senior-citizen status up front** when booking hotel reservations (not when checking out) and before you're seated in restaurants (not when paying the bill). When renting a car, ask about promotional car-rental discounts, which can be cheaper than senior-citizen rates.

➤ EDUCATIONAL PROGRAMS: **Elderhostel** (⊠ 11 Ave. de Lafayette, Boston, MA 02111-1746, ☎ 877/426–8056, FAX 877/426–2166, WEB www. elderhostel.org). **Folkways Institute** (⊠ 14600 S.E. Aldridge Rd., Portland, OR 97236-6518, ☎ 503/658–6600 or 800/225–4666, FAX 503/658–8672, WEB www.folkwaystravel.com). **Interhostel** (⊠ University of New Hampshire, 6 Garrison Ave., Durham, NH 03824, ☎ 603/862–1147 or 800/733–9753, FAX 603/862–1113, WEB www.learn.unh.edu).

SHOPPING

If you buy and ship home Chinese lacquer or other breakable keepsakes, **buy an all-risk insurance policy.** Ivory has long been a prized souvenir of trips to the Orient, but in 1990 the Hong Kong government imposed a stringent policy on the import and export of this bone derivative. As a result, you must get an import license from your country of residence, as well as an export license to take ivory out of Hong Kong. Failure to comply may result in a fine and forfeiture of the purchase. If you're considering buying ivory, check with the **Hong Kong Department of Agriculture and Fisheries** (☎ 2708–8885), as well as your home consulate or trade commission, for the latest regulations. Remember that all goods—with the exceptions of alcohol, tobacco, petroleum, perfume, cosmetics, and soft drinks—are duty-free everywhere in Hong Kong, not just in "duty-free" stores. Bargaining, even at street markets, has become increasingly rare.

Beware of merchants who claim to be giving you a "special" price; you may not get what you actually pay for.

SIGHTSEEING TOURS

The HKTB offers walking and exploring tours in Hong Kong, many of which can be personalized, including a very informative Feng Shui tour of Central. In addition to standard tours of Hong Kong, Splendid Tours & Travel offers tailor-made trips that can take you hiking through the jungle—or through a jungle of shops.

➤ SIGHTSEEING TOURS: **HKTB Visitor Hot Line** (☎ 2508–1234). **Splendid Tours & Travel** (⊠ 26/F Lockville Commercial Bldg., 25–27 Lock Rd., TST, Kowloon, ☎ 2316–2151, FAX 2312–2031, WEB www. splendidtours.com).

STUDENTS IN HONG KONG

To save money, **look into deals available through student-oriented travel agencies.** You need only a valid student ID card to qualify. Members of international student groups are also eligible.

➤ I.D.s & SERVICES: **Council Travel** (CIEE; ⊠ 205 E. 42nd St., 15th floor, New York, NY 10017, ☎ 212/822–2700 or 888/268–6245, FAX 212/822–2699, WEB www.councilexchanges.org) for mail orders only, in the United States. **Travel Cuts** (⊠ 187 College St., Toronto, Ontario M5T 1P7, Canada, ☎ 416/979–2406; 800/667–2887 in Canada, FAX 416/979–8167, WEB www.travelcuts.com).

SUBWAY TRAVEL

The four-line Mass Transit Railway (MTR) links Hong Kong Island to Kowloon (the shopping area Tsim Sha Tsui) and parts of the New Territories. Trains run frequently and are safe and easy to use. Station entrances are marked with a simple line symbol resembling a man with arms and legs outstretched. You buy tickets from ticket machines; change is available at the stations' Hang Seng Bank counters and from the machines themselves. Fares range from HK$4 to HK$26.

DISCOUNT PASSES

The special Tourist Ticket (HK$25) can save you money. Another bulk-value possibility is the Stored Value Ticket, which also provides access to the aboveground Kowloon Canton Railway (KCR). Tickets are HK$70, HK$100, and HK$200.

➤ SUBWAY INFORMATION: **HKTB Visitor Hot Line** (☎ 2508–1234). **Mass Transit Railway** (MTR; ☎ 2881–8888).

TAXES

Hong Kong levies a 10% service charge and a 3% government tax on hotel rooms.

TAXIS

Taxis in Hong Kong and Kowloon are usually red. A taxi's roof sign lights up when the car is available. Fares in urban areas are HK$15 for the first 2 km (1 mi) and HK$1.20 for each additional ⅕ km (⅒ mi). There is luggage surcharge of HK$5 per large piece, and surcharges of HK$20 for the Cross-Harbour Tunnel, HK$30 for the Eastern Harbour Tunnel, and HK$45 for the Western Harbour Tunnel. The Tsing Ma Bridge surcharge is HK$30. The Aberdeen, Lion Rock, and Junk Bay tunnels also carry small surcharges (HK$3–HK$8). Taxis cannot pick up passengers where there are double yellow lines. Note that it's hard to find a taxi around 4 PM when the drivers switch shifts.

Many taxi drivers do not speak English, so you may want to **ask someone at your hotel to write out your destination in Chinese.**

Backseat passengers must **wear a seatbelt or face a HK$5,000 fine.** Most locals do not tip; however, if you do—HK$5–HK$10—you're sure to earn yourself a winning smile from your underpaid and overworked taxi driver.

Outside the urban areas, taxis are green (blue on Lantau Island). Cabs in the New Territories cost less than urban taxis: HK$11.80 for the first 2 km (1 mi) and HK$1.10 for each additional ⅕ km (⅒ mi). Urban taxis may travel into rural zones, but rural taxis must not cross into urban zones. There are no interchange facilities for the two, so **do not try to reach an urban area using a green taxi.**

COMPLAINTS

Taxis are usually reliable, but if you have a problem **note the taxi's license number,** which is usually on the dashboard. The complaint hot line is ☎ 2577–6866 or 2889–9999.

TELEPHONES

Hong Kong phone numbers are comprised of eight digits. The local telephone system is efficient and telephone owners pay a flat monthly fee, not a per-call tariff; international calls are inexpensive relative to those in the United States. You can expect a clear-sounding connection. Directory assistance is helpful.

AREA & COUNTRY CODES

The country code for Hong Kong is 852. When dialing a Hong Kong number from abroad, drop the initial 0 from the local area code. The country code is 1 for the United States and Canada, 61 for Australia, 64 for New Zealand, and 44 for the United Kingdom.

The country code for Macau is 853; for China, 086.

DIRECTORY & OPERATOR ASSISTANCE

Dial 1081 for directory assistance from English-speaking operators. If a number is constantly busy and you think it might be out of order, call 109 and the operator will check the line. The operators are very helpful, if you talk slowly and clearly. However, do not be surprised if you call a local business and they simply hang up on you; often when local, nonnative English speakers don't understand you, they simply hang up rather than stammer through a conversation and lose face.

LOCAL CALLS

Given that your hotel will likely charge you for a local call, you might consider simply walking out of your hotel, stopping at the nearest shop, and asking the shopkeeper if you can use the phone. Most locals will not charge you to you use their phone for a local call since the phone company does not charge for individual local calls.

LONG-DISTANCE CALLS

You can dial direct from many hotel and business centers, but always with a hefty surcharge. Dial 013 for international inquiries and for assistance with direct dialing. Dial 10010 for operator-assisted calls to most countries, including the United States, Canada, and the United Kingdom. Dial 10011 for credit-card, collect, and international conference calls.

You can also make long-distance calls from **Hong Kong Telecom International** (✉ Hong Kong Trade Centre, Des Voeux Rd., Central, ☎ 2543–0603; ✉ TST Hermes House, Kowloon, ☎ 2888–7184 or 2888–7185). Here you dial direct from specially marked silver-color phone booths that take phone cards (available from Hong Kong Telephone Company's retail shops and 7-Eleven convenience stores throughout the island). The cards have values of HK$25, HK$50, and HK$100, and multilingual instructions for their use are posted in the phone booths.

LONG-DISTANCE SERVICES

AT&T, MCI, and Sprint access codes make calling long distance relatively convenient, but you may find the local access number blocked in many hotel rooms. First ask the hotel operator to connect you. If the hotel operator balks, ask for an international operator, or dial the international operator yourself. One way to improve your odds of getting connected to your long-distance carrier is to travel with more than one company's calling card (a hotel may block Sprint, for example, but not MCI). If all else fails, call from a pay phone.

➤ ACCESS CODES: **AT&T Direct** (☎ 800/435–0812). **MCI WorldPhone** (☎ 800/444–4141). **Sprint International Access** (☎ 800/877–4646).

PUBLIC PHONES

To make a local call from a pay phone, use a HK$1 coin or, at some phones, a credit card. Pay phones are not hard to find, but locals generally pop into a store and ask to use the phone there, as local calls are free on residence and business lines. Many small stores keep their telephone on the counter facing the street.

To make international calls from a pay phone, stop by a 7-Eleven or other convenience store and purchase a prepaid phone card.

Watch for multimedia Powerphones, whose touch screens allow you to check e-mail and send faxes as well as phone home.

TIME

Hong Kong is 12 hours ahead of Eastern Standard Time and 7 hours ahead of Greenwich Mean Time. Remember during daylight savings time to add an hour to the time difference.

TIPPING

Hotels and major restaurants usually add a 10% service charge; however, almost in all cases, this money does not go to the waiters and waitresses. Proprietors will tell you it goes to the cost of replacing broken crockery, napkins, and so on. If you want to tip a waiter or waitress, be sure to give it directly to that person and no one else. It is generally not the custom to leave an additional tip in restaurants, taxis, and beauty salons; but, if you do choose to tip, you'll receive more attentive service and make the usually not-very-well-paid employees immensely happy. If you buy your newspaper from a corner vendor, consider searching for one of the numerous octogenarians who are sadly still working for a living—leaving your extra change with these people is also another much appreciated tip.

TOURS & PACKAGES

Because everything is prearranged on a prepackaged tour or independent vacation, you'll spend less time planning—and often get it all at a good price.

BOOKING WITH AN AGENT

Travel agents are excellent resources. But it's a good idea to collect brochures from several agencies as some agents' suggestions may be influenced by relationships with tour and package firms that reward them for volume sales. If you have a special interest, **find an agent with expertise in that area**; ASTA (☞ Travel Agencies, *below*) has a database of specialists worldwide.

Make sure your travel agent knows the accommodations and other services of the place they're recommending. Ask about the hotel's location, room size, beds, and whether it has a pool, room service, or programs for children, if you care about these. Has your agent been there in person or sent others whom you can contact?

Do some homework on your own, too: local tourism boards can provide information about lesser-known and small-niche operators, some of which may sell only direct.

BUYER BEWARE

Each year consumers are stranded or lose their money when tour operators—even large ones with excellent reputations—go out of business. So **check out the operator.** Ask several travel agents about its reputation, and try to **book with a company that has a consumer-protection program.** (Look for information in the company's brochure.) In the United States, members of the National Tour Association and the United States Tour Operators Association are required to set aside funds to cover your payments and travel arrangements in the event that the company defaults. It's also a good idea to choose a company that participates in the American Society of Travel Agents' Tour Operator Program (TOP); ASTA will act as mediator in any disputes between you and your tour operator.

Remember that the more your package or tour includes the better you can predict the ultimate cost of your vacation. Make sure you know exactly what is covered, and **beware of hidden costs.** Are taxes, tips, and transfers included? Entertainment and excursions? These can add up.

➤ TOUR-OPERATOR RECOMMENDATIONS: **American Society of Travel Agents** (☞ Travel Agencies, *below*). **National Tour Association** (NTA; ✉ 546 E. Main St., Lexington, KY 40508, ☎ 859/226–4444 or 800/682–8886, WEB www.ntaonline.com). **United States Tour Operators Association** (USTOA; ✉ 342 Madison Ave., Suite 1522, New York, NY 10173, ☎ 212/599–6599 or 800/468–7862, FAX 212/599–6744, WEB www.ustoa.com).

TRAIN TRAVEL

The **Kowloon–Canton Railway** (KCR) has 13 commuter stops on its 34-km (22-mi) journey through urban Kowloon (from Kowloon to Lo Wu) and the new cities of Shatin and Taipo on its way to the Chinese border. The main station is at Hung Hom, Kowloon, where you can catch express trains to China. Fares range from HK$7.50 to HK$40, and no reservations are required. The KCR meets the MTR at the **Kowloon Tong** station. In the New Territories, the **Light Rail Transit** connects Tuen Mun and Yuen Long.

➤ TRAIN INFORMATION: **Light Rail Transit** (☎ 2468–7788). **Kowloon–Canton Railway** (KCR; ☎ 2947–7888). **Kowloon Tong station** (☎ 2602–7799).

TRAVEL CARD

The electronic Octopus Card (HK$100) is accepted on the MTR, Kowloon Canton Railway (KCR), Kowloon Motor Bus (KMB), and Citybus. You can buy the card at ticket offices and HKTB outlets; you place a refundable deposit of HK$50 on it, then reload it with HK$50 or HK$100 increments at Add Value machines or at one of the service counters inside the station. For more information, call **HKTB** (✉ The Center, 99 Queen's Rd., Central; ✉ Star Ferry Concourse, Kowloon; ☎ 2508–1234).

TRAMS

STREET TRAMS

Trams run along the north shore of Hong Kong Island from Kennedy Town (in the west) all the way through Central, Wanchai, Causeway Bay, North Point, and Quarry Bay, ending in the former fishing village of Shaukiwan. A branch line turns off in Wanchai toward Happy Valley, where horse races are held in season. Destinations are marked on the front of each tram; the fare is HK$2. **Avoid trams at rush hours,** which are generally 7:30–9 AM and 5–7 PM each weekday. Trams are generally quite slow, and a great way to inhale a lung full of car fumes, but they also give you an opportunity to see the city from a slow-moving vehicle.

PEAK TRAM

Dating from 1888, this railway rises from ground level to Victoria Peak (1,305 ft), offering a panoramic view of Hong Kong. Both residents and tourists use it; most passengers board at the lower terminus between Garden Road and Cotton Tree Drive. (The tram has five stations.) The fare is HK$18 one-way, HK$28 round-trip, and the tram runs every 10–15 minutes daily from 7 AM to midnight. A free shuttle bus runs between the lower terminus and the Star Ferry.

TRANSPORTATION
AROUND HONG KONG

Comprising a collection of islands in the South China Sea and a chunk of the Chinese mainland, Hong Kong may have more varieties of transportation than any other city in the world.

Buses (☞ Bus Travel Around Hong Kong, *above*) run throughout Hong Kong Island, Kowloon, and the New Territories, and along a number of routes linking the two sides of the harbor.

Ferries (☞ Boat & Ferry Travel, *above*) and a **subway system** (☞ Subway Travel, *above*) connect Hong Kong Island with the Kowloon peninsula and the Outer Islands.

Trains (☞ Train Travel, *above*) travel north from Kowloon serving cities all the way to the Chinese border. You can also opt for a limousine (the Mandarin and the Peninsula hotels rent chauffeur-driven Rolls-Royces), a car with driver (☞ Car Rental, *above*), or a touristy rickshaw (☞ Rickshaws, *above*).

Hong Kong Island has two kinds of **trams** (☞ Trams, *above*): a street-level tram that runs across the north shore, and the Peak Tram, a funicular railway that climbs Victoria Peak.

TRAVEL AGENCIES

A good travel agent puts your needs first. Look for an agency that has been in business at least five years, emphasizes customer service, and has someone on staff who specializes in your destination. In addition, **make sure the agency belongs to a professional trade organization.** The American Society of Travel Agents (ASTA), with more than 26,000 members in some 170 countries, is the largest and most influential in the field. Operating under the motto "Without a travel agent, you're on your own," it maintains and enforces a strict code of ethics and will step in to help mediate any agent-client disputes if necessary. ASTA also maintains a Web site that includes a directory of agents. (If a travel agency is also acting as your tour operator, *see* Buyer Beware *in* Tours & Packages, *above*.)

➤ LOCAL AGENT REFERRALS: American Society of Travel Agents (ASTA; ☎ 800/965–2782 24-hr hot line, FAX 703/739–7642, WEB www.astanet. com). Association of British Travel Agents (✉ 68–71 Newman St., London W1T 3AH, U.K., ☎ 020/7637–2444, FAX 020/7637–0713, WEB www. abtanet.com). Association of Canadian Travel Agents (✉ 130 Albert St., Ste. 1705, Ottawa, Ontario K1P 5G4, Canada, ☎ 613/237–3657, FAX 613/237–7502, WEB www.acta.net). Australian Federation of Travel Agents (✉ Level 3, 309 Pitt St., Sydney, NSW 2000, Australia, ☎ 02/9264–3299, FAX 02/9264–1085, WEB www.afta.com. au). Travel Agents' Association of New Zealand (✉ Box 1888, Wellington 10033, New Zealand, ☎ 04/499–0104, FAX 04/499–0827, WEB www. taanz.org.nz).

VISITOR INFORMATION

For general Hong Kong and Macau information before you go, contact the **Hong Kong Tourist Board (HKTB)** and **Macau Government Tourist Office** locations below. When you arrive, stop by an HKTB information center in Hong Kong.

➤ IN THE U.S.: HKTB (✉ 590 5th Ave., Suite 590, New York, NY 10036, ☎ 212/869–5008, FAX 212/730–2605; ✉ 610 Enterprise Dr., Suite 200, Oak Brook, IL 60521, ☎ 630/575–2828, FAX 630/575–2829; ✉ 10940 Wilshire Blvd., Suite 1220, Los Angeles, CA 90024, ☎ 310/208–4582, FAX 310/208–1869). Macau Government Tourist Office (✉ Box 350, Kenilworth, IL 60043, ☎ 847/251–6421 or 800/331–7150, FAX 847/256–5601).

➤ IN CANADA: HKTB (✉ 9 Temperance St., 3rd floor, Toronto, Ontario M5H 1Y6, ☎ 416/366–2389, FAX 416/366–1098).

➤ IN THE U.K.: HKTB (✉ 6 Grafton St., London W1X 3LB, ☎ 0711/530–

7100, FAX 020/7/533–7111). **Macau Government Tourist Office** (✉ 1 Battersea Church Rd., London SW11 3LY, ☎ 020/7/771–7006, FAX 020/7/771–7059).

➤ IN AUSTRALIA: **HKTB** (✉ Level 4, Hong Kong House, 80 Druitt St., Sydney NSW200, ☎ 612/928–3083, FAX 612/929–3383).

➤ IN HONG KONG: **HKTB** (✉ Star Ferry Concourse, Kowloon; ✉ The Center, 99 Queen's Rd. Central, Central, Hong Kong Island; ✉ Hong Kong International Airport). For round-the-clock phone assistance, call the multilingual **Visitor Hot Line** (☎ 2508–1234). For a printout of specific details, contact the 24-hour fax information service (FAX 900/6077–1128).

➤ U.S. GOVERNMENT ADVISORIES: **U.S. Department of State** (✉ Overseas Citizens Services Office, Room 4811 N.S., 2201 C St. NW, Washington, DC 20520, ☎ 202/647–5225 for interactive hot line, WEB travel.state.gov/travel/html).

WALKING

If you're not defeated by heat, Hong Kong is a pleasant place to stroll. On Hong Kong Island you might enjoy a walk through the very traditional Western district, where life has changed little over the years. If you really like to roam, **take a long hike in the New Territories or on Lantau Island.** The HKTB has self-guided tours of these distinct areas; each includes a map and detailed instructions for connecting the dots.

WEB SITES

Do check out the World Wide Web when you're planning your trip. You'll find everything from weather forecasts to virtual tours of famous cities. Be sure to **visit Fodors.com** (www.fodors.com), a complete travel planning site. You can research prices and book plane tickets, hotel rooms, rental cars, vacation packages, and more. In addition, you can post your pressing questions in the Travel Talk section. Other planning tools include a currency converter and weather

reports, and there are loads of links to other travel resources.

For a comprehensive guide to what's happening in Hong Kong, check out the HKTB's excellent site, www.discoverhongkong.com. For the latest political information plus news and interesting business links try the official Hong Kong government site at www.info.gov.hk. Hong Kong iMail Newspaper's site at www.hk-imail.com has the day's news and a look at what's happening in Hong Kong and the region. For an overview of tourism information and sites in Macau, visit www.macautourism.gov.mo.

WHEN TO GO

Hong Kong's high season, October through late December, is popular for a reason: the weather is pleasant, with sunny days and cool, comfortable nights. January, February, and sometimes early March are cold and dank, with long periods of overcast skies and rain. March and April can be either cold and miserable or sunny and beautiful. By May the temperature is consistently warm and comfortable.

June through September is typhoon season, when the weather is hot, sticky, and very rainy. Typhoons (called hurricanes in the Atlantic) must be treated with respect, and Hong Kong is prepared for these blustery assaults; if a storm is approaching, the airwaves will crackle with information, and your hotel and various public institutions will post the appropriate signals. When a No. 8 signal is posted, Hong Kong and Macau close down completely. Head immediately for your hotel and stay put. This is serious business—bamboo scaffolding can come hurtling through the streets like spears, ships can be sunk in the harbor, and large areas of the territory are often flooded.

Macau's summers are slightly cooler and wetter than Hong Kong's.

➤ FORECASTS: **Weather Channel Connection** (☎ 900/932–8437), 95¢ per minute from a Touch-Tone phone.

Smart Travel Tips A to Z

CLIMATE

The following are average daily maximum and minimum temperatures for Hong Kong.

Jan.	64F	18C	May	82F	28C	Sept.	85F	29C
	56	13		74	23		77	25
Feb.	63F	17C	June	85F	29C	Oct.	81F	27C
	55	13		78	26		73	23
Mar.	67F	19C	July	87F	31C	Nov.	74F	23C
	60	16		78	26		65	18
Apr.	75F	24C	Aug.	87F	31C	Dec.	68F	20C
	67	19		78	26		59	15

1   DESTINATION: HONG KONG

FROM CHINA TO CHINA

WHEN YOU FLY to Hong Kong, try to get a window seat. As you approach the coast of China you'll see a few small, rocky islands, tiny fishing boats, and sailboats in the channels leading into Hong Kong Harbour—one of the most spectacular harbors in the world.

Hong Kong is Cantonese for "fragrant harbor," a name inspired either by the incense factories that once dotted Hong Kong Island or by the profusion of scented pink *Bauhinias,* the national flower (whose representation has recently replaced colonial insignias).

Hong Kong is on the southeast coast of China, at the mouth of the Pearl River, on the same latitude as Hawaii and Cuba. By air, it's 2¾ hours from Beijing, 18 hours from New York, 12¼ hours from San Francisco, and 13 hours from London. It consists of three parts: Hong Kong Island, roughly 82 square km (32 square mi); Kowloon, 9 square km (3½ square mi); and the New Territories, about 945 square km (365 square mi). Its land mass grows, however, through land-reclamation projects, causing Hong Kong Harbour to narrow.

The name Hong Kong refers to the overall territory as well as to the main island, which is across the harbor from Kowloon. The island's principal business district is officially named Victoria, but everyone calls it Central. The island also contains the districts of Wanchai, Causeway Bay, Repulse Bay, Stanley, and Aberdeen. Kowloon includes Tsim Sha Tsui, Tsim Sha Tsui East, Hung Hom, Mong Kok/Yau Ma Tei, and the area north to Boundary Street. The New Territories begin at Boundary Street and extend north to the border with mainland China, encompassing the container port, the former Kai Tak airport, most of the major factories, and the outlying islands.

Hong Kong is 98% Chinese. Although the territory's official languages are English and Cantonese, the use of Mandarin (or *Putonghua*), China's official language, is on the rise. Many other languages and dialects are spoken here, including Hakka (the language of a group of early settlers from China), Tanka (the language of the original boat people who came here some 5,000 years ago), and Shanghainese. Among the nationalities living in Hong Kong, some 150,000 Filipinos make up the largest foreign community; most are women working as maids and nannies (*amahs* in local parlance), and can be seen socializing en masse in Statue Square on their day off, usually Sunday.

The three great strands of Chinese thought—Buddhism, Taoism, and Confucianism—together with Christianity make up Hong Kong's major religions, and you'll see signs of them everywhere. Chinese people tend toward eclecticism in their beliefs, so the distinctions between faiths are often blurred. It's not uncommon for the same person to put out food and incense for his departed ancestors at Spring Festival time, invite a Taoist priest to his home to exorcise unhappy ghosts, pray in a Buddhist temple for fertility, and take communion in a Christian church.

Hong Kong's earliest visitors are believed to have been people of Malaysian-Oceanic origin who came here by boat about 5,000 years ago. Their geometric-style drawings are still visible on rocks in Big Wave Bay (on Hong Kong Island) and on Po Toi Island. The earliest structure found so far is the 1,600-year old Han Dynasty tomb at Lei Cheng Uk Museum. More than 600 years later, the Tang Dynasty left lime kilns full of seashells—an archaeological mystery, as there are no clues indicating how or why the lime was used.

Records from the 13th century tell us Sung Dynasty loyalists fled China with their child emperor to escape the invading Mongols. The last of the Sung Dynasty emperors, a 10-year-old boy, is said to have spent a night in the late 1270s near the site of Hong Kong's former airport. One of his men is credited with naming Kowloon, which means "nine dragons" (he counted eight mountain peaks that resembled dragons and added one for the emperor, who was also considered a dragon). The boy was the only Chinese emperor believed to have set foot in what is now Hong Kong. Today, anyone visiting Po Lin Monastery, high in the mountains of Lantau Island, will pass Shek Pik Reservoir, where innumerable Sung Dynasty coins were found during the reservoir's excavation.

Western traders first appeared in the Hong Kong area in 1513. The first were Portuguese, but they were soon followed by the Spanish, Dutch, English, and French. All were bent on making fortunes trading porcelain, tea, and silk. Until 1757 the Chinese restricted all foreigners to neighboring Macau, the Portuguese territory 64 km (40 mi) across the Pearl River estuary. After 1757, traders (but not their families) were allowed to live just outside Canton for about eight months each year. Canton—also known by its Chinese name, Guangzhou—is only 30 minutes from Hong Kong by plane or three hours by train or hovercraft.

Trading in Canton was frustrating for the foreigners: It took at least 20 days for messages to be relayed to the emperor; local officials had to be bribed; and Chinese justice seemed unfair. For Western traders, life in Canton consisted of a lot of buying and little selling. At that time China was the world's premier source of silk, tea, porcelain, and textiles—they wanted nothing from the West except silver, until the British started offering opium.

T HE SPREAD OF the opium habit and the growing outflow of silver alarmed high Chinese officials as early as 1729. They issued edicts forbidding importation of the drug, but these rules were regularly circumvented. Then, in 1839, a heroic and somewhat fanatical imperial commissioner, Lin Ze-xu (Lin Tse-hsu), laid siege to the foreign factories in Canton and detained the traders until they surrendered more than 20,000 chests of the drug, almost a year's worth of trade. The Westerners also signed bonds promising to desist from dealing opium forever, upon threat of death. The opium was destroyed. The British continued to press the issue, however, and the resulting tension between the government and foreign traders led to the Opium Wars and a succession of unequal treaties enforced by superior British firepower. The most important of these treaties required China to cede the island of Hong Kong to Britain; later, another treaty added Kowloon. Finally, in 1898, China leased the New Territories to Britain for 99 years—it was the expiration of this lease that led to the handover in 1997.

British-ruled Hong Kong flourished from the start of trade, especially the trade in opium, which was not outlawed in Hong Kong until after World War II. The population grew quickly, from 4,000 in 1841 to more than 23,000 in 1847, as Hong Kong attracted anyone anxious to make money or to escape the fetters of feudalism and family.

Each convulsion on the Chinese mainland—the Taiping Rebellion in the mid-1800s, the 1911 republican revolution, the rule of warlords of the 1920s, the 1937 Japanese invasion—pushed another group of refugees into Hong Kong. Then Japan invaded Hong Kong itself. The population, 1.4 million just before the Japanese arrived, dropped to a low of 600,000 by 1945. Many Hong Kong residents were forced to flee to Macau and the rural areas of China. Older locals still remember the Japanese period with bitterness.

The largest group of Chinese refugees came in the wake of the Chinese civil war between the Nationalists and the Communists, which ended with a Communist victory in 1949. Many refugees, especially the Shanghainese (including the shipping family of Hong Kong's new chief executive, Tung Chee-hwa), brought capital and business skills. Hong Kong's population was 1.8 million in 1947; by 1961 it stood at 3.7 million. And for 25 days in 1962, when food was in short supply in China, Chinese border guards allowed 70,000 Chinese to walk into Hong Kong.

During China's antilandlord, anticapitalist, and antirightist campaigns, and especially during the Cultural Revolution (1967–76), more and more refugees risked both imprisonment and the sharks in Mirs Bay to reach Hong Kong. In 1967, inspired by the leftist fanaticism of the Red Guards in China, local sympathizers and activists in Hong Kong set off bombs, organized labor strikes, and demonstrated against the British rulers and Hong Kong's Chinese policemen. They taunted the latter by asking, "Will the British take you when they go?" But the revolutionaries did not have popular support, and the disruptions in Hong Kong lasted less than a year.

In the 30 years after the establishment of the People's Republic of China in 1949–50, about a half million mainlanders came to Hong Kong, disillusioned with communism and eager for a better standard of living for themselves and their families.

Until October 1980 the Hong Kong government had a curious "touch-base" policy—a critical game of hide-and-seek, or survival of the fittest. Any Chinese who managed to get past the barbed wire, attack dogs, and tough border patrols to the urban areas was allowed to stay and work. Local industries needed labor then. At first, a similarly lenient policy was applied to Vietnamese refugees who arrived between 1975 and 1982: more than 100,000 were allowed to work in Hong Kong pending transfer to permanent homes abroad, and 14,000 were given permanent-resident status. As the number of countries willing to take the Vietnamese dwindled, however, Hong Kong detained the 20,000 most recent arrivals in closed camps resembling prisons, in the hope that no more boat people would choose to make the trip. Amid much controversy and the dismay of human rights groups, all of the detained Vietnamese were returned to Vietnam before the handover.

In the early 1980s a worldwide recession made jobs harder to find. As the population continued to increase, the standard of services in Hong Kong began to deteriorate. After consulting China, the government decreed that everyone had to carry a Hong Kong identification card. Now, after the handover, mainlanders can apply to the Chinese government to request settlement in Hong Kong, but entries are restricted.

The fate of Hong Kong after the expiration of the New Territories lease on June 30, 1997, was the question hanging over the colony from the moment British Prime Minister Margaret Thatcher set foot in Beijing in September 1982 to start talks with China's paramount leader Deng Xiaoping. Stating from the outset that he intended to take back all of Hong Kong, Deng set the tone for a series of acrimonious talks at which no negotiations were possible. Though only the New Territories (NT) lease was due to expire, Hong Kong was not a viable entity without it: the NT consists of 97% of the land. Since Deng would not countenance a partial solution, a full re-

turn was inevitable. Discussions between China and Britain lasted for nearly two years, with China applying pressure by announcing in early 1984 that if no solution were found by September 1984 it would declare one unilaterally. With that, British resistance buckled; so the final agreement was broadly in line with China's wishes: Hong Kong would become a Special Administrative Region (SAR) under the Chinese flag, with a Chinese leader (called a chief executive) and a 50-year guarantee of autonomy, effective July 1, 1997. The deal was labeled "One Country, Two Systems."

HONG KONG'S ECONOMY did not react well to this political uncertainty. Land prices fell. The stock market plunged by as much as 50% from late 1981 to late 1983. The Hong Kong dollar plummeted in value, careening from HK$5.7 to the U.S. dollar at the end of 1981 to almost HK$10 in September 1983. This forced the government to intervene, albeit reluctantly. For stabilization's sake, the currency was pegged at HK$7.80 to the U.S. dollar with a unique Exchange Rate Mechanism, and this peg still stands, though it does make Hong Kong vulnerable to overseas inflationary pressures.

One of the greatest concerns for Hong Kongers was the issue of post-handover citizenship, since the British, fearful of a wave of Chinese moving to the United Kingdom, offered them only a British Nationals Overseas (BNO) passport, a kind of second-class document that allowed Hong Kongers to travel as British citizens but did not give them the right of abode in the United Kingdom. As a result, emigration—mainly to Canada, Australia, Britain, the United States, New Zealand, and Singapore—reached record levels, topping out at some 60,000 skilled Hong Kongers (and their families) annually, from doctors and architects to computer technicians and teachers, as they sought to acquire a foreign passport that would give them a sanctuary in the event that post-handover Hong Kong became intolerable. Many of them continued to do business in the territory, however, so as soon as they acquired their passports the flow reversed and they returned—along with their new-found prowess in English and experience abroad, making them one of the most sought-after groups for headhunters seeking to fill executive positions.

When the handover finally came, it was beamed live around the world and watched by hundreds of millions. At the stroke of midnight ushering in July 1, 1997, Prince Charles, representing his mother, Queen Elizabeth II, officially handed over this British Crown Colony 156 years, 5 months, and 10 days after Royal Navy captain Charles Elliot claimed Hong Kong Island for Queen Victoria. The recipient was China's President Jiang Zemin, the late Deng Xiaoping's chosen heir, who claimed the prize for the motherland in the vast Hong Kong Convention and Exhibition Centre in front of 5,000 specially invited guests (among them British Prime Minister Tony Blair and U.S. Secretary of State Madeleine Albright). Those watching also saw the heavens open—more rain fell that week than Hong Kong normally gets in a year—and a rain-soaked Prince Charles, accompanied by an equally drenched Chris Patten, the last British governor, sailed away in the Royal Yacht *Britannia* in the wee hours of July 1. Royal standards flying high, the royal yacht sailed slowly through the harbor, trailed by a Royal Navy destroyer, to join the waiting British fleet and lead it away from what had often been called the last jewel in Britain's colonial crown. Back in the Convention Centre, celebrations continued.

The rain itself inspired local commentary: were the gods washing the Brits away or weeping for them? In any case, the downpour ruined the grand entrance of the People's Liberation Army, which had timed the arrival of its main body of troops for 6:30 AM July 1—just in time for live, prime-time coverage in the United States. The soldiers duly arrived, standing at rigid attention in the backs of open trucks in a watery deluge, but the rain put a damper on the intended visual effect.

The new Special Administrative Region (SAR) government convened the Provisional Legislative Council (LegCo; Hong Kong's parliament) in the first few hours of its rule to swear in its members. The first step taken by the LegCo, at the behest of the Central Government, was to repeal the Bill of Rights that the last British governor, Chris Patten, had managed to get passed in order to calm those apprehensive of the future. As draconian as the repeal sounds, what was implemented instead was the original, long-standing British law concerning assembly. Under political pressure, the SAR Government eased the restrictions on police notification, so Hong Kong still has its annual Tiananmen memorial demonstrations and other anti-Chinese events. Demonstrations, sit-ins, marches, signature campaigns, and petitions are frequent events, as one group or another tries to influence or complain about an SAR law or proposed legislation. The protest events are always covered live and uncensored by the media, and the only police in evidence are traffic police. The traditional Sunday outdoor forum, in which issues are debated openly—and often with the participation of top government officials and legislators—is still avidly covered and reported by the local media. Not anticipated before the handover was mainland China's acceptance of some of its own dissidents' living freely in Hong Kong. Labor leader Han Dongfang, for example, was expelled in 1993 after being imprisoned for his part in the June 4, 1989, Tiananmen Square demonstrations. Though marooned here, he is nonetheless free to give speeches, comment openly on events here and on the mainland, edit his own labor bulletin, and host his own radio show. (The SAR government did bar dissident exiles such as Wang Dan from coming to Hong Kong in spring 1999 for a 10th-anniversary Tiananmen memorial gathering.)

WITH THE BENEFIT of a few years' hindsight, the handover looks anticlimactic. The rest of the world was always more apprehensive about Chinese rule than were most Hong Kongers. For most Hong Kongers, business takes precedence over all other issues and it was the Asian crisis, which hit within a month of the handover, that became the real news of 1997 and the years that followed. The very month Hong Kong came into being, Thailand experienced a run on its currency, the baht, the defense of which eventually cost the country most of its foreign exchange. Malaysia was next, then Indonesia, exacerbated by the fall of Suharto. Hong Kong's banks were heavily exposed in all of these markets. By autumn 1997, with a prestigious World Bank–IMF Conference in town, Hong Kong was busy defending its currency and its 15-year-old peg against the U.S. dollar, which now had become not just a financial mechanism but a political symbol of stability. China, despite economic problems of its own, helped Hong Kong's defense by promising not to devalue the yuan. Unlike some of its neighbors, the SAR had ample foreign reserves and, most important, virtually no debt; still, Hong Kong's stock and futures markets reeled with each currency attack from the big hedge funds. The side effects were high interest rates and high inflation, making Hong Kong one of the most expensive places in the world to live and do business. On August 24, 1998, the SAR Government purchased HK$15 billion (US$1.92 billion) worth of stock to drive prices up; the hedge funds retreated, cutting their losses. In June 1998, the government put forth an economic rescue package, its third, that froze land sales, the major source of government income, until March 31, 1999.

But for all the uncertain moments, the SAR pulled through it (as, now, has much of Asia) and with the stock market soaring it is easy to forget the economy was ever imperiled. Indeed, except for a few other small differences—the increasing use of Mandarin on television and in the streets, the Hong Kong Jockey Club's decision to drop the "Royal" that once preceded its name—the changes wrought by the handover are mostly ones of increasing integration between the local and mainland economies, a process that has been under way for at least two decades. Culturally, Hong Kong Chinese have long been akin to the southern Chinese, but these ties have been strengthened since Hong Kong's terrestrial TV stations have been received in south China, displaying Hong Kong's lifestyle for all to see. The rest of China may have been protected from the outside world, but southern China was not. Hong Kong went to bat for China time and time again with the U.S. government to obtain and keep China's Most Favored Nation status, arguing that if it were denied, Hong Kong's economy would be more adversely affected than China's.

Ironically, the biggest post-handover controversy surrounded the issue of Right of Abode—not, this time, about who from Hong Kong gets to live in the United Kingdom but who from the mainland can move to Hong Kong. The Basic Law guarantees this right to certain groups of people who have connections here, mainly children of Hong Kong residents who were not eligible for residency under the British. Most of these children—numbering between 200,000 and 1.6 million, depending on the estimate—live in China. Their waiting time for a one-way permit (i.e., authorized emigration) is 10 years, and corruption among those waiting is rampant. The Hong Kong courts ruled that these children had the right to move to the territory but amid much controversy the SAR executive, Tung Chee-hwa, appealed to the mainland to overrule, which it did. While most Hong Kongers were relieved not to face inundation by a million mainland children, many were concerned that this establishes a bad precedent that would erode local judicial autonomy.

ANOTHER CHALLENGE that put Hong Kong on the front pages of the world press was the bird flu that struck in January 1998. The U.S. Centers for Disease Control had a virologist in Hong Kong just 24 hours after hearing the news. With the memory of previous flu pandemics this century still fresh—Hong Kong's 1968 flu claimed 700,000 lives—microbiologists and virologists sought to isolate the new strain when it jumped species (from chickens to humans). This one claimed nine lives out of 18 victims; to control the disease, 1.5 million chickens were slaughtered on the Hong Kong side of the border alone, and every market, street stall, and farm was scoured. Eight weeks later, the return of this staple food to the markets and to the restaurant and dining-room tables was cause for Hong Kong–wide celebration.

The issue of Hong Kong's deteriorating natural environment has managed to unite all sides of the political spectrum. Water quality has long been a problem, with beaches being periodically closed due to pollution. But what has drawn renewed and unwelcome attention is the severe deterioration in air quality. (Foreigners' main complaints about Hong Kong are high prices and pollution.) When the SAR was finally forced by public opinion to place pollution meters at street level for more accurate readings, the results were shocking. Pollution levels are now reported like the weather, with warnings issued on bad days. The main culprits are diesel taxis, minibuses, buses, and trucks, whose industries have lobbied against environmental legislation. When the SAR's chief executive convened an International Advisory Board (with stars such as Rupert Murdoch and retired Federal Reserve Board chairman Paul Volker) to collect advice on keeping Hong Kong competitive in the new millennium, they spoke not of economics but of the outdoors.

Indeed, perhaps the greatest sign that Hong Kong is operating quite comfortably under Chinese rule is the very fact that political debate has, for the most part, centered on such quotidian issues as chickens and pollution rather than the much-feared crackdown on individual liberty. Graves are still swept on the Ching Ming and Chung Yeung holidays. The Buddha's birthday has been added to the official holiday list but the four-day Easter weekend and the two-day Christmas–Boxing Day respite remain on the calendar as well. The local press, though subject to some self-censorship, still thrives; international reporting, publishing, and broadcasting continue unabated. Great debates rage in the local print and electronic media, both pro and con the SAR's, or China's, latest action or pronouncement. And everyone has time to check up on the stock market.

—By Jan Alexander and Saul Lockhart;
updated by Eva Chui

WHAT'S WHERE

Hong Kong Island
Hong Kong is a dazzling melee of human life and enterprise. From the harbor, the city's latest architectural wonders stand against a green-mountain backdrop, while on the other side of the island beaches and quieter villages slow the pace considerably. Moving clockwise, beginning with the harbor districts, Western and Central are two of the liveliest areas, full of markets, other shopping, restaurants, businesses—you name it. South of these, Midlevels, with its agglomeration of apartment towers, and Victoria Peak rise above the din of downtown. Wanchai, the next district east, was once of ill repute but is now a popular locale for a night on the town. After that is Causeway Bay, a spectacular shopping haven. North Point is on the northeast corner; its principal tourist offerings are a market and a ferry pier. Shek O lies at a distant remove on the southeastern peninsula, a pleasant village with a beach for an afternoon's escape.

At the bottom of Hong Kong Island, Stanley was a fishing village in the 19th century. Now mostly residential, it, too, has a pleasant beach whose foreshores crowd with spectators during the annual dragon-boat races, a lively market, and restaurants that make a trip here worthwhile. Working your way back to the western part of the island you'll find the amusements of Ocean Park (with its Middle Kingdom and impressive aquarium sections) and the large town of Aberdeen (largely a fishing vessel shelter, as well as being home to many luxury yachts), followed by Repulse Bay, named for the HM *Repulse*, which the British used to break the ring of pirates that occupied this area. A large stretch of beach ends at the east side with large, colorfully tacky religious figures.

Kowloon
Bustling Kowloon occupies the tip of the peninsula across from Hong Kong Island. Tsim Sha Tsui, at the bottom of the peninsula, is crammed full of shops, restaurants, and businesses. Yau Ma Tei, on the western side of Kowloon, is noted for two temples, more practical shops, and great markets, such as the Jade Market and the Temple Street night market.

New Territories
Because of its distance (which in fact is not great) from the commercial hubs of Hong Kong Island and Kowloon, travelers often overlook the attractions of the New Territories. Parts of the area retain their isolated, rural character, even if to find them you must make your way past massive housing developments called new towns, built to house the burgeoning population. Shatin is one of these towns, with its ultramodern racecourse belonging to the Hong Kong Jockey Club and the very old Temple of Ten Thousand Buddhas. To the east, the village of Sai Kung has wonderful restaurants, and its Country Park is one of the most spectacular in the SAR.

Outer Islands

As popular getaways for locals and tourists alike, the islands around Hong Kong in the South China Sea have unique charms of their own, from beaches and old fishing villages to hiking trails and remote, ancient Buddhist monasteries. There are three main islands. Lantau is the largest, larger actually than Hong Kong Island, and has the Polin Monastery, with the largest reclining Buddha in the world. Lamma Island is famous for its seafood restaurants, Cheung Chau for its quaint shops.

Macau

A tiny geographical remnant of the 16th-century Portuguese spice trade, Macau provides a pleasant respite from the non-stop bustle of Hong Kong, 65 km (40 mi) to the east. Construction has taken away some of the island's quieter charms, but Portuguese influence—especially in the food—is yet another fascinating Eurasian variation played out in the South China Sea. Macau is a peninsula, connected by bridge to Taipa Island, which is in turn connected to Coloane Island by a causeway. Both islands are easy to reach and have many attractions of their own.

PLEASURES AND PASTIMES

Beaches

Surprising as it may seem, splendid beaches are all over the area, some of which are well maintained by the government and served by lifeguards. **Repulse Bay** is a sort of Chinese Coney Island. Around the corner is the smaller and less crowded **Deep Water Bay**; **Turtle Cove** is isolated and beautiful; Shek O's **Big Wave Bay** has a Mediterranean feel; and among New Territory and Outer Island beaches, **Pak Sha Chau** has lovely golden sands, while **Lo Sho Ching** is popular with local families.

Chinese Culture

There are so many ways of taking in day-to-day Chinese phenomena—at restaurants, in street markets where the very sense of an individual's personal space is so dramatically different than in the West, in ancient Chinese temples, in a karaoke bar, at the hands of a fortune teller, or in

parks watching the morning tai-chi-chuan ritual. Embrace as much of Hong Kong as you can. You'll never forget it.

Restaurants

Aside from New York, no other city in the world can match the distinct variety and integrity of cuisines consumed in Hong Kong. One of the most exciting aspects of being on Chinese soil is the opportunity to eat authentic Chinese food. While Cantonese is the main fare, Sichuan, Shanghainese, Peking, and Chiu Chow are among the other Chinese styles just a taste bud away. At the same time, at a cultural crossroads like Hong Kong, the steamy, aromatic tastes of pan-Asian cuisine are another unique culinary opportunity. Approach menus with a spirit of adventure, and you might enjoy some foods you otherwise might shy away from.

Shopping

Hong Kong has the best shopping in the world, if you work at it. Although the thought of crowded streets, mind-boggling choices, and endless haggling can be daunting, no place makes big spending easier than this center of international commerce. Even self-declared nonshoppers are tempted to part with their money, and some have admitted to enjoying the experience.

The variety of goods is astonishing: international designer products, expensive treasures, handcrafted folk items from all over Asia, electronic goods and luxury accessories. Just as remarkable is the physical array of places to shop, from sophisticated boutiques-lined malls to open-air markets and shadowy alleyways.

GREAT ITINERARIES

You could easily expand this itinerary to two weeks if you spend time shopping, visiting museums, exploring the New Territories, or by adding a few nights in the peaceful outer islands of Lantau, Lamma, or Cheung Chau.

If You Have 3 Days

Hong Kong is a complex city. On the surface it seems that every building is a high-rise sculpture of glass and steel and that every pedestrian is hurrying to a business meeting. But if you look past the shiny surface, you'll see the culture, heritage, and people that give this city its exotic flavor and unique outlook. To get a perspective on all the bustle, start your first day with a trip to the top of **Victoria Peak** by taking the **Peak Tram,** the steepest funicular railway in the world. From here you'll be able to get a bird's-eye view of Central's sparkling high-rises, the densely packed streets of Hong Kong Island, the harbor, and all the way to the outer edges of Kowloon. Descend back into **Central** and spend the rest of your first day checking out the centers of activity on Hong Kong Island: the harbor districts of **Central** and **Western** with their upscale shopping and landmark skyscrapers, the **Midlevels** with its series of outdoor escalators leading up the steep mountainside, the hustling **Wanchai** district, and **Causeway Bay** and **Admiralty** with their megamalls and department stores. If you finish up your day in Admiralty, consider getting dinner at one of the great restaurants in the Pacific Place shopping complex.

If you're staying on Hong Kong Island, start your second day with a ride on the **Star Ferry** to arrive in the **Tsim Sha Tsui** neighborhood at the tip of Kowloon (if you're staying in Kowloon, use the ferry to arrive on Hong Kong Island on your first day). The view of the towering city from the water is always an impressive one. Not far from the **Star Ferry Terminal** are the Hong Kong Space, Science, Art, and History museums. Continuing up Nathan Road you'll come upon the **Peninsula Hotel,** one of the true landmarks of Hong Kong. Take a peek at the palatial lobby, stop in for a cup of coffee, or come back later for the justifiably popular afternoon high tea. Continue up **Nathan Road,** crammed with stores big and small, on your way to the temples of **Tin Hau,** the oldest in Hong Kong, and **Wong Tai Sin,** an explosively colorful and noisy spot with a full concourse of fortune tellers. Also take this opportunity to visit some of the diverse markets that are unique to Hong Kong. The **Bird Garden,** with birdcages lining the walkways and busy vendors selling cricket treats for their beloved songbird pets, particularly stands out. Other markets in the area include the enclosed **Jade Market,** the **Flower Market** (most interesting

in the time leading up to the New Year), and the **Ladies** and **Night** markets (the latter starts around 6 PM). Wrap up your day in Kowloon with a drink or dinner at the Peninsula's **Felix** restaurant for unparalleled views of neon-lit Central.

On your third day, take a hair-raising bus ride from Central to the south side of Hong Kong Island. You'll have an unforgettable view of the island's coastline as the double-decker bus descends from the peaks of the busy shopping and business districts into the sandy coves of **Stanley** and **Repulse Bay.** Try to sit in the front of the upper deck for a ride more exciting than any amusement park. Start your day in **Stanley,** wandering through the market before it gets too crowded. If you haven't bought souvenirs yet, this is the best, and cheapest, place to do it. When you're ready for a break from the frenetic market, wander along the waterfront and choose a spot for lunch. In the afternoon, take the bus to the beachfront town of Repulse Bay for a relaxation break on the sunny sand. Then hop the bus back to Central in time for dinner.

If You Have 5 Days

Spend your first three days as laid out above, and on your fourth day venture out to the New Territories. You can easily spend several days exploring the area, but if you'd like to see a lot in a short time, perhaps the easiest way is through an organized tour sponsored by the Hong Kong Tourism Bureau (HKTB). You can also rent a car or taxi and driver and explore on your own, or if you'd like to use public transportation, the KCR train will take you to the eastern territories to visit **Shatin,** home of both a very modern **racetrack** and the time-honored **Temple of Ten Thousand Buddhas.** In the western new territories, you can reach the **Sam Tung Uk Museum,** a walled village, by MTR, and **Ching Chung Koon Taoist Temple** by train.

On your fifth day take a ride out to **Lantau Island.** Once again, you could spend several days exploring the outer islands, but if your time is limited, take the ferry from Central to the western side of **Lantau Island.** From here take a bus (or hike) to **Po Lin Monastery** where **Tin Tan Buddha,** the world's tallest outdoor bronze Buddha, is located. From here take the bus to **Tai O,** a quaint fishing village where you can have a seafood lunch. In the afternoon, take the bus back to the harbor and **Silvermine Bay** where you can rent bikes to explore the small village of **Mui Wo** before taking the ferry back to Central.

If You Have 7 Days

Spend your first five days in Hong Kong as suggested above, then pack a small bag and head out to **Macau** for an overnight stay. While Macau can easily be seen in one day, and is easy to reach on the superfast ferry, to really get a feel for its old-world charm you should spend the night. Give yourself time to explore the **Old Citadel** section of the city where you'll find the fascinating **Museum of Macau** and the landmark structure of the church of **São Paulo**. This Portuguese-influenced neighborhood also has reasonably priced shops that sell everything from furniture to polo shirts. You'll also want to set aside time to explore **Peninsular Macau** where you can visit the picturesque **A-Ma Temple** and the informative **Maritime Museum**. While you're in this neighborhood, stop by the **Pousada de São Tiago**, a tranquil inn built into the ruins of a 17th-century fort, for a meal or a drink. For dinner make sure to sample the unique and tasty Macanese cuisine, at night you can entertain yourself in a casino, and the next day perhaps lay on the white sands of a Macau beach to end your stay in this part of the world.

FODOR'S CHOICE

Dining

Petrus. A superb view, a fine selection of wine, and sumptuous dishes with artistic flair have earned this French restaurant's prestigious reputation. $$$$

Yü. A creative East-and-West menu and posh decor make this the best seafood restaurant in town and arguably the best restaurant in Hong Kong. $$$$

Cafe Deco Bar and Grill. Combining Hong Kong chic and pan-Asian cuisine with panoramic views from atop Victoria Peak, this has become an island favorite. $$$

The Verandah. Classical colonial elegance with contemporary European cuisine await you at this restaurant overlooking Repulse Bay. $$$

Yung Kee. What you expect from Cantonese dining—lightning-fast preparation, high-energy service, and reasonable prices—is what you get at Yung Kee, which is why so many people keep coming back. $$–$$$

Afonso III, Macau. Try this simple café for a unique experience of Portuguese cuisine, where the chef prepares food the way his grandmother did. $$

Great Shanghai Restaurant. This restaurant wins no awards for its decor, but it's excellent for culinary adventurers and those who prefer the bold flavors of Shanghai food to the more delicate flavors of local Cantonese fare. $$

Wu Kong. Friendly service with authentic cooking in this traditional Shanghainese restaurant ensures you a delightful northern Chinese meal. $$

Lodging

Island Shangri-La, Hong Kong Island. This hotel, which towers above the Pacific Place complex, has spacious rooms and spectacular views of the Peak and Victoria Harbour. $$$$

Mandarin Oriental, Hong Kong Island. The Mandarin matches convenience with luxury, making it one of the world's great hotels. Celebrities and VIPs agree. $$$$

Peninsula, Kowloon. The Pen is the ultimate in colonial elegance, with its mix of European ambience and Chinese details. $$$$

Pousada de São Tiago, Macau. This traditional Portuguese inn is built into the ruins of a 17th-century fortress and incorporates ancient trees and natural springs into its design. The furnishings were custom-made in Portugal and Hong Kong. $$$

Garden View International House, Hong Kong Island. This small, attractive hotel overlooks the botanical gardens and the harbor. $

Parks, Gardens, and Walks

Dragon's Back in Shek O Country Park. Bring your hiking boots and canteen and escape the urban madness on a moderately hilly trail where banana leaves grow to lengths of 3 ft and the view of the sea is nothing short of spectacular.

Lantau Island, Shek Pik to Tai O. If you're a seasoned hiker, try this wondrous all-day stretch of the Lantau Trail, which passes the Shek Pik Reservoir and a half dozen tucked-away monasteries on its way down to the pristine seaside village of Tai O.

Coloane Park, Macau. On the southernmost of Macau's three islands, Coloane Park has a remarkable walk-in aviary with more than 200 bird species (some quite rare), a nature trail, and a fascinating collection of exotic trees and shrubs.

Lou Lim Ioc Garden, Macau. For a lovely respite in Macau, stroll through this Soochow-style enclosed garden, a miniature bamboo forest, a lake, and a traditional nine-turn bridge.

Excursions
The view of the coastline from the **Ocean Park cable car.** From here you'll think you're riding over the Mediterranean as you gaze down at a panorama of mountains, pastel villas, and the vast blue sea.

Crossing the harbor on the **Star Ferry,** first class. Feeling the wind of the South China Sea is vital to any experience of Hong Kong, whose very existence owes itself to the crossing of seas—not to mention today's stunning views.

A 30-minute **junk trip** through Macau's Inner Harbour, organized by the Maritime Museum, brings up close the life of the fishing population and the booming Chinese suburb on the opposite shore.

Street Markets
Bird Garden, Kowloon. The bird garden consists of various courtyards filled with trees and 70 stalls selling birds, cages, and such accoutrements as tiny porcelain feeders and fresh grasshoppers.

Rua de Cinco de Outubro, Macau. Here in traditional Chinese Macau, street markets offer incredible bargains in namebrand clothing, made under license in local factories.

Temples and Shrines
The Temple of Ten Thousand Buddhas, Shatin. You have to climb nearly 500 steps to reach this wonder, but with its 13,000 statues and gilded, mummified holy man, in addition to views of Amah Rock and a restaurant serving traditional Buddhist meals, it's worth the effort.

Po Lin Buddhist Monastery, Lantau Island. Built on a grander scale than most temple complexes in Hong Kong, Po Lin Monastery is home to Southeast Asia's tallest bronze Buddha, more than 100 ft high.

A-Ma Temple, Macau. Named for a sea goddess who, according to custom, saved a humble junk from a storm, A-Ma is the oldest and perhaps the most beautiful temple in Macau.

Museums
Hong Kong Museum of Art. This is the place in town to see ancient Chinese scrolls and sculpture along with the work of the Territory's own contemporary masters.

Hong Kong Museum of History. See what Hong Kong looked like more than 6,000 years ago, when tigers and other animals ranged over the islands. Scenes of Neolithic life, life-size dioramas, military displays, and artifacts trace the territory's development up to the present.

The Maritime Museum, Macau. From its dragon boats to pirate-chasing *lorchas,* Portuguese voyage charts, and navigation equipment, the ship-shape Maritime Museum provides a fascinating view of seagoing Macau.

Nightlife
The tiny streets of Central's **Lan Kwai Fong** area hide more than 100 restaurants and bars of every description and ethnic orientation, with celebrants often spilling out onto the streets with their drinks. It's a superb way to start, spend, or end an evening.

Crazy Paris Show at Hotel Lisboa, Macau. Girls, girls, girls (wait, was that a boy in there?)—if that's what you're after, this Paris- and Vegas-style show is the best around.

Taste Treats
Dim sum for lunch anywhere. Since you've come to the source, this is one tradition you can't pass up.

A market-stall Chinese breakfast of **congee** (rice porridge) at Kowloon Park Road and Haiphong Road, Kowloon. Some of these foods are so exotic that we can't recommend them to everyone, but this is a quintessential Hong Kong experience.

Afternoon tea in the grand lobby of the Peninsula Hotel. Dignified and utterly civilized, this legacy of the British presence in Hong Kong can lift you beyond the Peninsula's own elegance to another era entirely.

Special Events

Candlelight parades. Two parades, one in honor of the mid-autumn moon and another at the Dragon Boat Festival in June, are both resplendent with traditional costumes, music, and general merrymaking.

Bun Festival (May) on Cheung Chau. To placate vengeful spirits of the dead, villagers offer fresh-baked buns in the form of three 50-ft-high bun towers outside the Pak Tai Temple. Bring a camera to capture the parade of elaborate floats and an altar of papier-mâché gods.

Fringe Festival. Experience the best of Hong Kong's avant-garde theater, music, and art at the unique Fringe Club, housed in a historic building that used to be a dairy depot. The festival is held on various dates in January and February.

The Good Friday Passion Parade, Macau. A statue of Christ is carried through the streets in procession on the first weekend of Lent, with the stations of the cross erected along the way.

Horse racing. All of Hong Kong loves to gamble, and there's no better way to see a cross section of the population, from the boxes to the bleachers, than taking your chances. Whether you win or not, you'll find the mood contagious. The HKTB runs tours to both racecourses.

FESTIVALS AND SEASONAL EVENTS

Top seasonal events in Hong Kong include the Chinese New Year, the Hong Kong Arts Festival, the Hong Kong Food Festival, and the Dragon Boat Festival. The most colorful shindigs of all are the many lunar festivals celebrated throughout the year. Contact the HKTB for exact dates and more information.

WINTER

JAN.➤ The Fringe Club's **City Festival** showcases an assortment of international and local drama, dance, music, and light entertainment.

JAN.➤ In the **Swimming World Cup,** top-ranked swimmers compete in one of the legs of the international short courses series. World records have been set in previous years at the Kowloon Park indoor swimming pool.

LATE JAN.–EARLY FEB.➤ The **Hong Kong Marathon** consists of three hot races—a full marathon, a half-marathon, and a 10K race. The event attracted nearly 7,000 athletes last year, including many well-known foreign distance runners.

FEB.➤ The **Chinese New Year** has the city at a virtual standstill as shops shut down for three days and people don their best to visit friends and relatives.

FEB.➤ For the **Spring Lantern Festival,** streets and homes are decorated with brightly colored lanterns for the last day of Chinese New Year celebrations.

LATE FEB.–EARLY MAR.➤ The **Hong Kong Arts Festival** showcases four weeks of world-class music, dance, and drama from around the globe. HKTB offices worldwide have schedules and information.

EARLY MAR.➤ The **Hong Kong Open Golf Championship** is held at the Hong Kong Golf Club.

SPRING

MID-MAR.➤ The annual **Hong Kong Food Festival** is a two-week smorgasbord of events, including cooking classes with world-renowned chefs, tours of famous restaurants and teahouses, and an amusing waiters' race and cheerleading competition.

LATE MAR.–EARLY APR.➤ The **Rugby Sevens** is the world's premier seven-a-side rugby tournament usually held over Easter weekend in a sold-out 40,000-seat stadium.

EARLY APR.➤ The **Ching Ming Festival,** literally "bright and clear" is when families visit the burial plots of ancestors and departed relatives.

APR.➤ The **Hong Kong International Film Festival** focuses on hot spots in global cinema as well as special sections on restored Mandarin classics, commendable locally made films, and many other Asian productions.

APR.➤ The **Hong Kong Open** tennis tournament attracts some of the biggest names in the sport.

LATE APR.➤ For the **Birthday of Tin Hau,** goddess of the sea, fishermen decorate their boats and converge on seaside temples to honor her, especially around the Tin Hau Temple in Junk Bay.

MAY➤ The **Birthday of Lord Buddha** is celebrated on the eighth day of the fourth moon. The devout flock to major Buddhist shrines like the Temple of 10,000 Buddhas at Shatin or Po Lin Monastery on Lantau.

MAY➤ The **Bun Festival** on Cheung Chau Island attracts thousands for a three-day rite dedicated to placating the spirits of the dead. It culminates in a grand procession.

MAY➤ **Le French May Festival of Arts** attracts some of the best Gallic dance, music, and theater groups to the territory. There's also a smorgasbord of French films plus art exhibitions at venues across Hong Kong.

JUNE➤ The **Dragon Boat Festival** pits long, multi-oared dragon-head boats against one another in races to commemorate the hero Chu Yuen, a 4th-century scholar who supposedly threw himself into a river to protest the corruption of government officials, causing local fishermen to race to save him.

SUMMER

JULY 1 ➤ **Return to Motherland Day** marks the day that Hong Kong reverted to Chinese sovereignty in 1997.

AUG. ➤ The **Hungry Ghosts Festival** is a time when food is set out and elaborate ceremonies are performed to placate the angry roaming spirits of those buried without proper funeral rites, forgotten by their families, or deceased with no descendents to care for their grave sites.

MID-AUG. ➤ The **Seven Sisters (Maiden) Festival** is a celebration for lovers, and a time when young girls pray for a good husband.

MID-AUG. ➤ The **Women's Beach Volleyball Tour** is part of the FIVB's (Federation of International Volleyball) world tour

that has top-ranked players from around the globe competing on a man-made beach at Victoria Park. Dubbed "Sportainment," the five-day event has a carnival-like atmosphere alongside the action.

AUTUMN

SEPT. ➤ The **Chinese Opera Fortnight** presents traditional Cantonese, Peking, Soochow, Chekiang, and Chiu Chow operas in the City Hall Theatre, Concert Hall, and Ko Shan Theatre.

SEPT. ➤ The **Mid Autumn Festival,** also known as the Lantern or Moon Festival, sees crowds with candle lanterns gather in parks and other open spaces sharing *yue bing* or "moon cakes," which are stuffed with red-bean or lotus-seed paste. Such

hearty foods are said to symbolize happiness and completion.

LATE SEPT. OR EARLY OCT ➤ The **Birthday of Confucius** honors the revered philosopher.

MID-OCT. ➤ The **Chung Yeung Festival** commemorates a Han Dynasty tale about a man taking his family to high ground to avoid disaster. Like the Ching Ming festival, this is a time to clean family graves and make offerings.

LATE OCT. OR EARLY NOV. ➤ The **Chinese Arts Festival** showcases more than 150 artistic events (dance, music, and theater) from as far afield as Australia, Bhutan, Hawaii, and Mongolia. It is held biennially, in even-numbered years.

LATE NOV. ➤ The **Macau Grand Prix** takes over the city streets for a weekend.

MID-DEC. ➤ The **Hong Kong Judo Championship** takes place at Queen Elizabeth Stadium.

2 EXPLORING HONG KONG

Hong Kong is back: the buzz, energy, and reckless optimism of fortunes being made (and occasionally lost) have returned after a brief lull sparked by the Asian economic crisis. Yet the audacity of this city, which was crafted out of barren rock and political turmoil, still inspires—and its streets once again surge and swirl with enterprise, hitting the visitor like a shot of adrenaline.

Updated by
Eva Chui

T O STAND ON THE TIP OF KOWLOON PENINSULA and look out across the harbor to the full expanse of the Hong Kong island skyline—as awesome in height as Manhattan's, but only a few blocks deep and strung along the entire north coast—is to see the triumph of ambition over fate. Whereas it took Paris and London 10 or 20 generations to build the spectacular cities we know today, and New York six, Hong Kong built almost everything you see before you in the time since today's young investment bankers were born. It is easy to perceive this tremendous creation of wealth as an inevitable result of Hong Kong's strategic position, but at any point in the Territory's history things might have happened slightly differently, and the island would have found itself on the margins of world trade rather than at the center.

When the 30-square-mi (78-square-km) island of Hong Kong was ceded to the British after the Opium War of 1841, it consisted, in the infamous words of the British minister at the time, of "barren rock" whose only redeeming feature was the adjacent deep-water harbor. For the British, though, it served another purpose: Hong Kong guards the eastern edge of the Pearl River delta, and with it access to Guangzhou (Canton), which in the mid-19th century was China's main trading port. By controlling Hong Kong, Britain came to control the export of Chinese products such as silk and tea, and to corner the Chinese market for Western manufactured goods and opium. The scheme proved highly profitable.

If British trade were all Hong Kong had going for it, however, its prosperity would have faded with said empire. No, the real story of Hong Kong begins in the 1920s, when the first wave of Chinese refugees settled here to avoid civil unrest at home. They were followed in the '30s and '40s by refugees fleeing in advance of invading Japanese soldiers. But the biggest throngs of all came after the 1949 Communist revolution in China—mostly from the neighboring province of Guangdong, but also from Fujian, Shanghai, and elsewhere. Many of these new arrivals came from humble farming backgrounds, but many others had been rich, and had seen their wealth and businesses stripped away by the revolutionaries. They came to Hong Kong poorer than their families had been in generations, yet by virtue of their labor their descendants are the wealthiest generation yet.

Hong Kong has always lived and breathed commerce, and it is the territory's shrines to Mammon that will make the strongest impression when you first arrive. The Central district has long been thick with skyscrapers bearing the names of banks and conglomerates, and yet more continue to be built, squeezed into irregular plots of land that would seem insufficient for buildings half the size. When that doesn't work, the city simply reclaims more land from the harbor and builds on it almost before it dries. For a few years it will be obvious which land is new and which is old as the ground is turned and foundations laid, but soon enough the two will meld into one, just as they have before: you now have to walk four blocks from the Star Ferry terminal, through streets shaded by office towers, to reach Queen's Road Central, the former waterfront. A visitor may well ask what one can know for sure in this world if not where the earth ends and the oceans begin, but Hong Kongers have gotten used to such vagaries.

Watching young investment bankers out on a Friday night in Hong Kong's nightspot haven of Lan Kwai Fong, reveling in their outrageous good fortune at being in this place at this time in history, one can't help

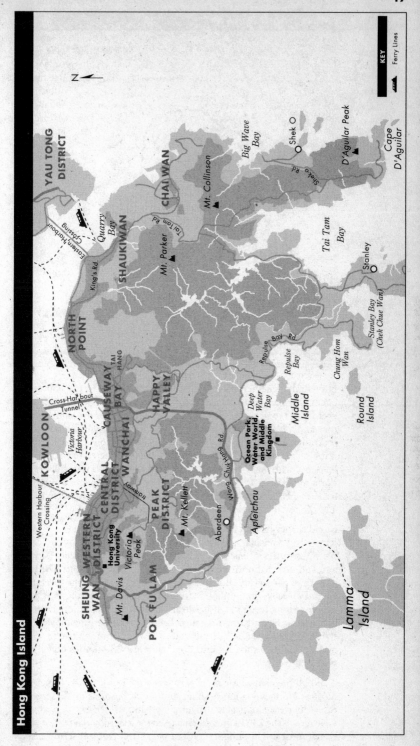

Hong Kong Island

KEY

Ferry Lines

N

YAU TONG DISTRICT

Eastern Harbour Crossing

Quarry Bay

King's Rd

NORTH POINT

SHAUKIWAN

CHAI WAN

Mt. Collinson

Big Wave Bay

Shek O

Shek O Rd

D'Aguilar Peak

Cape D'Aguilar

Tai Tam Bay

Mt. Parker

Tai Tam Rd

Stanley

Stanley Bay (Chek Chue Wan)

Chung Hom Wan

Round Island

Repulse Bay Rd

Cross-Harbour Tunnel

KOWLOON

Victoria Harbour

CAUSEWAY BAY

TAI HANG

WANCHAI

HAPPY VALLEY

Repulse Bay

Deep Water Bay

Middle Island

Western Harbour Crossing

CENTRAL DISTRICT

(Tramway)

PEAK DISTRICT

Mt. Kellett

Wong Chuk Hang Rd

Ocean Park, Water World, and Middle Kingdom

SHEUNG WAN

WESTERN DISTRICT

Hong Kong University

Victoria Peak

Aberdeen

Apleichau

Mt. Davis

POK FU LAM

Lamma Island

18

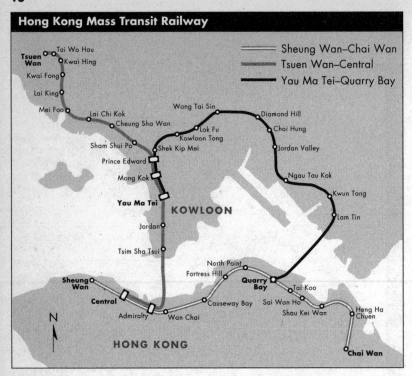

Hong Kong Mass Transit Railway

Sheung Wan–Chai Wan
Tsuen Wan–Central
Yau Ma Tei–Quarry Bay

Tsuen Wan · Tai Wo Hau · Kwai Hing · Kwai Fong · Lai King · Mei Foo · Lai Chi Kok · Cheung Sha Wan · Sham Shui Po · Shek Kip Mei · Prince Edward · Mong Kok · **Yau Ma Tei** · Jordan · Tsim Sha Tsui · Wong Tai Sin · Lok Fu · Kowloon Tong · Diamond Hill · Choi Hung · Jordan Valley · Ngau Tau Kok · Kwun Tong · Lam Tin · **KOWLOON**

North Point · Fortress Hill · **Quarry Bay** · Tai Koo · Sai Wan Ho · Shau Kei Wan · Heng Ha Chuen · Causeway Bay · Wan Chai · Admiralty · **Central** · **Sheung Wan**

N

HONG KONG

Chai Wan

but wonder whether this can possibly last. There's a heady, end-of-an-era exuberance to it all—a decadence that portends doom ahead. Yet visitors to Hong Kong have felt this same sentiment for almost a century and a half and, save for the rare economic downturn, the day of reckoning has not come. One of those rare exceptions came in 1997—not with the handover to China, which many expected to create problems, but with the Asian crisis, which took almost everyone by surprise. For a moment in 1997 and '98, it seemed Hong Kongers would have to permanently scale back their ambitions. But then the moment passed and the usual breakneck growth returned.

Rapid change has not been limited to Hong Kong Island or the crowded Kowloon Peninsula, but extends up through the "new towns" of the New Territories. Some of these, like Shatin, were rice paddies 20 years ago and now form thriving cities of a half million people. The most ambitious project of all is the one you see on arrival: the leveling of Chek Lap Kok, an uninhabited island of rock and scrub, that made way for Hong Kong's stylish, ultraefficient new international airport. Arriving in Hong Kong may now lack the rooftop-grazing shock of flying into the old Kai Tak, but you're whisked through the airport in no time and can then zip into Central in just 23 minutes on the Airport Express train.

Amid all the change it can be easy (even for residents) to forget that most of Hong Kong has nothing to do with business or skyscrapers: three-quarters of it is actually rural land and wilderness. A bird's-eye view reveals the 236 islands that make up the lesser-known part of Hong Kong; most are nothing but jagged peaks and tropical scrub, just as Hong Kong Island itself once was. Others are time capsules of ancestral China, with tiny temples, fishing villages, and small vegetable farms. Even Hong Kong Island, so relentlessly urban on its north coast, consists mostly of rolling green hills and sheltered bays on its south side. So whether you're looking for the hectic Hong Kong or the relaxed one, both are easy enough to find—indeed, sometimes only a few minutes apart.

HONG KONG ISLAND

Just 77 square km (30 square mi), Hong Kong Island is where the action is, from high finance to nightlife to luxury shopping. As a result—even though Kowloon is just a short ride away—many residents feel little reason to ever leave the island. One of Hong Kong's unexpected pleasures is that, despite what sometimes feels like unrelenting urbanity, property development has actually been restricted to a few small areas. As a result, a 20-minute taxi ride from downtown Central can have you breathing fresh air and seeing only lush green vegetation.

Hong Kong has few historical landmarks (largely because soaring property values have long since caused most older buildings to be torn down and replaced) and no more than a handful of cultural sights, but it pulses with an extraordinarily dynamic contemporary life. In general, the commercial and shopping districts are on the island's north coast, interspersed with the ubiquitous apartment blocks, while the towns on the rest of the island tend to be more residential. Each district has a name (and the name of its MTR stop usually corresponds) and a slightly distinct character, but the borders tend to blur together.

Central Hong Kong, in the middle of the island's north side, is a gleaming modern business enclave containing the stock exchange, dozens of banks, deluxe hotels, and upmarket shops.

The **Western** district lies, sure enough, to the west of the Central district and consists primarily of small shops, markets, small, interconnected ladder streets, and rows of traditional shop houses.

The **Midlevels** area runs halfway up the Peak behind Central and consists of high-rise luxury apartment blocks soaring straight out of the tropical bush.

Victoria Peak, an exclusive residential area, is the highest (1,805 ft) of a small range of hills in the middle of the island, high above Midlevels. Reached via the Peak Tram or zigzagging roads, it offers spectacular views, a selection of restaurants, and more shopping.

Wanchai, east of Central, was once famed for its nightlife, as immortalized in Richard Mason's novel *The World of Suzie Wong* and the ensuing movie. It still has plenty of bars, but it's now better known for its convention center, smart offices, and wide range of restaurants.

Causeway Bay, just east of Wanchai, was once a middle-class Chinese community but is now primarily a business and tourist area filled with offices, hotels, and restaurants, and is undoubtedly one of the busiest shopping hubs in the city.

Deep Water Bay, Repulse Bay, and Stanley are prestigious residential areas on the south side of the island with a few beaches and the famous souvenir-hunter's paradise, Stanley Market.

Shek O, a pleasant seaside village on the southeast coast, has a mixture of modest village houses and baronial mansions.

Central and Western Districts

The office towers and opulent shopping centers of Hong Kong's core business district occupy one of the most expensive stretches of land on earth. It may be fitting, then, that Central also houses nearly every major investment and commercial bank, fashion designer, and luxury-goods boutique the world has yet produced. The streets are often so crowded with bankers and shoppers that a pedestrian can feel like a salmon trying to swim upstream to spawn. Fortunately, most of the buildings are connected by elevated covered walkways that can also be handy in the rain. Bear in mind that on Sunday, many Central shops close and the district teems with thousands of maids, mostly Filipinas, who, with nowhere else to spend their day off, congregate en masse in the public gardens, sidewalks, and plazas of the area.

The Western district is gradually becoming more like Central, but it still retains a traditional feel that many other areas have lost. Most of the buildings are high-rises (and older and more run-down than those in Central), but it's in some of the small alleys off Western's main streets that the old China Coast comes alive. Traditional shops sell dried sea horses, curled snakes, salted fish, aromatic mushrooms, herbal medicines, steaming noodles, and, of course, tea, by the glass or by the bushel.

Numbers in the text correspond to numbers in the margin and on the Central and Western Districts map.

A Good Walk

Walking is by far the best way to get around Central and Western, and orientation is easy since the harbor is always north. Start at the **Star Ferry Terminal** ①, where sturdy green-and-white boats deposit passengers arriving from Kowloon. With your back to the harbor (and stepping out from the awning to get a better view), you can see many of Hong Kong's most significant buildings, as well as a number of practical landmarks. Just in front of you is a parking garage, to the east (left) of which is the double decker, open-air shuttle to the Peak Tram and the unattractive City Hall complex. To your right is the General Post Office, a squat white building, and behind it is the towering **Jardine House** ② with its many round windows, and on its right the marble-and-mirrored-glass stripes of Exchange Square, which houses the stock exchange and the American Club and has a bus terminal underneath. Just north of Exchange Square are the new Airport Express terminal and, along the water, the piers for ferries to the outlying islands.

Follow the awnings to the right and go through the underground walkway to **Statue Square** ③. The intriguing Victorian/Chinese hybrid building on the east side of the square is the **Legislative Council Building** ④. Along the southern end of the square are the buildings of Hong Kong's three note-issuing banks: the Art Deco former headquarters of the **Bank of China** ⑤, the spectacular strut-and-ladder facade of the **Hongkong & Shanghai Bank (HSBC)** ⑥, and, pressing up against it, the rose-color wedge of Standard Chartered Bank. The HSBC building is one of the most important buildings in 20th-century architecture; walk under it and look up into the atrium through the curved glass floor, or go inside for a view of its details. Exiting HSBC on the south side, cross the street (Queen's Road Central) and turn left past the giant yet unimaginative Cheung Kong building (on your right) and Chater Garden (on your left) until you come to the triangle-scheme Bank of China Tower, with its adjacent Chinese waterfall garden. This is the headquarters of the largest mainland-Chinese bank and was built a few years before the handover in an effort to architecturally one-up its local rival, HSBC.

Head back on Queen's Road Central toward HSBC and walk until you get to the intersection with Pedder Street, where you'll find **The Landmark** ⑦, the mother of all luxury shopping centers. Having paid your respects, exit and turn left (south) on Pedder Street and walk straight

FENG SHUI AT WORK

THERE'S A SUBTLE BATTLE going on in Central, a battle between good and evil forces created by feng shui (pronounced "fung suoy" and literally translated as "wind" and "water"). Feng shui, for the uninitiated, is the traditional Chinese art that determines the placement of objects by their relationship to natural elements to enhance the natural yin/yang balance. The feng shui principles governing positioning are highly complex. The most popular school of thought in Hong Kong emphasizes general geographic orientation, such as the relationship to nearby mountains or bodies of water. Another school of thought focuses on the symbolic importance of shapes in the surrounding environment, with triangles (such as those on the headquarters of the Bank of China) giving off particularly bad feng shui. In general, the principles of both schools relate to the flow of energies in nature. Some are considered beneficial (thus an entrance will be positioned to allow them to enter) and others are considered to be negative (in which case objects such as metal bars can be introduced to deflect them). Mercifully, these flows often correspond to more prosaic preferences: the ideal orientation of a building, for example, is facing out to sea with a mountain behind—which also happens to afford the best view and a cooling breeze. Even in modern Central, where feng shui is regarded as something akin to superstition, most developers figure it's better to be safe than sorry, so it's the rare skyscraper that's built without consulting a feng shui expert. Indeed, rumor has it that when the HSBC headquarters were built in the mid-1980s (at a cost of at a cost of nearly US$1 billion) the escalators were reset from their original straight position so that they would be at an angle to the entrance of the building. Because evil spirits can only travel in a straight line, this realignment was thought to prevent waterborne spirits from flowing in off Victoria Harbor. The escalators are also believed to resemble two whiskers of a powerful dragon, sucking money into the bank.

The Bank of China Tower with its many triangular angles, however, is not believed to have such good feng shui. A popular notion is that the building, which thins at the top, resembles a screwdriver that is drilling the wealth out of Hong Kong. Another is that buildings facing the sharp edges of the building will encounter negative feng shui and resulting problems. One example given by critics is the Lippo Centre which faces one of the triangles. The Lippo Centre was formerly the Bond Centre, owned by disgraced Australian businessman Allen Bond who was forced to sell the building after experiencing financial troubles. Another example is the Government House, originally considered to be one of the best feng shui locations in Hong Kong, with clear, uninterrupted views of the mountains and sea. However, one of the angles of the Bank of China Tower bisects the Government House, resulting in, critics say, among other things, a nasty fall taken by Margaret Thatcher when the former British Prime Minister was on an official visit. The building is considered to be in such an unlucky position that it now sits empty most of the year.

If you look up at the HSBC building, you'll notice two metal rods on top that look like a window-washing apparatus. Look more closely and you'll see that the rods are pointed at the Bank of China, a classic feng shui technique to protect the building from the negative energy of the dreaded triangles.

If you'd like to learn more about the feng shui power struggles of Central, the HKTB leads interesting weekly tours on the subject. Contact any HKTB bureau for more details.

Central and Western Districts

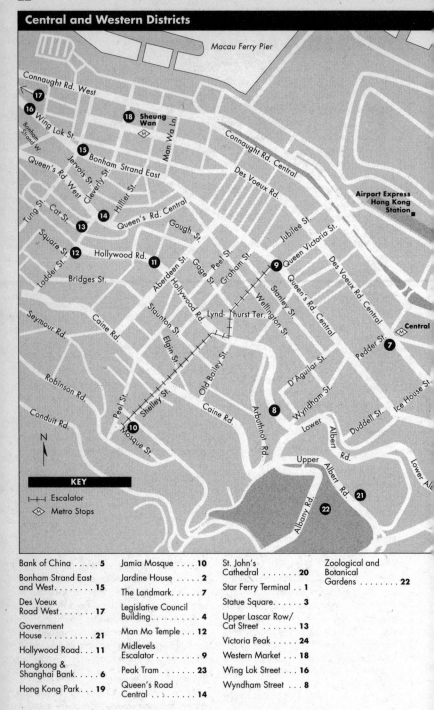

Macau Ferry Pier

Connaught Rd. West

17

16 Wing Lok St.

18 **Sheung Wan**

Man Wa Ln.

Bonham Strand W

15 Bonham Strand East

Connaught Rd. Central

Des Voeux Rd.

Queen's Rd. West

Jervois St.

Cleverly St.

Hillier St.

13 14

Queen's Rd. Central

Gough St.

Jubilee St.

Airport Express Hong Kong Station

Tung St.

Cat St.

Square St.

12 Hollywood Rd.

11

Aberdeen St.

Hollywood Rd.

Gage St.

Peel St.

Graham St.

9 Queen Victoria St.

Queen's Rd. Central

Des Voeux Rd Central

Bridges St.

Ladder St.

Staunton St.

Elgin St.

Lynd- hurst Ter.

Wellington St.

Stanley St.

Central

Seymour Rd.

Caine Rd.

D'Aguilar St.

Pedder St.

7

Ice House St.

Robinson Rd.

Peel St.

Shelley St.

Old Bailey St.

Caine Rd.

Arbuthnot Rd.

Wyndham St.

8

Duddell St.

Conduit Rd.

10 Mosque St.

Lower

Albert Rd.

Lower Al

N

Upper

Albert Rd.

21

KEY

Escalator

Metro Stops

Albany Rd.

22

Bank of China **5**	Jamia Mosque **10**	St. John's Cathedral **20**	Zoological and Botanical Gardens **22**
Bonham Strand East and West **15**	Jardine House **2**	Star Ferry Terminal . . **1**	
	The Landmark **7**	Statue Square **3**	
Des Voeux Road West **17**	Legislative Council Building **4**	Upper Lascar Row/ Cat Street **13**	
Government House **21**	Man Mo Temple . . **12**	Victoria Peak **24**	
Hollywood Road . . **11**	Midlevels Escalator **9**	Western Market . . . **18**	
Hongkong & Shanghai Bank **6**	Peak Tram **23**	Wing Lok Street . . . **16**	
Hong Kong Park . . . **19**	Queen's Road Central **14**	Wyndham Street . . . **8**	

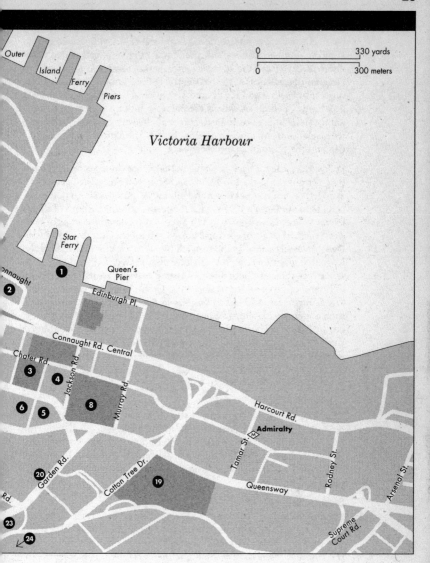

Outer

Island

Ferry

Piers

Victoria Harbour

0 — 330 yards
0 — 300 meters

Star
Ferry

onnaught

❶

Queen's
Pier

❷

Edinburgh Pl.

Connaught Rd. Central

Chater Rd.

❸

❹

Jackson Rd.

❻ ❺

❽

Murray Rd.

Harcourt Rd.

Admiralty

Tamar St.

Rodney St.

Arsenal St.

❷⓪

Garden Rd.

Cotton Tree Dr.

❶⑨

Queensway

Rd.

❷③

❷④

Supreme
Court Rd.

up the steep hill until you pass the colonial red-and-white-striped building on the left that hosts the Fringe Club, an avant-garde arts center. At the five-street intersection, a sharp right takes you into Lan Kwai Fong, a prime entertainment district, but veering right gets you to **Wyndham Street** ⑧ and the start of a breathtaking series of antiques and Oriental-rug galleries. At the old Central Police Station, Wyndham Street turns into Hollywood Road, and you'll see an overpass that forms a link in the open-air **Midlevels Escalator** ⑨. Join up with it by turning left up an incline; once aboard, take it all the way up the hill until you see an elaborate metalwork gate on the left. The gate hides a small garden and the tranquil **Jamia Mosque** ⑩, built in 1915.

Follow the escalator back downhill to **Hollywood Road** ⑪, perhaps stopping for a meal in the hip Elgins and Staunton Street areas en route. Turn left on Hollywood Road and follow the antiques shops to the colorful **Man Mo Temple** ⑫. To reach the curio and trinket shops of **Upper Lascar Row** ⑬ (also known as Cat Street), walk down the steps of Ladder Street, just across from Man Mo Temple. Continue down to **Queen's Road Central** ⑭ and turn left (west) to see a bit of the old Hong Kong that may otherwise seem to have disappeared. Turn right on Cleverly Street, then left. Both **Bonham Strand East and West** ⑮ have plenty of little shops to explore, as does the adjacent **Wing Lok Street** ⑯. Follow Bonham Strand West to **Des Voeux Road West** ⑰ to see the dried food and medicine shops. When you're just about ready to turn back, head toward the harbor and follow Connaught Road east until you come to the cream-and-brown **Western Market** ⑱, built in 1906 and lovingly restored. From here it's an easy tram ride back to Central. The quaint trams are known commonly as "ding ding," for the sound the bell makes when starting and stopping.

TIMING

Allow a full day, perhaps two if you want to spend any appreciable time shopping for antiques. It's physically possible to walk from the Star Ferry Terminal to Cat Street in three hours, but you won't be able to see anything in depth. The Man Mo Temple will add 20 minutes. The second half of the walk, from Cat Street to Western Market, will take an hour or two.

Sights to See

❺ **Bank of China.** In the politics of Hong Kong architecture, the stylish Art Deco building that served as the old Bank of China headquarters was the first trump: built after World War II, it was 20 ft higher than the adjacent Hongkong & Shanghai Bank (HSBC). It is now one of the smallest buildings in Central, utterly dwarfed by the imposing new structure HSBC built in the mid-1980s. The Bank of China refused to take this challenge lying down, however, and commissioned the Chinese-American architect I. M. Pei to build a new headquarters nearby. The result, the **Bank of China Tower,** completed in 1990, is a masterful twisting spire of replicating triangles, and was the first building to break the ridgeline of Victoria Peak. It may not be as innovative as the new HSBC building, but it dominates Hong Kong's urban landscape and embodies the post-handover balance of power. For a panoramic, and uncrowded, viewing spot of Central head to the 43rd floor. The observation deck is open weekdays from 9 to 5 and Saturday 9 to 1. And best of all, it's free. The old building now houses Sin Hua Bank and, on the top floor, David Tang's exclusive China Club, which manages to be both postmodern and nostalgic for pre-Communist Shanghai. ✉ *Garden Rd.*

★ ⑮ **Bonham Strand East and West.** A major thoroughfare in one of Hong Kong's most charmingly traditional areas, Bonham Strand is lined with shops selling goods that evoke the old China Coast trade merchants. A few shops sell live snakes, whose meat is used in winter soups to ward off colds and whose gallbladders reputedly improve vigor and virility. Bonham Strand West, in particular, is known for its Chinese medicines and herbal remedies. Many of its old shops have their original facades, and inside, the walls are lined with drawers and shelves of jars filled with hundreds of pungent ingredients such as wood barks and insects. These are consumed dried and ground up, infused in hot water or tea, or taken as powders or pills.

⑰ **Des Voeux Road West.** You'll recognize the tram tracks when you get to the west end of Bonham Strand West. On the left (south) side of the street are a cluster of shops selling preserved foods—everything from dried and salted fish to black mushrooms to vegetables—and herbal medicines. This is a good area for lunchtime dim sum.

⑪ **Hollywood Road.** Many of Hong Kong's best antiques, furniture, and classical-art galleries are concentrated on Wyndham Street, at the road's eastern end. As the road heads west, the shops gradually move down-market, selling mostly porcelain, curios, and not-very-old trinkets masquerading as ancient artifacts. Look to the left for a sign saying POSSESSION STREET, where Captain Charles Elliott of the British Royal Navy stepped ashore in 1841 and claimed Hong Kong for the British empire. It's interesting to note how far today's harbor is from this earlier shoreline—the result of a century of aggressive land reclamation.

OFF THE BEATEN PATH
HONG KONG MUSEUM OF MEDICAL SCIENCES – Tucked away in an Edwardian-style building behind a small park in Midlevels, this museum is worth the climb through tiny backstreets for anyone interested in the history of Chinese medicine in Hong Kong. Exhibits compare the uses of Chinese and Western medicines and show Chinese medicines of both animal and herbal origin as well as a traditional Chinese medical practitioner's equipment. Several other rooms are devoted to Western medical subjects. To get here from Hollywood Road, follow Ladder Street behind Man Mo Temple, going south and uphill to Square Street, which veers right, then left to Caine Lane. Follow a circular path up about 300 ft around Caine Lane Garden, a park with colorful stucco structures, until you reach Number 2. ✉ 2 Caine La., Midlevels, Hong Kong, ☎ 2549–5123, FAX 2559–9458. ☑ Free. ☉ Tues.–Sat. 10–5, Sun. 1–5.

★ ⑥ **Hongkong & Shanghai Bank (HSBC).** With its distinctive ladder facade, this striking building is a landmark of modern architecture. Designed by Sir Norman Foster as the headquarters of Hong Kong's premier bank (you'll see it depicted on most of the paper money) and completed in 1985, the building sits on four props, which allow you to walk under it and look up through its glass belly into the soaring atrium within. Imposing as that may be, the building is most interesting for its sensitive use of high-tech details: the mechanics of everything from the elevators' gears and pulleys to the electric signs' circuit boards are visible through smoked glass. In addition to its architectural triumph, the building served a symbolic function as well: built at a time of insecurity vis-à-vis China at a cost of almost US$1 billion, it was a powerful statement that the bank had no intention of taking its money out of the Territory. ✉ 1 Queen's Rd., Central, across from Statue Sq.

⑩ **Jamia Mosque.** This attractive gray-and-white mosque was built by HMH Essack Elias of Bombay in 1915, and it shows its Indian heritage in the perforated arches and decorative work on the facade. The mosque itself is not open to non-Muslims, but it occupies a small, verdant enclosure that offers a welcome retreat from the city. It once had a nice view down toward the water, but that was disrupted by an apartment tower—one of many now ringing this site. ⊠ *30 Shelley St., just off Midlevels Escalator.*

❷ Jardine House. To the west of the Star Ferry Terminal, recognizable by its signature round windows, this 1973 building was once the tallest in Central. It houses Jardine, Matheson & Co., the greatest of the old British *hongs* (trading companies) that dominated trade with imperial China. Jardines has come a long way from the days when it trafficked opium, and its investment-banking arm, Jardine Fleming, is one of the most respected in Asia. ⊠ *Connaught Pl., across from the Central Post Office.*

❼ The Landmark. Few fashion designers, watch craftsmen, or other makers of luxury goods do not have—or do not crave—a boutique in the Landmark. The building is no longer the city's poshest, but its Pedder Street location is still priceless, and it has its own MTR entrance. Live concerts are occasionally performed near the fountain in the high-ceiling atrium. ⊠ *Des Voeux Rd. between Ice House and Pedder Sts.* ☉ *Building, daily 9 AM–midnight; most shops, daily 10–6.*

❹ Legislative Council Building. Built for the Supreme Court in 1912 and now home to the Legislative Council (known as LegCo), this building is one of the few grand Victorian structures left in this area. Note the Chinese-style eaved roof, a modest British concession to local culture. The council had no real power in the British days, but starting in 1991 it did have a majority of elected members who challenged the administration every Wednesday. Since the handover in 1997, mainland attempts to muzzle LegCo's pro-democracy members have been only moderately successful, so it continues to serve as a forum for debate, if not as an organ of political power. In front of the Council Building is the **Cenotaph,** a monument to all who lost their lives in the two world wars. ⊠ *Statue Sq. at Jackson Rd.*

⓬ Man Mo Temple. Built in 1847 and dedicated to the gods of literature and of war—Man and Mo, respectively—this is Hong Kong Island's oldest temple. It now serves primarily as a smoke-filled haven for elderly women paying respects; ashes flutter down onto your clothes from the enormous spirals of incense hanging from the beams. The statue of Man is dressed in green and holds a writing brush, while Mo is dressed in red and holds a sword. To their left is a shrine to Pao Kung, god of justice, whose face is painted black; to the right is Shing Wong, god of the city. The temple bell, cast in Canton in 1847, and the drum next to it are sounded to attract the gods' attention when a prayer is being offered. To check your fortune, stand in front of the altar, take one of the small bamboo cylinders available there, and shake it until one of the sticks falls out. The number on the stick corresponds to a written fortune. The English translation of said fortune is in a book that the temple will happily sell you. ⊠ *Hollywood Rd. at Ladder St.* ☉ *Daily 8–6.*

❾ Midlevels Escalator. Completed in 1993, this is actually a 1-km-long (½-mi-long) combination of escalators and walkways that provide free, glass-covered transport up or down the steep incline between Central and Midlevels. The painless uphill climb provides a view of small Chinese shops and gleaming residential high-rises, as well as the Jamia Mosque (built in 1915), at Shelley Street. **Staunton Street,** one level above Hollywood Road, is now known as Hong Kong's SoHo (South of Hollywood), with an eclectic collection of cafés and bars, including the Sherpa Himalayan Coffee Shop and the hole-in-the-wall Le Rendezvous French crepery.

Plan to ride the escalators up between 10:20 AM and midnight. From 6 to 10 AM the escalators move downhill, so commuters living in Midlevels can get to work, or to the public transportation, down in Central; and after 11:30 they shut down. You can get off at any point and explore the side streets, whose vendors sell porcelain, clothes, and antiques (not necessarily authenticated). Almost every building has a tiny makeshift altar to the ancestors, usually made of red paper with gold Chinese characters, with offerings of fruit and incense. ⊠ *Enter across from Central Market, at Queen's Rd. Central and Jubilee St.* ⊙ *Daily 6 AM–11:30 PM.*

⑭ **Queen's Road Central.** This street once ran along the waterfront. It is, at various points, one of Hong Kong's most prestigious shopping addresses and among its quaintest and most traditional streets.

Of the countless shops and market stalls selling dried herbs, live snakes, and everything else imaginable to treat the body's vital energies, the **Eu Yan Sang Medical Hall** (⊠ 152 Queen's Rd., Central) is the one to visit for an education in traditional Chinese medicines. Glass cases display reindeer antlers, dried fungi, ginseng, and other standard medicinal items; English-language cards explain some of the items' uses, and men behind the counters will happily sell you purported cures for anything from the common cold to impotence (the cure for the latter is usually slices of reindeer antler boiled into tea). A note of caution: look all you want, but remember that Chinese medicines are not regulated by the Hong Kong government, and anything that sounds dubious or dangerous might be just that.

★ ❶ **Star Ferry Terminal.** Since 1898 the ferry terminal has been the gateway to the island for commuters and travelers coming from Kowloon. First-time visitors are all but required to cross the harbor on the Star Ferry at least once and ride around Hong Kong Island on a double-deck tram. In front of the terminal you will usually see a few red rickshaws; once numbering in the thousands, these two-wheel man-powered taxis are all but gone. ⊠ *Enter terminal through tunnel next to Mandarin Hotel, Connaught Rd. and Connaught Pl.* ⊡ *1st class HK$2.20, 2nd class HK$1.70.* ⊙ *Daily 6 AM–midnight.*

OFF THE BEATEN PATH

HONG KONG DOLPHIN WATCH – The Chinese white dolphin (actually from pink to dark gray, and found in waters from South Africa to Australia) is on its way to extinction in the South China Sea, mainly because of dredging for the new airport. Hong Kong Dolphin Watch sponsors a Dolphin Discovery Cruise three or four times a week—there's no guarantee, but on most trips you'll catch one or two dolphins playing in the water. The trip, which departs from Queen's Pier (next to City Hall), makes for an enjoyable day at sea, and tickets help raise money to build a sanctuary that would ensure the dolphins' survival. The cost includes a buffet lunch. Try to reserve at least two weeks in advance. ⊠ *Box 4102, Central, Hong Kong,* ☎ *2984–1414,* FAX *2984–7799.* ⊡ *HK$320.*

❸ **Statue Square.** This piece of land was gifted to the public by the Hongkong & Shanghai Bank (whose headquarters dominate the southern end), with the proviso that nothing built on it could block the bank's view of the water. The square is named for the statue of Sir Thomas Jackson, Bart. (1841–1915), who was the bank's chief manager for more than 30 years in the late 19th century. The square is surrounded by some of the most important buildings in Hong Kong, including those housing the Hong Kong Club, the Legislative Council, and the Bank of China, and has an entrance to the Central MTR station. On Sunday it becomes the hub for thousands of Filipina maids enjoying their day off.

NEED A
BREAK?

On the west side of Statue Square is the **Mandarin Oriental Hotel** (✉ 5 Connaught Rd., ☎ 2522–0111), one of the finest hotels in the world. The mezzanine coffee lounge is a pleasant place to have a drink (they also have an excellent high tea), or you can people-watch at the Captain's Bar, where billion-dollar deals are consummated over cognac.

⑬ Upper Lascar Row. Cat Street, as Upper Lascar Row is often called, is a vast flea market. You won't find Ming vases here—or anything else of significant value—but you may come across an old Mao badge or an antique pot or teakettle.

More worthwhile for the art or antiques collector is the section of shops and stalls known as **Cat Street Galleries** (✉ 38 Lok Ku Rd.), adjacent to the flea market, open 10–6 every day but Sunday. This is a new and growing complex, with galleries selling every kind of craft, sometimes old but more often new. You can rest your feet and have coffee in the convenient little European café Somethin' Brewin'.

⑱ Western Market. Erected in 1906, this is the only surviving segment of a larger market building built in 1858. It functioned as a produce market for 83 years and included living quarters for coolies and inspectors in the four corner towers. Threatened with demolition, it was exquisitely restored and turned into a unique shopping outlet. Alas, they've never gotten the retail mix quite right, filling the place with souvenir and trinket shops on the ground floor, fabrics on the middle floor, and a Chinese restaurant on the top floor. The building, however, gorgeously decorated with Chinese bunting, is worth a trip. ✉ 323 Connaught Rd. W. ☉ Daily 10 AM–11:45 PM.

⑯ Wing Lok Street. You can still find fascinating traditional items on this street (off Queen's Road Central), as it's lined with Chinese shops selling dried fish and seafood, rattan goods, medicines, and the engraved seals called chops. You can have your initials engraved in Roman letters or Chinese characters on a chop made of plastic, bone, or jade. (Ivory is also available all over Hong Kong, but it's illegal to bring it into the United States.) It takes about an hour to engrave a chop, which you can pick up later or the following day.

★ ⑧ Wyndham Street. The galleries that pack the curving block of Wyndham Street from the Fringe Club to where Wyndham becomes Hollywood Road can be approached more as a collection of miniature museums than as mere shops. Their showrooms hold some spectacular antique furniture, art, and artifacts (albeit perhaps smuggled out of their countries of origin) at prices that, while not cheap by any means, are a fraction of what they would be outside the region. Most stores are open daily from 10 to 7, though some have shorter hours or close altogether on Sunday. Here is a rough guide, starting from the western end: the **Oriental Rug Gallery** and **Oriental Carpets Gallery** specialize in rugs from the Middle East and Central Asia. **Artemis** has gorgeous but expensive furniture, along with statuary and stonework. **MinGei Antiques** has Chinese furniture and an interesting collection of birdcages. **Zitan** has chests and old doors, many in a more authentic state than the restored pieces sold elsewhere. **Zee Stone Gallery** specializes in Tibetan arts, including silverwork, silk hangings, and robes. **Ad Lib** has kiln work, statues, and the ubiquitous Ming and Qing Dynasty reproduction furniture. **Teresa Coleman Fine Arts,** opposite the police station at the corner of Pottinger Street, is among the premier galleries in Asia, with an ability to find little treasures others miss, like embroidered dragon robes and collars or vibrant-blue "kingfisher" jewelry. **Chu's** focuses on artifacts from Tibet, including carpets and chests.

Schoeni is actually on Hollywood Road, near the police station, and is better known as a promoter of contemporary mainland Chinese art, but has an antiques gallery on nearby Old Baily Street. For more on shopping, *see* Chapter 7.

From Central to the Peak

Midlevels is the wide band of land south of Central that runs halfway up Victoria Peak. Long one of Hong Kong's most desirable residential districts, it is now lined with towering apartment blocks that cling precariously to the hillside. Bisecting it is the **Midlevels Escalator** (☞ *above*), which connects Central Market with some of the area's main residential roads. Free of charge and protected from the elements, the escalator has proved a great way to move commuters and tourists through the congested city without destroying the landscape. The Midlevels is also worth a visit to see Hong Kong University, the Botanical Gardens, and some of Hong Kong's few remaining examples of Victorian apartment architecture, though the latter are disappearing rapidly.

Victoria Peak, high above Midlevels, is known simply as the Peak, and soars 1,805 ft above sea level. Residents here take special pride in the positions to which they have, quite literally, risen; theirs is the most exclusive residential area on the island—perhaps in all of Asia.

Numbers in the text correspond to numbers in the margin and on the Central and Western Districts map.

A Good Tour

Start your walk at 2 Queen's Road Central, diagonally across the street from Chater Garden. Head uphill on Garden Road and cross the street at the pedestrian overpass to Cotton Tree Drive. You should be facing **Hong Kong Park** ⑲, where you'll find the **Museum of Tea Ware** and a large aviary and conservatory.

Leave the garden and return to Garden Road. On the right heading up Garden Road is **St. John's Cathedral** ⑳. Continue up the road and turn right on Upper Albert Road, passing the former **Government House** ㉑. Farther up Garden Road are the United States Consulate General and the **Zoological and Botanical Gardens** ㉒.

Stroll through the gardens, zoo, and aviary. Swing back down Garden Road, cross it, and go to the **Peak Tram** ㉓, just behind St. John's Building (not to be confused with the cathedral). Take the tram to **Victoria Peak** ㉔.

For a scenic alternative to the Peak Tram, you can catch Bus 15 or a cab from Central. Both go through the steep roads of the residential areas of Midlevels, a route just as beautiful as the tram's. You can also get to the Peak on the Number 1 minibus from the terminal behind the former HMS *Tamar* site (now occupied by the People's Liberation Army), next to the City Hall complex.

TIMING

This walk is largely uphill and is complicated somewhat by the elaborate road system that crisscrosses the area. The entire route takes about four hours. Allow about 40 minutes for the Museum of Tea Ware and at least 45 minutes to stroll through Hong Kong Park's greenhouses and aviary, both of which can get crowded. Add another half hour or more for the zoo at the Zoological and Botanical Gardens. The tram ride up the mountain will take about 20 minutes. Allow about an hour for the Peak.

Sights to See

㉑ Government House. Constructed in 1855, this handsome white Victorian building was the official residence of the British governor. During the Japanese Occupation it was significantly rebuilt, so it now exhibits a subtle Japanese influence, particularly the eaved roof. The SAR's chief executive, Tung Chee Hwa, had no wish to reside here—some say because of perceived negative feng shui—so Government House is used periodically for state occasions. It is not open to the public. ✉ *Upper Albert Rd., just west of Garden Rd.*

★ ☺ **⑲ Hong Kong Park.** Hoarding 25 acres of prime real estate, this park has to be one of the world's most valuable. Built by the Hong Kong Jockey Club with the abundant revenues from its racetracks, it comprises lakes, gardens, sports areas, a café, a rain-forest aviary with 500 species of birds, and a greenhouse with 200 species of tropical and arid-region plants. Although some of the artificial rocks and waterfalls in the lower gardens can feel a little unnatural, the park is a blessedly quiet and lush oasis within the urban melee.

The park also contains Flagstaff House, the former official residence of the commander of the British forces and the city's oldest colonial building (built in 1846). The house is now the **Museum of Tea Ware,** which has a fascinating exhibit chronicling the history of tea and its various accessories (including the famous Yixing tea ware) from the 7th century on. Who knew, for example, that Tibetan cream tea could be made with cheese by-products, or that the method of steeping leaves in water came relatively late, following a preference for whipped tea? ✉ *Cotton Tree Dr. at park entrance,* ☎ *2869–0690.* 🎫 *Free.* ☉ *Park, daily 6:30 AM–11 PM. Museum, Tues.–Sat. 10–5.*

㉓ Peak Tram. Housed in the Lower Peak Tram Terminus is the world's steepest funicular railway. It passes five intermediate stations on its way to the upper terminal, 1,805 ft above sea level. The tram was opened in 1880 to transport people to the top of Victoria Peak, the highest hill overlooking Hong Kong Harbour. Before the tram, the only way to get to the top was to walk or take a bumpy ride up the steep steps in a sedan chair. The tram has two 72-seat cars, which are hauled up the hill by cables attached to electric motors. A shuttle bus to and from the Peak Tram leaves from Edinburgh Place, next to City Hall. ✉ *Between Garden Rd. and Cotton Tree Dr.* ☎ *2522–0922.* 🎫 *HK$20 one way, HK$30 round-trip.* ☉ *Daily every 10–15 mins 7 AM–midnight.*

⑳ St. John's Cathedral. Completed in 1849, this Anglican cathedral was built with Canton bricks in the shape of a cross. It serves as a good example of both Victorian-Gothic and Norman architecture. ✉ *4–8 Garden Rd., up from Queen's Rd. Central, on west side of the street just past the large parking lot.* ☉ *Daily 9–5, Sun. services.*

★ **㉔ Victoria Peak.** Known in Chinese as Tai Ping Shan, or Mountain of Great Peace, the Peak is Hong Kong's one truly essential sight. On a clear day, nothing rivals the view of the dense, glittering string of skyscrapers that line Hong Kong's north coast and the carpet of buildings that extend to the eight mountains of Kowloon. It's well worth timing your visit to see the view both by day and at night, perhaps by taking in a meal at one of the restaurants near the upper terminus. The Peak is more than just a view, however; it also contains extensive parkland, perfect for a picnic or a long walk.

With the opening of the **Peak Tower,** the commercial complex of shops, restaurants, and diversions up top, the site's developers have tried to rebrand a visit to the Peak, spectacular enough in the old days, as "the Peak Experience," complete with shopping, amusement parks, and restaurants. This has been a mixed success, but children might enjoy some of the activities; The Peak Explorer is a virtual-reality ride through outer space, while the Rise of the Dragon takes you on a railcar through a series of animated scenes from Hong Kong's history, including a frighteningly accurate rendition of the 1907 typhoon that devastated the territory. There's also a Ripley's Believe It or Not Museum.

🐾 ㉒ **Zoological and Botanical Gardens.** A visit here is a delightful way to escape the city's traffic and crowds. In the early morning the spectacle of people practicing tai chi chuan (the ancient art of meditative shadow boxing) is an interesting sight. The quiet pathways are lined with semitropical trees, shrubs, and flowers. The zoo has jaguars and gorillas, which for years were a source of friction between the government and animal-rights groups, but the cages have been expanded to better simulate the animals' natural habitats; as a result, you can usually see the jaguars swimming in their pool or sunbathing. There is also an aviary with more than 300 species of birds, including a spectacular flock of pink flamingos. ⊠ *Upper Albert Rd., opposite Government House; enter on Garden Rd.,* ☎ *2530–0155.* 🎫 *Free.* ⊙ *Daily 6:30 AM–7 PM.*

OFF THE BEATEN PATH	**YAN YUEN SHEK –** Also known as Lovers' Rock, Yan Yuen Shek is a shrine that some Chinese women visit daily, burning joss sticks and making offerings in hopes of finding a husband. The 6th, 16th, and 26th days of each lunar month are the most popular times, and during the Maidens' Festival, in August, fortune-tellers set up shop for the lovelorn. A visit here is best combined with a visit to the Zoological and Botanical Gardens. Leave the gardens by the upper exit, east of the aviaries; cross Garden Road and take the left fork (Magazine Gap Road) at the traffic circle. Take a sharp left onto Bowen Road, a pleasant, tree-lined street that becomes a traffic-free path all the way to Happy Valley. From there Lovers' Rock is a 20- to 30-minute stroll. To get back to town, walk to the Wong Nai Chung Gap Road traffic circle at the end of Bowen Road, where you can catch Bus 15 or 15B to the Peak or Bus 6 or 61 back to Exchange Square, or you can take a taxi.

Wanchai

Wanchai was once one of the five *wan*—areas the British set aside for Chinese residences—but it developed a reputation for vice and became a magnet for sailors on shore leave, as during the Vietnam War. How times have changed: Wanchai is still as risqué an area as Hong Kong has to offer, but that says more about the city's overall respectability than it does about its available indulgences. For all its bars and massage parlors, Wanchai is now so safe that it seems a pale version of the "Wanch" of Richard Mason's novel *The World of Suzie Wong.*

The city's high real-estate prices have inevitably turned parts of Wanchai into an area of office towers, but it comes as a pleasant surprise to see how many crowded little alleys remain. A chance wrong turn can lead you into an outdoor wet market, a tiny furniture maker's shop, or an age-old temple. At night, the area comes alive (☞ Chapter 5) with bars, restaurants, and discos, as well as establishments offering some of Wanchai's more traditional services.

Numbers in the text correspond to numbers in the margin and on the Wanchai, Causeway Bay, Happy Valley, and North Point map.

A Good Walk

Walking is the best way to get around Wanchai, as the district's charms are more in its atmosphere than in specific sights. Take a circular walking tour starting from the junction of Queensway and **Queen's**

| 0 | | 330 yards |
| 0 | | 300 meters |

KEY

Ⓜ Metro Stops

Victoria Harbour

③

⑥

Wanchai Ferry Pier

Hung Hing Rd.

Seafront Rd.

②

Harbour Rd.

④

Harbour Dr.

Gloucester Rd.

Stewart Rd.

Tonnochy Rd.

Marsh Rd.

Jaffe Rd.

O'Brien Rd.

Fenwick St.

Luard Rd.

Lockhart Rd.

Fleming Rd.

Wanchai Rd.

Bowrington Rd.

Ⓜ **Admiralty**

Hennessy Rd.

Ⓜ **Wanchai**

Southorn Playground

Thomson Rd.

①

Queen's Rd. East

Johnston Rd.

Morrison Hill

Spring Garden Ln.

Cross St.

Wanchai Rd.

Queen's Rd. East

Academy for
Performing Arts
and Hong Kong
Arts Centre 2

Aw Boon Haw
(Tiger Balm)
Gardens 12

Cargo Handling
Basin. 6

Causeway Bay
Typhoon Shelter 8

Central Plaza 4

Happy Valley
Racetrack. 13

Hong Kong
Convention and
Exhibition Centre . . . 3

Hong Kong
Yacht Club. 5

Kwun Yum
Temple. 11

Noonday Gun 7

Queen's Road East . . 1

Tin Hau Temple. . . . 10

Victoria Park 9

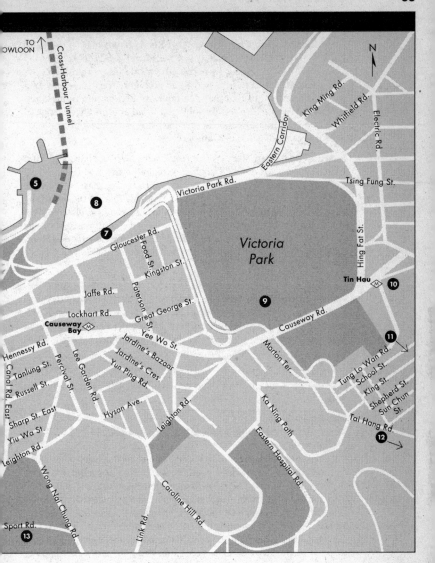

TO
KOWLOON

Cross-Harbour Tunnel

King Ming Rd.

Whitfield Rd.

Electric Rd.

Eastern Corridor

Tsing Fung St.

Victoria Park Rd.

5

8

7

Gloucester Rd.

Food St.

Kingston St.

Hing Fat St.

Victoria Park

Jaffe Rd.

Paterson St.

Great George St.

9

Tin Hau **10**

Lockhart Rd.

Causeway Bay M

Yee Wo St.

Jardine's Bazaar

Causeway Rd.

11

Hennessy Rd.

Tanlung St.

Lee Garden Rd.

Jardine's Cres.

Yun Ping Rd.

Morton Ter.

Tung Lo Wan Rd.

School St.

King St.

Shepherd St.

Sun Chun St.

Canal Rd. East

Russell St.

Percival St.

Hysan Ave.

Leighton Rd.

Ka Ning Path

Tai Hang Rd.

Sharp St. East

Yiu Wa St.

12

Leighton Rd.

Wong Nai Chung Rd.

Link Rd.

Caroline Hill Rd.

Eastern Hospital Rd.

Sport Rd.

13

Road East ① (a 10-minute ride from Central by tram or Bus 5, or a few blocks from the Admiralty MTR stop). Continue on Queen's Road East and turn left onto Wanchai Road, a busy market area selling a variety of foods, clothing, and household goods. This is a good place for browsing, especially in the narrow side alleys. To the left, several small lanes lead to Johnston Road and more tram lines; this area contains many shops that make rattan furniture, picture frames, and curtains to order. Turn left on Johnston Road and follow the edge of Southorn Playground, a popular meeting place, especially for those looking for a game of cards or Chinese chess.

Luard Road—along with cross streets Hennessy, Lockhart, and Jaffe roads—is the heart of Old Wanchai. At night the area is alive with multicolor neon signs and a lively trade in bars, pubs, massage parlors, and restaurants. Hennessy Road, which roughly follows the line of the original harborfront, is another good place to browse. Walk east on Hennessy Road to Fleming Road and turn north. Continue to Harbour Road, then head west to the **Academy for Performing Arts and Hong Kong Arts Centre** ②, in two adjacent buildings that function as the core of Hong Kong Island's cultural activity.

Continue on Harbour Road to Seafront Road and the **Hong Kong Convention and Exhibition Centre** ③. Circle back to Harbour Road and head east for a look at the **Central Plaza** ④, one of the world's tallest buildings. From here you can taxi back to your hotel, catch the MTR at the Wanchai station, or continue walking along the harborfront to the Wanchai Ferry pier for a ferry to Kowloon.

TIMING

If you stop to take in views and exhibits, this walk takes about two hours.

Sights to See

❷ **Academy for Performing Arts and Hong Kong Arts Centre.** Hong Kong is often maligned, not least by its foreign residents, as a cultural desert, but these two adjacent buildings help defuse this charge, with excellent facilities for both exhibits and the performing arts. Find out about the busy schedule of activities—dance, classical music, and theater by local and visiting artists—in local newspapers or at the ticket reservations office. While you're at the Arts Centre, visit the **Pao Gallery** (fourth and fifth floors), which hosts both local and international exhibits. The Academy for Performing Arts was financed with horse-racing profits donated by the Hong Kong Jockey Club. ⊠ *2 Harbour Rd., Wanchai,* ☏ *2582–0256.* ⊠ *Free.* ☉ *Daily 10–8.*

NEED A
BREAK?

Open Kitchen, on the sixth floor of the Hong Kong Arts Centre, serves delicious meals in a self-serve-style environment. ⊠ *2 Harbour Rd., Wanchai,* ☏ *2827–2923.* ☉ *Daily 11–11.*

❹ **Central Plaza.** In Asia's ongoing race to build ever-taller skyscrapers, this office complex (completed in 1992) briefly held the title as the region's tallest. It has long since been surpassed, but at 78 stories it's still quite striking. ⊠ *Harbour Rd. and Fleming Rd.*

❸ **Hong Kong Convention and Exhibition Centre.** The original center opened in 1988 as one of the largest and best-equipped meeting facilities in the world, but—in typical Hong Kong fashion—it was quickly deemed insufficient. Needing a suitable venue for the 1997 handover ceremonies, the city decided to build, in a mad, furious dash, the extension that now sits prominently on a spit of reclaimed land jutting into the harbor. With its glass walls and swooping curved roof, it's an outstanding venue for annual international trade fairs, regional conferences, and hundreds of local events. An exceptionally long walk through the center yields a few celebratory sculptures commemorating the handover and a waterfront promenade with views of a not-very-distant Kowloon. It forms the core of the complex that includes the Convention Plaza office tower, a block of service apartments, and two hotels, the Grand Hyatt and the Renaissance Harbour View. ⊠ *Enter on Harbour Rd. between Fenwick Rd. and Fleming Rd.*

NEED A BREAK? Next to the Convention and Exhibition Centre is the **Grand Hyatt Hotel.** From its polished marble and enormous Chinese vases to the jungle-size flower displays and grand staircases, this hotel just manages to stay on the tasteful side of opulence. The second-floor lounge is an exceptionally relaxing place to sit and chat over a drink or two.

① **Queen's Road East.** It's choked with traffic day and night, but this busy shopping street is packed with diversions. You'll pass rice and food shops and stores selling rattan and traditional furniture, curtains, picture frames, paper lanterns, and Chinese calligraphic materials. Shortly before reaching the Hopewell Centre, you may notice the altar of the **Tai Wong Temple** and smell its smoldering joss sticks.

Causeway Bay, Happy Valley, and North Point

Causeway Bay, one of Hong Kong's best shopping areas, also has a wide range of restaurants and a few sights. Much of the district is easily reached from Central by the tram that runs along Hennessy Road, or by the MTR to the Causeway Bay station.

The areas east of Victoria Park offer little for first-time visitors. North Point and Quarry Bay are both undeniable parts of the "real" Hong Kong, which means they're full of offices, apartment blocks, and factories. From Causeway Bay you can ride the tram for a few miles through these areas, perhaps the best way to get a feel for the environment.

Numbers in the text correspond to numbers in the margin and on the Wanchai, Causeway Bay, Happy Valley, and North Point map.

A Good Tour

If you come by taxi, a good starting point is the **Hong Kong Yacht Club** ⑤, which overlooks the **Cargo Handling Basin** ⑥. Stroll around the harbor and have a look at the **Noonday Gun** ⑦ and the boats in the **Causeway Bay Typhoon Shelter** ⑧. From Gloucester Road, which runs by the Noonday Gun, you can walk to **Victoria Park** ⑨, where you can roam at leisure and, on a nice day, have lunch or beverages in the outdoor restaurant. Exit from there onto Causeway Road, and walk or take a taxi to **Tin Hau Temple** ⑩. Take another taxi to **Kwun Yum Temple** ⑪. Continue uphill on Tai Hang Road (a 15-minute walk or a brief ride by taxi or Bus 11) to **Aw Boon Haw (Tiger Balm) Gardens** ⑫, then taxi to the **Happy Valley Racetrack** ⑬. Happy Valley is an interesting area with pockets of large middle-class housing, a legacy of life in less hectic, more spacious times. While the racetrack is the center point of the valley, there are several quaint *dai pai dong* or tea cafés and restaurants and shops to wander through.

TIMING

Allow four to five hours so you'll have plenty of time to stroll around the park, catch taxis, and find the museum. Try to set out late in the morning, just after rush hour, as the traffic in Causeway Bay—both pedestrian and vehicular—can be extremely daunting. The busiest intersection is right in front of the Sogo department store, which, with its skyscraper-size advertisements, looks a bit like an Asian Times Square.

Sights to See

★ ☺ ⑫ **Aw Boon Haw (Tiger Balm) Gardens.** Built in 1935 with profits from sales of a popular menthol balm, the gardens were the pet project of two Chinese brothers, who also built a mansion here. Eight acres of hillside are pocked and covered with grottoes and pavilions filled with garishly painted statues and models of Chinese gods, mythical animals, and scenes from fables and parables. An ornate seven-story pagoda contains Buddhist relics and the ashes of monks and nuns. It's great fun to explore, especially for children. Be forewarned: some Taoist and Buddhist scenes are decidedly gruesome. There are plans in the works for parts of the gardens to be renovated, but at press time there was no official word on developments. ⊠ *Tai Hang Rd., Happy Valley.* ☜ *Free.* ☉ *Daily 9:30–4.*

⑥ **Cargo Handling Basin.** West of the Yacht Club and east of the Wanchai Ferry pier (which sends ferries to Kowloon), you can watch the unloading of boats bringing cargo ashore from ships anchored in the harbor. ⊠ *Hung Hing Rd.*

⑧ **Causeway Bay Typhoon Shelter.** This boat basin was originally built as a bad-weather haven for sampan dwellers. In the 1960s and '70s, tourists could have dinner on a sampan, but this is no longer possible, as the number of fishing families who live in those small open-air boats has dwindled and the basin has filled with pleasure craft. A few traditional sampans, crewed primarily by elderly toothless women, still putter around ferrying owners to their sailboats.

⑬ **Happy Valley Racetrack.** Hong Kong punters are the world's most avid horse-racing fans, and the track in Happy Valley—opened soon after the British first arrived in the territory—is one of their headquarters (the other being the newer, larger track in Shatin, in the New Territories). Races alternate between the tracks but are generally held in Happy Valley on Wednesday night or weekends from September through June. The joy of the Happy Valley track, even for those who aren't into horses, is that it's smack in the middle of the city and surrounded by towering apartment blocks—indeed, people whose balconies hang over the back-stretch often have parties on racing days. There are members-only stands, but the Hong Kong Tourist Board (HKTB) organizes special day-tours that allow visitors to experience the exclusive high-roller lounges. However, if you're game, it's just HK$10 to join in at the public stands where feverish gamblers wave their newspapers madly during races. ⊠ *Hong Kong Jockey Club, 2 Sports Rd., Happy Valley,* ☎ *2966–8111 or 2966–8364.* ☜ *HK$50 for entrance badge.*

⑤ **Hong Kong Yacht Club.** The yacht club is worth a visit, but it's not open to the public, so try to find a local who is a member (or knows one) to give you guest privileges. If you belong to a yacht club at home, you may have reciprocal guest privileges. Once inside, you're surrounded by display cabinets full of silver prize trophies and welcomed by a delightfully old-fashioned bar with magnificent views of the harbor. On weekends the place hums with activity, especially when there are races, common from spring through fall. The South China Sea Race to Manila is held every two years at Easter time; call the race office (☎ 2891–0013) for details. ⊠ *Kellet Island, off Hung Hing Rd.,* ☎ *2832–2817.*

⑪ **Kwun Yum Temple.** A shrine to the goddess of mercy has stood on this site for 200 years, but the current structure is mostly new, dating from 1986. Constructed on top of a huge boulder, it has a high ceiling and gallery and is very popular with local worshipers. ⊠ *Lin Fa Kung St. W.* ☉ *Daily 9–nightfall.*

❼ Noonday Gun. "In Hong Kong they strike a gong and fire off a noonday gun," wrote Noël Coward in his song "Mad Dogs and Englishmen." They still fire that gun at noon each day from a small enclosure overlooking the Yacht Club Basin and Typhoon Shelter, which is reached via a long walk (follow the signs) through the parking garage next to the Excelsior Hotel. The tradition was started by Jardine Matheson and Co., the great hong that inspired James Clavell's novels *Taipan* and *Noble House*: Jardine would fire a salute each time their *taipan*, who ruled over the company like a lord, would enter or leave the harbor. This angered the local governor, who ordered the company to use a gun instead of a cannon, and to fire it only as a noontime signal. The gun itself, with brass work polished bright, is a 3-pound Hotchkiss that dates back to 1901. ⊠ *Across from Excelsior Hotel, 281 Gloucester Rd.*

NEED A BREAK?
Have coffee or lunch in the first-floor coffee shop of the **Excelsior Hotel** (⊠ 281 Gloucester Rd., ☎ 2894–8888), overlooking the Yacht Club, and gaze at the yachts docked in the harbor.

❿ Tin Hau Temple. Located on a street of the same name off Causeway Road (behind Park Cinema on the southeast side of Victoria Park), this temple is one of several in Hong Kong similarly named and dedicated to the goddess of the sea. Its decorative roof and old stone walls are worth a peek; the date of construction is unknown, but the temple bell was made in 1747. ⊠ *Tin Hau St. off Causeway Rd.*

❾ Victoria Park. Beautifully landscaped with trees, shrubs, flowers, and lawns, the park has an aviary and recreational facilities for swimming, lawn bowling, tennis, roller-skating, and even go-cart racing. The Lantern Carnival is held here in mid-autumn, with the trees a mass of colored lights. Just before Chinese New Year (late January–early February), the park hosts a huge flower market. Early every morning the park fills with hundreds of tai chi chuan practitioners. ⊠ *Gloucester Rd.*

OFF THE BEATEN PATH
LAW UK FOLK MUSEUM – It's worth a trip to the end of the MTR line to see this 200-year-old house, which belonged to a family of Hakkas, the farmers who originally inhabited Hong Kong Island and the peninsula all the way into what is now southern Guangdong. Decorated in period style, the museum displays rural furniture and farm implements. Photos show you what bustling, industrial Chai Wan looked like in the 1930s, when it was a peaceful bay inhabited only by fishermen and squatters. ⊠ 14 Kut Shing St., 1 block from Chai Wan station; outside station turn left and follow Kut Shing St. as it turns to the right, ☎ 2896–7006. ☜ Free. ☉ Tues.–Sat. 10–1 and 2–6, Sun. 1–6.

South Side

One of Hong Kong's unexpected pleasures is that, for all the unrelenting urbanity of the north coast of the island, the south side consists largely of rolling green hills and a few residential areas that have sprung up around picturesque bays. A few points of interest nestle within the rolling hills. You can't cover this area on foot, but you can take a city bus or taxi from Central to either Stanley or Shek O (a 20- to 30-minute ride) and walk around.

Numbers in the text correspond to numbers in the margin and on the South Side map.

A Good Tour

Start the tour at **Hong Kong University** ①, which you can easily reach by taxi from Central; visit the **Fung Ping Shan Museum** on campus. From here take a taxi around the western end of the island to **Ab-**

erdeen ②, with its teeming harbor full of sampans. Take a bus or a sampan to **Apleichau (Duck's Tongue) Island** ③.

If you have children in tow, you might want to take a taxi east of Aberdeen to **Ocean Park** and **Middle Kingdom** ④ and spend the day here; or you can skip the theme parks and taxi from Aberdeen along the scenic coastal road to **Deep Water Bay** ⑤ and **Repulse Bay** ⑥. Taxi or bus from there to **Stanley** ⑦, where the main attraction is shopping at Stanley Market. Finally, stop at **Shek O** ⑧, the easternmost village on the island's south side.

From Shek O the round-island route continues back to the north, to the housing and industrial estate of Chai Wan, where you can choose between a fast journey back to Central on the MTR or a slow ride to Central on the double-deck tram that crosses the entire north side of the island via Quarry Bay, North Point, and Causeway Bay.

TIMING

If your time in Hong Kong is short, you can see all of these sights in a day, though it might make sense to limit yourself to, say, Stanley and Shek O. If you want to squeeze everything in, set out early in the morning and plan to make Shek O your dinner stop. Alternatively, you could easily spend an entire day shopping in Stanley and another day on the beach at Shek O or hiking through Shek O Country Park.

Shek O is worth visiting only in good weather. You can hike there year-round, although the beach is best from June through November.

Sights to See

❷ **Aberdeen.** Named after an English lord, not the Scottish city, Aberdeen got its start as a refuge for pirates some 200 years ago. After World War II Aberdeen became fairly commercial as the *tanka* (boat people) attracted tourists to their floating restaurants. You'll notice the famous Jumbo restaurant just offshore, its faux-Chinese decorations shrouded in lights. The tanka continue to live on houseboats, and although they may appear picturesque to passersby, their economic conditions are depressing.

You can still see much of traditional Aberdeen, such as the **Aberdeen Cemetery** (⊠ Aberdeen Main Rd.), with its enormous gravestones, and side streets where you'll find outdoor barbers at work and any number of dim sum restaurants. In the harbor, some 3,000 junks and sampans are interspersed with floating restaurants, and you will undoubtedly be invited on board for a ride through the harbor. Use one of the licensed operators, which depart on 20-minute tours daily from 8 to 6 from the main Aberdeen seawall opposite Aberdeen Centre. Groups can bargain: A trip for four to six people should cost from HK$100 to HK$150. Individual tickets are HK$40.

Also in Aberdeen is a famous **Tin Hau temple,** whose ancient original bell and drum are still used at its opening and closing each day. Currently in a state of decline, this is one of several shrines to the goddess of the sea celebrated in the Tin Hau Festival in April and May, when hundreds of boats converge along the shore.

❸ **Apleichau (Duck's Tongue) Island.** To get here, take a bus across the bridge or arrive by sampan. Apleichau Island has a boatbuilding yard where junks, yachts, and sampans are constructed, almost all without formal plans. Look to your right when crossing the bridge for a superb view of the harbor and its countless junks. Vehicles are not allowed to stop on the bridge, so you'll have to walk back if you want to take a picture.

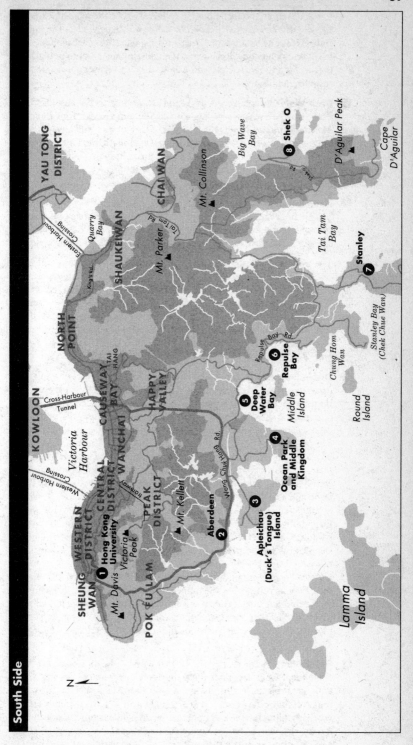

N

YAU TONG
DISTRICT

KOWLOON

Eastern Harbour Crossing

Cross-Harbour
Tunnel

Western Harbour Crossing

Victoria
Harbour

SHEUNG
WAN

WESTERN
DISTRICT

CENTRAL
DISTRICT

WANCHAI

CAUSEWAY
BAY

NORTH
POINT

King's Rd.

Quarry
Bay

SHAUKEIWAN

CHAI WAN

Mt. Collinson ▲

Big Wave
Bay

8 Shek O

D'Aguilar Peak
▲ D'Aguilar

Cape
D'Aguilar

Shek O Rd.

Tai Tam Rd.

Mt. Parker ▲

HAPPY
VALLEY

TAI
HANG

Tai Tam
Bay

Stanley

7

Stanley Bay
(Chek Chue Wan)

Chung Hom
Wan

Repulse
Bay

Repulse Bay Rd.

6 Repulse Bay

5 Deep
Water
Bay

Middle
Island

Round
Island

PEAK
DISTRICT

Mt. Kellett ▲

Wong Chuk Rd.

Tramway

Aberdeen

2

3

4 Ocean Park
and Middle
Kingdom

POK FU LAM

1 Hong Kong
University

Victoria
Peak ▲

▲ Mt. Davis

Apleichau
(Duck's Tongue)
Island

Lamma
Island

On your left are boats belonging to members of the Marina Club and the slightly less exclusive Aberdeen Boat Club, as well as the famous Jumbo Floating Restaurant. Quiet and unspoiled just a decade ago, Apleichau is now bursting at the seams with development—both public housing and a number of gleaming new private residential estates and shopping malls.

⑤ Deep Water Bay. Situated on Island Road, just to the east of Ocean Park, this bay was the setting for the William Holden film *Love Is a Many Splendored Thing* (1955), and its deep coves are still lovely. Nearby are the manicured greens of the exclusive Hong Kong Golf Club. Not surprisingly, the area has become a multimillionaires' enclave and is home to Hong Kong's richest man, Li Ka-shing, a very private real-estate tycoon.

❶ Hong Kong University. Established in 1911, the university has almost 10,000 undergraduate and graduate students. Most of its buildings are spread along Bonham Road, the most interesting of which is the 19th-century University Hall, designed in a hybrid Tudor Gothic style.

The university's **Fung Ping Shan Museum** has an excellent collection of Chinese antiquities (ceramics and bronzes, some dating from 3000 BC, fine paintings, lacquerware, and carvings in jade, stone, and wood). It also has the world's largest collection of Nestorian crosses from the Yuan Dynasty (1280–1368), and some superb ancient pieces: ritual vessels, decorative mirrors, and painted pottery. The museum is a bit out of the way, but it's a must for the true Chinese art lover. ✉ *94 Bonham Rd.*, ☎ 2859–2114. ✆ *Free.* ⊙ *Mon.–Sat. 9:30–6.*

☞ ❹ Ocean Park and Middle Kingdom. The Hong Kong Jockey Club built these two large attractions, just east of Aberdeen. One of the world's largest oceanariums, **Ocean Park** (☎ 2873–8888) occupies 170 acres overlooking the sea. On the lowland side are gardens, parks, and a children's zoo. A cable car with spectacular views of the entire south coast can take you to the headland side and to Ocean Theatre, the world's largest marine-mammal theater, where dolphins and a killer whale perform for crowds of up to 4,000. There are also various carnival rides, including a mammoth roller coaster and the gravity defying Abyss Turbo Drop and a new Adventure Bay development is scheduled for completion in 2003. The park is open daily 10–6 and charges HK$150 for adults. Originally a theme park representing 5,000 years of Chinese history, **Middle Kingdom** (2873–8583) is undergoing redevelopment. Some say the move is to compete with Disney's $3 billion theme park on Lantau Island due for completion in 2005. Middle Kingdom's new plan aims to create a retail, dining, and entertainment facility, although at the moment you can see the dinner-theater production, "The Glory of the Forbidden City." The colorful theatrical performance has Chinese acrobats, Sichuan opera, and *bian lian* or quick face change acts. Note that Water World, which used to adjoin the site, has closed. ✉ *Tai Shue Wan Rd.*

❻ Repulse Bay. Named after the British warship HMS *Repulse* (not, as some local wags say, after the pollution of its waters), the beach is a wonderful place to while away an afternoon. This was the site of the famed Repulse Bay Hotel, which gained notoriety in December 1941 when invading Japanese clambered over the hills behind it and entered its gardens, which were being used as headquarters by the British. After a brief battle, the British surrendered. The hotel was demolished in 1982 and eventually replaced with a luxury residential building, but replicas of its Repulse Bay Verandah Restaurant and Bamboo Bar were opened in 1986, run by the same people who operated the hotel.

NEED A
BREAK? To taste the experience of colonial pampering, treat yourself to British high tea at the **Repulse Bay Verandah Restaurant and Bamboo Bar.** Tea is served daily from 3 to 5:30. ✉ *109 Repulse Bay Rd.,* ☎ *2812–2722. AE, DC, MC, V.*

❽ Shek O. The easternmost village on the south side of Hong Kong Island is a popular weekend retreat. It's filled with old houses, great mansions, a superb golf course and club, a few simple restaurants, a pretty beach, and fine views, albeit marred by some ugly new housing developments. Leave the town square, full of small shops selling inflatable toys and other beach gear, and take the curving path across a footbridge to the "island" of **Tai Tau Chau,** really a large rock with a lookout for scanning the South China Sea. Little more than a century ago, this open water was ruled by pirates.

You can hike through **Shek O Country Park** in less than two hours. Look here for birds that are hard to find in Hong Kong, such as Kentish plovers, reef egrets, and black-headed gulls, as well as the colorful rufus-backed shrike and the ubiquitous, chatty bulbul.

NEED A
BREAK? A favorite place for lunch, drinks, or just alfresco lounging is Shek O's **Black Sheep Restaurant,** a small place with an eclectic menu and the kind of relaxed ambience that makes you wonder if you're still in Hong Kong. Clusters of palm fronds give it the feel of a tropical island hideaway. ✉ *From Shek O village, turn left at the Thai restaurant by the small traffic circle, continue down the road and around the corner on the right,* ☎ *2809–2021. AE, DC, MC, V.*

❼ Stanley. Notorious during World War II as the home of Japan's largest POW camps in Hong Kong, Stanley is now known for its picturesque beaches and its market, where casual clothing and tourist knickknacks are sold at wholesale prices. Hong Kong has dozens of shops offering similar bargains, but it's more fun to shop for them in Stanley's countrified atmosphere. You can also buy ceramics, paintings, and books. The old police station, built in 1859, is open to the public and now houses a restaurant. Past the market, on Stanley Main Street, a strip of restaurants and pubs faces the bay. On the other side of the bay is a Tin Hau temple, wedged between giant new housing estates.

KOWLOON

Kowloon Peninsula is the extension of mainland China just across the harbor from Central, bounded in the north by the string of mountains that give Kowloon its poetic name: *gau lung,* "nine dragons." Kowloon is closer to China than Hong Kong in more ways than just geography: although the island's glittering skyscrapers are suffused with international commerce, Kowloon's urban fabric is even denser but has an older look to it. The proximity of the old Kai Tak airport kept building heights down (though landings still made you feel like you were scraping Kowloon's rooftops), but with the opening of the new airport Kowloon will no doubt rival the heights of Hong Kong at some point. The peninsula boasts many of the territory's best hotels as well as a mindboggling range of shopping options; and no visit to Hong Kong is complete without taking on the commercial chaos of Nathan Road.

The southernmost part of Kowloon is called Tsim Sha Tsui, where such landmarks as the Star Ferry Pier and the elegant Peninsula Hotel stand proudly. A series of cultural buildings lines the waterfront, including the bold, parabolic curves of the Cultural Centre and the golf ball–shape Space Museum. North of Tsim Sha Tsui are the market districts of Jordan and Mong Kok, where you can buy everything from pirated videos to electronics to name-brand clothes at fire-sale prices. Tsim Sha Tsui is best reached by the Star Ferry, while the rest of Kowloon is easily accessible by MTR or taxi.

Numbers in the text correspond to numbers in the margin and on the Kowloon Peninsula map.

A Good Tour

From the Kowloon tip, wend your way into the urban jungle of Tsim Sha Tsui from the **Star Ferry Pier** ①, which is a 10-minute ferry ride from the pier on the Hong Kong side—and, incidentally, the most romantic way to see the harbor, day or night.

Stroll east along the pedestrian waterfront to the Victoria Clock Tower, then visit the **Hong Kong Cultural Centre** ②. Note the luxurious **Peninsula Hotel** ③, across from which you'll find the **Hong Kong Space Museum** ④. The **Hong Kong Museum of Art** ⑤ is behind the Space Museum.

Continue east on Salisbury Road and turn left on Chatham Road South and continue north to the corner of Cheong Wan Road, where you'll find the **Hong Kong Science Museum** ⑥ and the newly relocated **Hong Kong Museum of History** ⑦. Backtrack a bit on Chatham Road to Granville Road or Cameron Road and turn right. The next main boulevard will be **Nathan Road** ⑧. Head south a short way on Nathan Road, then turn right onto Haiphong Road to get to **Kowloon Park** ⑨.

Return to Nathan Road and continue north to Jordan Road, then make a left and then a right onto **Temple Street** ⑩. Follow Temple Street north to the **Kansu Street Jade Market** ⑪, to the west. Continue one block north of Kansu Street to the **Tin Hau Temple** ⑫.

From here you can either walk or take the MTR to Prince Edward to see the new **Bird Garden** ⑬, which replaced the old Bird Market.

The **Wong Tai Sin Temple** ⑭ is best reached by MTR. The Wong Tai Sin station is four stops from Prince Edward on the green Kwun Tong line; the temple is directly opposite the station.

TIMING

You can take this tour in one day, but it will be a tiring day, as Kowloon is crowded, noisy, and often frustrating to walk or drive through. Plan a half day to stroll from the Star Ferry Pier to the Tin Hau Temple, stopping to see sights and shops along the way. Allow at least an hour for the Space Museum and the Museum of Art, another 45 minutes for the Science Museum, and an hour for the Museum of History. Be flexible with your shopping time; you'll want to compare prices before you make decisions. If you have two days in Kowloon, take the walk from Star Ferry to Kowloon Park the first day, then start at Temple Street and continue to Wong Tai Sin Temple the next day.

Start around 10 AM to avoid rush-hour traffic. Note that all museums offer free admission on Wednesday, though they're quite inexpensive normally. For the avid museum goer, the Hong Kong Tourist Board (HKTB) offers a Museum Tour pass for HK$50 that includes visits to the Museum of Art and Space, Science, History, and Heritage museums. The pass also includes a shuttle bus to each location. Buses depart throughout the day so visitors can spend as much time in each place as they wish. For tickets and bus timetable, visit any HKTB Visitor Information Centre.

Sights to See

⑬ **Bird Garden.** Built in 1997 on Yuen Po Street, 10 minutes from the Prince Edward MTR station, this garden replaced the old Bird Market, whose

Bird Garden **13**

Hong Kong Cultural
Centre **2**

Hong Kong
Museum of Art **5**

Hong Kong
Museum of History . . . **7**

Hong Kong
Science Museum **6**

Hong Kong Space
Museum **4**

Kansu Street Jade
Market **11**

Kowloon Park **9**

Nathan Road **8**

Peninsula Hotel **3**

Star Ferry Pier **1**

Temple Street **10**

Tin Hau Temple **12**

Wong Tai Sin
Temple **14**

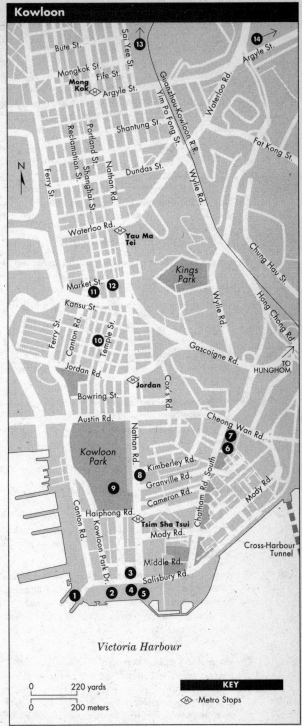

Kowloon

Victoria Harbour

0   220 yards

0   200 meters

KEY

Ⓜ Metro Stops

narrow streets of bird shops have been redeveloped. What the garden lacks in spontaneous tumult it makes up for with an attractive outdoor setting in the shadow of the KCR railroad tracks—and the rumble of each passing train sends the birds into a frenzy. The garden is composed of various courtyards filled with trees and surrounded by 70 stalls selling birds, cages, and such accoutrements as tiny porcelain feeders and fresh grasshoppers. Plenty of free birds also swoop in to gorge on spilled food and commiserate with their imprisoned brethren. If you walk from the MTR, you'll enjoy an aromatic approach through a street lined with flower shops. ⊠ *Yuen Po St.* 🖾 *Free.* ☉ *Daily 7 AM–8 PM.*

OFF THE
BEATEN PATH

CHI LIN NUNNERY – Considered a gem of Chinese monastic architecture, the nunnery was reopened in 2000 after a multimillion-dollar renovation completed in traditional Tang-era style—no nails were used in the construction, only wooden dowelling and brackets, a truly marvelous architectural achievement. The 8-acre site includes 16 Buddhist halls, a Zen-style rock garden, and a Ten Thousand Buddhas pagoda. ⊠ *5 Chi Lin Dr., Diamond Hill, 15-min walk from Diamond Hill MTR,* ☎ *2354–1770.* 🖾 *Free.* ☉ *Thurs.–Tues. 9–3:30.*

---

❷ **Hong Kong Cultural Centre.** This stark, architecturally controversial building (which looks better by its flattering nighttime lighting than by day) has tile walls inside and out, sloped roofs, and no windows—an irony, since the view of the harbor would be superb. Its concert hall and two theaters host almost every major artist who performs in the territory. Exhibits are occasionally mounted in the atrium, which has its own three-story metallic mural by Van Lau called *The Meeting of Yin and Yang.* In front of the center is a long, two-level promenade with plenty of seating and a view of the entire north coast of Hong Kong. ⊠ *10 Salisbury Rd.,* ☎ *2734–2010.*

★ ❺ **Hong Kong Museum of Art.** The exterior is unimaginative, but inside are five floors of innovatively designed galleries. One is devoted to historic photographs, prints, and artifacts of Hong Kong, Macau, and other parts of the Pearl River delta; other galleries feature Chinese antiquities, fine art, and visiting exhibits. ⊠ *10 Salisbury Rd.,* ☎ *2721–0116.* 🖾 *HK$20 for adults, half price Wed.* ☉ *Fri.–Wed. 10–6.*

❼ **Hong Kong Museum of History.** The museum, in an ungainly building adjacent to the Science Museum, covers a broad expanse of Hong Kong's past with life-size dioramas. Exhibits outline 6,000 years of the territory's cultural heritage and history. Special themed exhibits are often on display as well. ⊠ *100 Chatham Rd. S,* ☎ *2724–9042.* 🖾 *Free.* ☉ *Tues.–Sat. 10–6, Sun. 1–6.*

★ ☝ ❻ **Hong Kong Science Museum.** More than 500 scientific and technological exhibits—including an energy machine and a miniature submarine—emphasize interactive participation. The highlight is a series of experiments that test memory and cognitive ability. ⊠ *2 Science Museum Rd., corner of Cheong Wan Rd. and Chatham Rd.,* ☎ *2732–3232.* 🖾 *HK$25 for adults; HK$12.50 concession.* ☉ *Tues.–Fri. 1–9, weekends 10–9.*

☝ ❹ **Hong Kong Space Museum.** Across from the Peninsula Hotel, this dome-shape museum houses one of the most advanced planetariums in Asia. The museum has a variety of interactive models explaining basic aspects of space exploration (though some of these are less than lucid), as well as fly wires to let you experience weightlessness and such. It also contains the **Hall of Solar Science,** whose solar telescope permits visitors a close look at the sun, and the **Space Theatre** (seven shows daily from 2:30 to 8:30), with Omnimax movies on space travel, sports, and natural wonders. Children under three are not admitted.

✉ *10 Salisbury Rd.,* ☎ *2734–2722.* 🎫 *HK$10 for exhibits; Omnimax shows: HK$32 front row; HK$24 back row.* ☉ *Mon. and Wed.–Fri. 1–9, weekends 10–9.*

⑪ Kansu Street Jade Market. The old jade market was a sea of pavement trading, but this more orderly market has 450 stalls, selling everything from priceless ornaments to fake pendants. If you don't know much about jade, take along someone who does or you might pay a lot more than you should. Try to come between 10 and noon, as many traders close shop early. ✉ *Kansu and Battery Sts.* ☉ *Daily 10–3:30.*

☺ ⑨ Kowloon Park. The former site of the Whitfield Military Barracks is now a restful, green oasis. Signs point the way to gardens with different landscaping themes—the sculpture garden is particularly interesting, and the Chinese Garden has a lotus pond, streams, a lake, and a nearby aviary with a colorful collection of rare birds. The **Jamia Masjid and Islamic Centre** is in the south end of the park, near the Haiphong Road entrance. This is Hong Kong's principal mosque, albeit not its most graceful; built in 1984, it has four minarets, decorative arches, and a marble dome. At the northern end of the park sits an extraordinary public swimming complex built, like so much else in the city, by the Hong Kong Jockey Club with revenues from the races. ✉ *Just off Nathan Rd.*

⑧ Nathan Road. The densest shopping street in town, the so-called Golden Mile runs for several miles both north and south and is filled with hotels, restaurants, and shops of every description. To the left and right are mazes of narrow streets lined with even more shops crammed with every possible type of merchandise—jewelry, electronics, clothes, souvenirs, cosmetics, and so on (☞ Chapter 7). Expect to be besieged with street hawkers trying to sell you cheap "Rolexes."

③ Peninsula Hotel. The grande dame of Hong Kong hotels, the Peninsula is a local institution. The exterior of this sumptuous hotel is lined with a fleet of Rolls-Royce taxis and doormen in white uniforms, while the huge colonnaded lobby has charm, grandeur, string quartets, and the sedate air of excessive wealth tastefully enjoyed. Even if you're not staying here, stop inside to browse the upscale shopping arcade, partake of high tea, or just marvel at the architecture. ✉ *Salisbury Rd.,* ☎ *2366–6251.*

NEED A BREAK?	Tsim Sha Tsui is short on quiet cafés, but the **Peninsula Hotel** serves high tea—the perfect way to rest your shopping feet in style. Nibble on a majestic array of scones and pastries in the lobby (HK$165 per person) daily from 2 to 7. Or settle down for à la carte tea in the Verandah restaurant Friday to Sunday 3 to 5.

① Star Ferry Pier. The pier makes a convenient starting point for any tour of Kowloon. (It also has a bus terminal, which sends buses to all parts of Kowloon and to the New Territories.) As you face the bus station, Ocean Terminal, where luxury cruise ships berth, is on your left; inside this terminal, and in adjacent Harbour City, are miles of air-conditioned shopping arcades. To the right of the ferry pier is **Victoria Clock Tower**, which dates from 1915 and is all that remains of the old Kowloon–Canton Railway Station. (The new station, for travel within China, is 2 km [1 mi] to the east.)

OFF THE BEATEN PATH	**LEI CHENG UK MUSEUM –** This small museum in Sham Shui Po houses a 1,600-year-old vault and is worth a trip for its age alone. The four barrel-vaulted brick chambers form a cross around a domed vault, and the funerary objects are typical of the tombs of the Han Dynasty (AD 25–220). The vault was discovered in 1955 during excavations for the

huge housing estate that now surrounds it. To get here, take Bus 2 from Kowloon's Star Ferry terminal to Tonkin Street (drops you closer), or catch the MTR to the Cheung Sha Wan station (faster trip). ✉ *41 Tonkin St., Lei Cheng Uk Resettlement Estate.* ☎ *2386–2863.* 🎫 *Free.* 🕐 *Mon.–Wed. and Fri.–Sat. 10–1 and 2–6, Sun. 1–6.*

● **Temple Street.** The heart of a busy shopping area, Temple Street is ideal for wandering and people-watching. By day you'll find market stalls with plenty of kitsch and plenty of bargains in clothing, handbags, accessories, tapes, and CDs, but the best time to come is after 8 PM, when the streets become an open-air bazaar of fortune-tellers, prostitutes, street doctors offering cures for almost any complaint, and occasionally Chinese opera.

Such nearby lanes as **Shanghai Street** and **Canton Road** are also worth a peek for their shops and stalls selling everything from herbal remedies to jade and ivory. **Ning Po Street** is known for its paper kites and for the colorful paper and bamboo models of worldly possessions (boats, cars, houses) that are burned at Chinese funerals.

● **Tin Hau Temple.** One of Kowloon's oldest temples, this sensual site is filled with incense and crowds of worshipers. You'll probably be encouraged to have a try with the fortune sticks, known as *chim* sticks. Each stick is numbered, and you shake them in a cardboard tube until one falls out. A fortune-teller asks you your date of birth and makes predictions from the stick based on numerology. ✉ *Market St., 1 block north of Kansu St.* 🕐 *Daily 7–5:30.*

★ ● **Wong Tai Sin Temple.** Have your fortune told at this large, vivid compound, whose Buddhist shrine is dedicated to a shepherd boy who was said to have magic healing powers. In addition to the main altar, the pavilions, and the arcade—where soothsayers and palm readers are happy to interpret Wong Tai Sin's predictions for a small fee—there are two lovely Chinese gardens and a Confucian Hall. ✉ *2 Chuk Yuen Village, Won Tai Sin (in front of MTR stop),* ☎ *2327–8141.* 🎫 *Small donation expected.* 🕐 *Daily 7–5.*

THE NEW TERRITORIES

Until a generation ago, the expansive New Territories consisted almost exclusively of farmland and traditional walled villages. Today, following a government housing program that created "new towns" such as Shatin and Tsuen Mun with up to 500,000 residents, parts of the New Territories are beginning to feel more like the rest of Hong Kong. Within its expansive 518 square km (200 square mi), however, you'll still feel far removed from the congestion and urban rigors of Hong Kong Island and Kowloon. It's here you'll find many of the area's lushest parks and therapeutic nature walks. In addition, you'll be able to sneak glimpses of traditional rural life in the restored walled villages and ancestral clan halls scattered throughout the area.

The New Territories got its name when the British acquired this area. Whereas Hong Kong Island and Kowloon were taken outright following the Opium War of 1841, the land that now constitutes the New Territories was handed over much later on a 99-year lease. It was this lease that expired in 1997 and was the catalyst for the return of the entire colony to China. Because of its size, the New Territories can be difficult to explore without a car, but between the bus, MTR, and the Kowloon–Canton Railway, you can at least get close to many sights.

Perhaps the best way to see some of the smaller villages is to go on one of the HKTB's organized tours (even if you don't think of yourself as a tour type), which loop through the region. In addition to the tours' convenience, the guides are knowledgable and helpful. The Heritage tour focuses on the territory's fast-disappearing traditional walled villages and ancestral halls. The six-hour Land Between tour takes you through the rural countryside, including Chuk Lam Shim Yuen (Bamboo Forest Monastery) and Hong Kong's tallest mountain, Tai Mo Shan. Reserve through your hotel's tour desk or at an HKTB information center (☎ 2807–6390 Monday–Saturday, 2508–1234 Sunday and holidays).

Numbers in the text correspond to numbers in the margin and on the New Territories and the Outer Islands map.

Western New Territories

A Good Tour

Start at **Sam Tung Uk Museum** ①, an 18th-century walled village in Tseun Wan. From here take a taxi to the **Yuen Yuen Institute** ②, which brings together Buddhism, Taoism, and Confucianism. From there drive to **Ching Chung Koon Taoist Temple** ③, near the town of Tuen Mun, and then a little farther north to the **Miu Fat Buddhist Monastery** ④ on Castle Peak Road, which is a popular place for a vegetarian lunch. Drive from there to the **Kam Tin Walled Village** ⑤, a 17th-century enclave accessible by Bus 51.

After wandering the old village, you can drive east to go up to the peak of **Tai Mo Shan** ⑥ or drive north to visit the scenic town of **Lok Ma Chau** ⑦. End your tour at **Tai Fu Tai** ⑧, a 19th-century mansion that illustrates the conflicted political times during which it was built.

TIMING

Allow at least a full day for this tour, more depending on your pace. Plan to start in the morning and have lunch at the Miu Fat Monastery.

Sights to See

❸ **Ching Chung Koon Taoist Temple.** This huge temple near the town of Tuen Mun has room after room of altars, all filled with the heady scent of incense burning in bronze holders. On one side of the main entrance is a cast-iron bell with a circumference of about 5 ft—all large monasteries in ancient China rang such bells at daybreak to wake the monks and nuns for a day of work in the rice fields. On the other side of the entrance is a huge drum that was used to call the workers back in the evenings. Inside, some of the rooms are papered with small pictures; their relatives pay the temple to have these photos displayed so they can see their dearly departed as they pray. The temple also includes a retirement home, built from donations, which provides a quiet and serene atmosphere for the elderly. Colorful plants and flowers, hundreds of dwarf shrubs, ornamental fishponds, and pagodas bedeck the grounds. ⊠ *Adjacent to Ching Chung LRT station.*

❺ **Kam Tin Walled Village.** This village was built in the 1600s as a fortified town belonging to the Tang clan. Six walled villages surround Kam Tin, but **Kat Hing Wai** is the most popular. The original walls are intact, with guardhouses on the four corners and arrow slits for fighting off attackers; but the image of antiquity is somewhat marred by the modern homes and TV antennas looming over the ancient fortifications. Just inside the main gate is a narrow street lined with shops selling souvenirs and mass-produced oil paintings.

❼ **Lok Ma Chau.** Once, the hillside view from Lok Ma Chau was of bucolic rice paddies and duck ponds. Now it's the best vantage point in Hong Kong of mainland China and the high-rise urban developments

The New Territories and Outer Islands

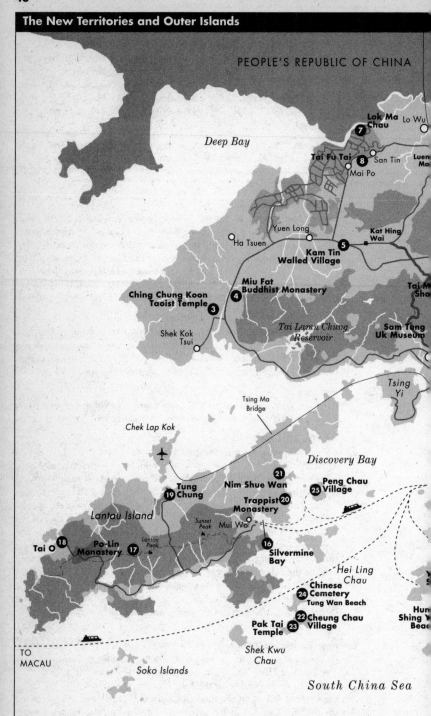

PEOPLE'S REPUBLIC OF CHINA

Deep Bay

Lok Ma Chau ⑦ Lo Wu

Tai Fu Tai ⑧ San Tin Luen Ma

Mai Po

Yuen Long

Kat Hing Wai

Ha Tsuen

Kam Tin Walled Village ⑤

Miu Fat Buddhist Monastery ④

Ching Chung Koon Taoist Temple ③

Tai M Sha

Shek Kok Tsui

Tai Lam Chung Reservoir

Sam Tung Uk Museum

Tsing Yi

Tsing Ma Bridge

Chek Lap Kok

Discovery Bay

Nim Shue Wan ㉑

Tung Chung ⑲

Peng Chau Village ㉕

Trappist Monastery ⑳

Lantau Island

Sunset Peak

Mui Wo

Lantau Peak

Tai O ⑱

Po-Lin Monastery ⑰

Silvermine Bay ⑯

Hei Ling Chau

Chinese Cemetery ㉔
Tung Wan Beach

Hun Shing Beac

Pak Tai Temple ㉓ ㉒ **Cheung Chau Village**

TO MACAU

Shek Kwu Chau

Soko Islands

South China Sea

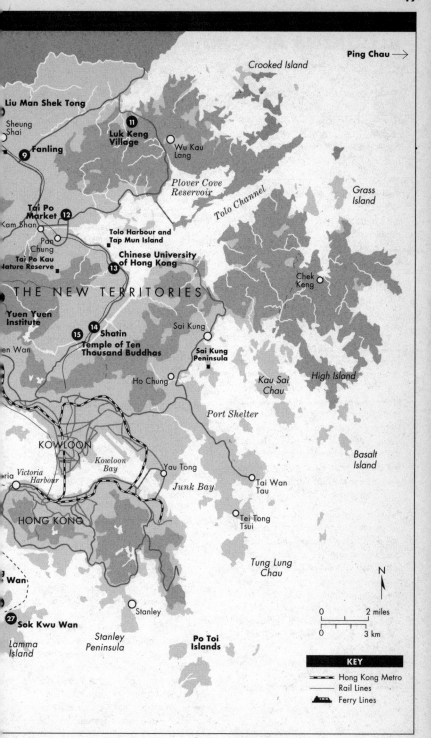

Ping Chau →

Crooked Island

Liu Man Shek Tong

Sheung
Shai

⑪ Luk Keng
Village

Fanling ⑨

Wu Kau
Lang

Plover Cove
Reservoir

Grass
Island

Tolo Channel

Tai Po
Market ⑫

Kam Shan

Pan
Chung

Tolo Harbour and
Tap Mun Island

Tai Po Kau
Nature Reserve

Chinese University
of Hong Kong ⑬

Chek
Keng

THE NEW TERRITORIES

Yuen Yuen
Institute

⑮ ⑭ Shatin
Temple of Ten
Thousand Buddhas

en Wan

Sai Kung

Sai Kung
Peninsula

High Island

Ho Chung

Kau Sai
Chau

Port Shelter

Basalt
Island

KOWLOON

Kowloon
Bay

Yau Tong

Junk Bay

Tai Wan
Tau

ria

Victoria
Harbour

HONG KONG

Tei Tong
Tsui

Tung Lung
Chau

N

Wan

⑳⑦ Sok Kwu Wan

Lamma
Island

Stanley

Stanley
Peninsula

Po Toi
Islands

0   2 miles
0   3 km

KEY

Hong Kong Metro
Rail Lines
Ferry Lines

RELIGIONS AND TRADITIONS

BUDDHISM AND TAOISM are the main religions followed in Hong Kong, while Confucianism is a set of moral codes that are widely held. Each complements the other and is present in daily life through traditions and festivals.

Buddhism In Hong Kong there are more than 400 Buddhist temples, ranging from the large Po Lin Monastery in Lantau—home to the world's largest, seated, outdoor bronze Buddha—to the small, smoky shrine covered with incense in a dead-end street near Lan Kwai Fong. Lord Buddha's birthday, the eighth day of the fourth moon, is a public holiday in Hong Kong, and worshippers visit temples, as well as participate in festive activities.

Buddhist devotees give offerings to the gods in return for luck, health, and of course, prosperity. One of the most popular is Tin Hau, Queen of Heaven and Protector of all Seafarers. She has an important place in Hong Kong due to the territory's maritime history. Her birthday is celebrated on the 23rd day of the third month of the Lunar calendar when fishermen colorfully decorate their boats and pray at temples for good catches in the coming year.

Taoism There is a long history of involvement by worshippers of Taoism in tai chi, or "shadow boxing." The graceful exercise combines thought and action, and is believed to stimulate the central nervous system, lower blood pressure, relieve stress, and gently tone muscles without strain. Tai chi's rhythmic movements also massage internal organs and improve their functionality. The essence of tai chi is a combination of control and balance, which embodies Taoist thought. Walking through any part of Hong Kong in the early morning, you'll no doubt encounter groups or individuals performing this ancient Chinese martial art.

One of the best known Taoist gods is Kwan Tai, the God of War and the patron of the Hong Kong police, and, ironically, of the Triads as well. Tai was a historical figure who lived during the Three Kingdoms period (AD 220–AD 265) and who was later deified as a Taoist symbol of loyalty and integrity. Visit the 19th-century Man Mo Temple on Hollywood Road, and you'll find an ever-burning lamp standing before his statue. Sung Dynasty general Che Kung is another god who was elevated to a Taoist deity. Legend has it that he saved the inhabitants of Shatin Valley from the plague centuries ago. Now, believers gather at his major temple in Shatin on his birthday, the third day of the Lunar New Year.

Confucianism The fundamental concerns of the Confucian tradition are learning to be human and filial devotion. Respecting elders is considered one of the most important values in families and this is reflected in the Ching Ming Festival or "Remembrance of Ancestors Day." This is a key holiday in the Chinese calendar, when families visit cemeteries to sweep their ancestors' graves and clean headstones in a sign of respect. The day is also known as "sweeping the graves" day.

The importance of the family gathering on Chinese New Year's Eve is equivalent to Christmas in the West. Just like in the West, this is a time for celebrations and a huge feast. Traditionally, *lai see*, or red pockets, with tokens of cash, are handed out from the elders to the young, and are considered lucky money. The period leading up to New Year's Day is very busy, too, with superstitious families taking steps to avoid any chance of bad luck in the coming year. It's believed that you must not wash your hair in the first few days of the new year, otherwise your life span will be shortened. Also, sweeping the floors during this same time is considered unlucky, because all the money and good fortune will be swept out the door.

— Eva Chui

of Shenzhen Special Economic Zone. This sleepy border town is now facing new development of its own with the construction of the Lok Ma Chau rail terminus, a $250 million (HK$2 billion) project, that will become the second cross-border facility in the territory. The project is expected to be completed in 2004.

4 **Miu Fat Buddhist Monastery.** On Castle Peak Road near Tuen Mun, Miu Fat is a popular place for a vegetarian lunch. The monastery itself is ornate, with large carved-stone animals guarding the front. Farther on is the former clan village of **Yuen Long**, now almost completely redeveloped as an industrial and residential complex. ⊠ *Castle Peak Rd.* ☞ *Free.* ☉ *Daily 10–6.*

1 **Sam Tung Uk Museum.** This walled village, built in 1786, looks more like a single large house with numerous interlocking chambers and white-washed interior courtyards. Set in a forested area incongruously amid the residential towers and chaotic commercial life of Tsuen Wan, its construction obeys a rigid symmetry, with the ancestral hall and two common chambers forming the central axis and the more private areas flanking it. The front door is angled to face west–southwest, in keeping with feng shui principles of alignment between mountain and water. The village is easily reached by MTR; it's a five-minute walk from the Tseun Wan stop to the museum.

★ **8** **Tai Fu Tai.** Built in 1865 by a scholar of the gentry class, this exquisitely preserved home reflects the European architectural influence on China, which was a result of the Western victory over China in the Opium War of 1841 and the gradual encroachment of colonialism. With loyalties divided, the scholar-gentry class decided to incorporate a few European design elements to indicate their open-mindedness. French rococo moldings and stained glass above the doorways belie the home's traditional Qing Dynasty style. Other charming idiosyncrasies include an upper floor that allowed women to watch guests unobserved and an enclosed courtyard called a "moon playing" chamber for examining the night sky.

6 **Tai Mo Shan.** Rising 3,230 ft above sea level, Tai Mo Shan—which translates as Big Hat Mountain—is Hong Kong's highest peak and the area around the peak has been cordoned off as a country park. Access is via a former military road (you can see the old British barracks, now occupied by the People's Liberation Army, en route), and a lookout about two-thirds of the way up gives you a chance to see both sides of the territory: rolling green hills in the foreground and dense urban development in the distance. On a clear day you can even see the spire of the Bank of China building in Central.

2 **Yuen Yuen Institute.** This complex of pavilions and prayer halls was built in the 1950s to bring together the three streams of Chinese thought: Buddhism (which emphasizes nirvana and physical purity), Taoism (nature and inner peace), and Confucianism (which follows the practical and philosophical beliefs of Confucius). The main three-tiered red pagoda is a copy of the Temple of Heaven in Beijing, and houses 60 statues representing the full cycle of the Chinese calendar—you can look for the one that corresponds to your birth year and make an offering of incense.

Central and Eastern New Territories

A Good Tour

Although parts of this tour are accessible by KCR train, you should consider renting a taxi and driver for the day for visiting some of the more remote sights. Otherwise, if you take a taxi to a sight you may not be able to find one to take you back.

Start from the north end of the tour and take the train to **Fanling** ⑨, then take a taxi from the KCR stop to the **Luen Wo Market.** From there, drive to the nearby village of Sheung Shui to see the ancestral hall of **Liu Man Shek Tong** ⑩, then head northeast to **Luk Keng village** ⑪, which is close to the Chinese border. It is a scenic drive past Plover Cove Reservoir to **Tai Po Market** ⑫, which runs along the streets near the Tai Po KCR stop. Wander around the market, then take the KCR south one more stop to the University station to find the **Chinese University of Hong Kong** ⑬. Take a campus bus or taxi to the **Art Gallery,** in the university's Institute of Chinese Studies Building.

Go back to the University station and take the train another stop south to the **Shatin Racecourse,** which adjoins the Racecourse station. Take a look around, then take the train one more stop south if you want to see the functional new town of **Shatin** ⑭. From here you can take a taxi or go to Shatin KCR station and walk to the **Temple of Ten Thousand Buddhas** ⑮, which provides a view of Amah Rock and Tai Mo Shan, Hong Kong's highest peak.

If you want to spend some time enjoying the outdoors, the Eastern New Territories has several attractive undeveloped areas: you can explore the beaches and fishing villages of **Tap Mun Island** or wander the forest and seaside trails of the **Sai Kung Peninsula.**

TIMING

Allow a couple of days for this tour. For a shorter tour, you may want to select sights that are geographically close together. If you want to visit Tap Mun Island or the Sai Kung Peninsula, set aside a separate day for each.

Sights to See

⑬ **Chinese University of Hong Kong.** The Art Gallery in the Institute of Chinese Studies Building is well worth a visit for its large exhibits of paintings and calligraphy from the Ming period to modern times. There are also important collections of bronze seals, carved jade flowers, and ceramics from South China. Take the KCR to University station, then a campus bus or taxi. ⊠ *Tai Po Rd., Shatin,* ☎ *2609–7416.* ☑ *Free.* ☉ *Mon.–Sat. 10–4:30, Sun. 12:30–4:30.*

NEED A
BREAK?
Across from the Chinese University campus is the popular restaurant **Yucca de Lac,** which serves meals outdoors in the green hills along Tolo Harbour, affording a pleasant view of the university. ⊠ *Tai Po Rd., Ma Liu Shui village,* ☎ *2691–1630.* ☉ *Daily 11–11. MC, V.*

OFF THE
BEATEN PATH
TOLO HARBOUR AND TAP MUN ISLAND – About a 15-minute walk from the Chinese University along Tai Po Road is the Ma Liu Shui Ferry pier, the starting point for a ferry tour of the harbor and Tap Mun Island. The ferry makes many stops, and if you take the 8:30 AM trip you'll have time to hike around Tap Mun Island and still turn back by late afternoon (☎ 2527–2513 for Tsui Wah Ferry schedule, ☑ weekdays HK$32, weekends HK$50 round-trip). Tap Mun has a small village with a few Chinese restaurants, but you can also bring a picnic lunch. This trip is better by far in sunny weather. The **New Fisherman's Village,** on the southern tip of the island, is populated mainly by Hakka fisherwomen. About 1 km (½ mi) north, near the western shore, is the ancient village of Tap Mun, where you'll see old women playing mah-jongg. The huge **Tin Hau Temple,** dedicated to the goddess of the sea, is one of the oldest temples in Hong Kong and is less than ½ km (¼ mi) north of the vil-

lage. It sits at the top of a flight of steps that leads down into the water of the harbor; inside are old model junks and, of course, a veiled figure of the goddess herself. Go to the east side of the island to see the Tap Mun Cave and some of the best-kept beaches in the territory.

⑨ Fanling. Although this town has the rather spare, functional feel of many of the new towns and may be of little interest to you, the nearby **Luen Wo Market** is one of the territory's most impressive and well worth a look. A grid of small stalls selling everything from T-shirts to pigs' lungs and the bustle and pungent aromas prove that local merchants can quickly make even a relatively newly built marketplace feel traditional.

⑩ Liu Man Shek Tong. Approached down a small, unmarked path in the village of Sheung Shui, this ancestral hall was built in 1751 and was one of few such halls that survived the antihistorical Cultural Revolution of the mid-1960s–mid-1970s. A recent restoration (completed in 1994) preserved the spectacular original roofs and ornamentation but substituted concrete walls to take the weight off the rickety pillars—at some cost to the site's aesthetic unity, unfortunately. It is interesting to note that the Liu clan, for whom this hall was built, was obsessed with education: the wood panels hung in the rear hall indicate the education levels achieved by various clan members under the old imperial civil-service-exam system of the Qing Dynasty. 🎫 *Free.* ⊙ *Wed., Thurs., weekends, and public holidays 9–1 and 2–5.*

⑪ Luk Keng village. This tiny Hakka village is home to fewer than 200 residents, most of them widows. While most of the existing buildings were constructed in the 1960s (the dates are marked above the entryways), the village abuts the Luk Keng Country Park, which is an egret sanctuary, lending the place a superbly tranquil air.

⑭ Shatin. Whether you enter Shatin by road or rail, you'll be amazed to find this metropolis smack dab in the middle of the New Territories. One of the so-called new towns, Shatin underwent a population explosion starting in the mid-1980s that transformed it from a town of 30,000 to a city of more than a half million in less than 15 years. It's home to the **Shatin Racecourse** (⊠ Racecourse stop on KCR), Hong Kong's largest and a spectacular place to watch a race. Also here is the **Hong Kong Heritage Museum** (⊠ 1 Man Lam Rd., ☎ 2180–8188, 🎫 HK$10, free Wed., ⊙ Tues.–Sun. 10–6) devoted to Chinese history, art, and culture. Exhibitions are housed in a five-story building surrounded by a traditional Chinese courtyard.

OFF THE **SAI KUNG PENINSULA** – To the east of Shatin, Sai Kung Peninsula is home
BEATEN PATH to a few small towns and Hong Kong's most beloved nature preserve. The hikes through the hills surrounding High Island Reservoir are spectacular, and the beaches are among the Territory's cleanest, largely because they are sheltered from the effluent that flows out of the Pearl River delta. A number of open-air seafood restaurants dot the area as well. (If you choose to eat in a seafood restaurant, note that physicians caution against eating raw shellfish here because of hepatitis outbreaks.) Take the MTR to Choi Hung and then Bus 92, Bus 96R, or Minibus 1 to Sai Kung Town. You can also take a taxi along **Clearwater Bay Road**, which will take you into forested areas and land that is only partially developed, with Spanish-style villas overlooking the sea. To cruise around the harbor, rent a *kaido* (pronounced "guy-doe"; one of the small boats run by private operators for about HK$130 round-trip), and stop at tiny **Yim Tin Tsai Island**, which has a rustic Catholic mission church built in 1890. **Sai Kung Country Park** has several hiking trails (☞ Chapter 6) that wind through majestic hills overlooking the water. This excursion will take a full day, and you should go only in sunny weather.

⑫ **Tai Po Market.** *Tai po* means "shopping place," and the town more than lives up to its name. In the heart of the region's breadbasket, Tai Po is fast becoming a utilitarian "new town," but its main open-air market is a feast for the eyes: baskets of lush green vegetables, freshly cut meat hanging from great racks overhead, fish swimming in tanks awaiting selection, and a variety of baked and steamed treats. Adjacent to the market is the 100-year-old **Man Mo Temple**; you'll smell the incense offered by worshipers. ⊠ *Take KCR to the Tai Po Market stop.* ⊘ *Daily 9–6.*

⑮ **Temple of Ten Thousand Buddhas.** You have to climb some 500 steps to reach this temple, nestled in the foothills of Shatin, but it's worth every step: inside the main temple are nearly 13,000 gilded ceramic statues of Buddha, all virtually identical. They were made by Shanghai craftsmen and donated by worshipers. From here you can also see the nearby Amah Rock. Amah means "nurse" in Cantonese, and the rock resembles a woman with a child on her back; it's popular with Chinese women. ⊠ *Shatin.* ⌨ *Free.* ⊘ *Daily 9–5.*

THE OUTER ISLANDS

It's easy to forget that Hong Kong is not the only island in these parts. But for residents, the Outer Islands are a popular and important chance to escape the city and enjoy the waterfront, good seafood, and a little peace and quiet. The islands' villages are very much up to speed (and, to the regret of many, cellular phones still work here), but they run at a more humane pace. For maximum relaxation, try to come on a weekday, as the Hong Kong weekenders often come in large numbers and bring their stresses with them.

In addition to Hong Kong Island and the mainland sections of Kowloon and the New Territories, 235 islands were under the control of the British until July 1997. The largest, Lantau, is bigger than Hong Kong Island; the smallest is just a few square feet of rock. Most are uninhabited. Others are gradually being developed, but at nowhere near the pace of the main urban areas. A few of the outlying islands are off-limits, occupied by prisons or military bases. The four that are most easily accessible by ferry—Lantau, Lamma, Cheung Chau, and Peng Chau—have become popular residential areas and welcome visitors.

You can reach the islands by scheduled ferry services operated by the **New World First Ferry** (☎ 2131–8181). The ferries are easy to recognize by the large letters HKF on their funnels. For most destinations you'll leave from the Outlying Districts Services Pier, in Central, on the land reclamation area just west of the Star Ferry Terminal. Boats to Discovery Bay on Lantau leave from the Star Ferry Terminal itself. Schedules are available at the information office on the pier; round-trip fares range from HK$15 to HK$50.

Numbers in the text correspond to numbers in the margin and on the New Territories and the Outer Islands map.

Lantau

The island of Lantau lies due west of Hong Kong. At 143 square km (55 square mi), it is almost twice the size of Hong Kong Island. Hong Kong's new airport, at Chek Lap Kok, and Walt Disney World, currently under construction at Penny's Bay and due for completion in 2005, may eventually change the face of Lantau, but for the time being it's sparsely populated and makes a nice getaway from the city.

A Good Tour

Because of Lantau's size, you should plan to see either the western half (Silvermine Bay, Po Lin Monastery, and Tung Chung) or the eastern half (Discovery Bay, the Trappist monastery, and perhaps Peng Chau) instead of combining both on a single visit. To do the western tour, take the ferry to the town of Mui Wo on **Silvermine Bay** ⑯, an area being developed as a commuter suburb of Hong Kong Island. Lantau is very mountainous, so for a tour of the outlying villages, plan to hike (☞ Chapter 6) or take a bus. From Mui Wo, the island's private buses head out to the **Po Lin Monastery** ⑰, home of a giant Buddha; **Tai O** ⑱, an ancient fishing village; and **Tung Chung** ⑲, which has a Sung Dynasty fort.

Although the **Trappist Monastery** ⑳ near **Nim Shue Wan** ㉑ can be reached by bus from Silvermine Bay, one alternative is to combine the monastery with other sights on the eastern end of the island by taking the ferry from Central to Discovery Bay. From there it is half-hour walk to the monastery. Ferries for Discovery Bay leave from the Star Ferry Terminal, and from the pier in Discovery Bay turn left and walk to Nim Shue Wan, then follow the signs to the monastery. You can also take a small passenger ferry, or kaido, between Peng Chau Island and Nim Shue Wan.

TIMING

The ferry ride from Central to Silvermine Bay takes about an hour, while the trip to Discovery Bay (via faster boats) takes about 25 minutes; after that, you can spend as long on Lantau as you like. The island is worth at least a full day's visit, even two; and you could easily spend a day on just one or two of the attractions listed below, so choose the ones that interest you most. The best overnight accommodations are at the Silvermine Beach Hotel (☞ Chapter 4); you can also stay at the Po Lin and Trappist monasteries. The HKTB has information on these and other Lantau lodgings.

Sights to See

㉑ **Nim Shue Wan.** For quiet and solitude, take the 90-minute hike through this old fishing village—where you might see fishermen's grandchildren talking on their cellular phones—and the unspoiled woods and hills beyond to the **Trappist Monastery** (✉ Grand Master, Trappist Haven, Lantau Island, Box 5, Peng Chau, ☎ 2987–6292) (☞ *below*), on eastern Lantau. On the way you'll see beaches that would be beautiful except for the astounding amount of trash thrown there or washed ashore. You can spend the night in the monastery's simple accommodations, but you must make reservations well in advance.

⑰ **Po Lin Monastery.** Within the Precious Lotus Monastery, in Lantau's mountainous interior, is the world's tallest outdoor bronze statue of Buddha, the **Tin Tan Buddha**—measuring more than 100 ft high and weighing 275½ tons. The statue is all the more impressive for its situation at the peak of a hill, which essentially forces pilgrims to stare up at it as they ascend. The adjacent monastery, gaudy and exuberantly commercial, is known for the vegetarian meals served in the temple refectory. ✉ *Take the bus marked* PO LIN MONASTERY *from Mui Wo and ask the driver to let you off at the monastery stop, from which you follow signs.* ☜ *Free.* ☉ *Daily dawn–dusk.*

⑯ **Silvermine Bay.** This area is being developed as a commuters' suburb of Hong Kong Island. You can rent bicycles in front of the **Silvermine Beach Hotel** (☞ Chapter 4) to ride around the village of Mui Wo, still surrounded by terraced fields.

⑱ Tai O. Divided into two parts connected by a modern drawbridge, the village still has many waterfront stilt houses and fishing shanties. However, part of the old village was devastated by a fire in 2000 which subsequently raised concerns about the safety of the traditional stilt houses. The fires reportedly spread quickly throughout the homes because of inadequate safety measures when they were built. Today there are plans to build new homes under modern safety guidelines, while the dwellings that were spared from the fire are a reminder of earlier village life. Visit the local temple dedicated to Kuanti, the god of war, and taste the local catch at one of Tai O's seafood restaurants. ✉ *Take the bus marked* TAI O *from Mui Wo village.*

⑳ Trappist Monastery. Despite its unexpectedly futuristic 1950s architecture, the monastery and its adjacent chapel exude a wonderfully placid air. Founded in 1951, the monastery is reached by a steep wooded path that ends at a footbridge suspended over a small stream. Like many Trappist monasteries, this one served as a working dairy for many years. The walk from Discovery Bay takes about 30 minutes, and you'll know you're on the right path if you find yourself walking through the backyards of the ramshackle huts en route. ✉ *Follow the poorly marked concrete path from the southwest end of Discovery Bay to the forest, where the signs become more useful.* 🎫 *Free.* ☉ *Daily dawn–dusk.*

⑲ Tung Chung. Here an ancient **Sung Dynasty fort** was evacuated by the Qing Dynasty army in 1898, when the New Territories was leased to Britain. The fort is now an elementary school. Tung Chung's other attraction is its view of **Chek Lap Kok Airport**. The government plans to build a "new town" here, similar to Shatin, which aims to move people from the crowded cities and into the New Territories.

Cheung Chau

Cheung Chau, southwest of Lantau and about one hour from Central by ferry, is Hong Kong's most crowded outlying island (all things being relative), with about 22,000 people. It is most well known as the home to Hong Kong's only gold medalist (in windsurfing), Lee Lai San, affectionately known to the locals as San San. At the tip of the beach is a lovely outdoor restaurant owned by relatives of San San, who have proudly hung a large framed picture of the athlete in her golden moment. The island community mostly live on the sandbar that connects the two hilly tips of this dumbbell-shape entity. Its Mediterranean flavor has attracted artists and writers from around the world, some of whom have formed an expatriate artists' colony here. Cheung Chau also draws Hong Kongers for another reason: its hotels rent by the hour (you'll see their booths in front of the ferry terminal), offering young lovers a brief escape from the congested living quarters and parental oversight of home.

There are no vehicles here—with the exception of a miniature red fire truck—so be prepared to walk around the island. As an alternative, you can take one of the small sampans that ferry year-round from Hong Kong Island to Cheung Chau's beaches, which are virtually deserted and have clear water.

TIMING

The ferry from Central takes an hour each way. You can make Cheung Chau a day trip, or you can stay in reasonable comfort at the **Cheung Chau Warwick** hotel (☞ Chapter 4), on East Bay at Tung Wan Beach, just north of Cheung Chau village.

Sights to See

22 **Cheung Chau village.** The entry into Cheung Chau's harbor, through lines of gaily bannered fishing boats, is an exhilarating experience. Cheung Chau is highly historical, with pirate caves and ancient rock carvings along the waterfront just below the Warwick hotel. Dining out here is also a joy, as there are dozens of open-air cafés on either side of the crowded sandbar township—both on the waterfront **Praya Promenade** and overlooking the main public beach at **Tung Wan.**

24 **Chinese cemetery.** These graves are generally modest and are set very close together, but each one bears a photo, etched onto a porcelain plate, of the person buried below. The ground is littered with fake money (belonging to the Bank of Hell, and denominated in the millions of dollars) that relatives burn to bring the deceased prosperity in the afterlife. ⊠ *1 km (½ mi) from ferry pier; turn right from pier and walk along waterfront until you leave town, then follow paths veering left up the hill.* 🎫 *Free.* ⊙ *Daily dawn–dusk.*

23 **Pak Tai Temple.** Dedicated to the protector of fishermen, this 200-year-old temple hosts the colorful, springtime Bun Festival, one of Hong Kong's most popular community galas. The festival originated in the 18th century as an appeasement for the spirits of people killed by pirates—spirits thought to wreak plagues upon the village. Beside the main altar are four whale bones from the nearby sea. ⊠ *½ km (¼ mi) from ferry pier; turn left from the pier and walk along the waterfront until you see the temple, a slight uphill walk.* 🎫 *Free.* ⊙ *Daily dawn–dusk.*

Lamma Island

What Lamma lacks in sights, it makes up for with an abundance of quaint, lackadaisically bustling port-side village charm. The waterfront is lined with restaurants offering alfresco dining and the pleasure of exquisitely fresh seafood plucked live from tanks and cooked on the spot. Once you've feasted, you can work off the meal by taking the hour-long walk through rolling green hills that connects the two main villages.

In addition to its other attractions, Lamma is as close to a 1960s bohemian scene as Hong Kong gets, full of laid-back expatriates driven out of Central by high rents. They have spawned a subculture of vegetarian restaurants and Tibetan crafts stores.

TIMING

The ferry from Central to either Sok Kwu Wan or Yung Shue Wan takes about 25 minutes and leaves from the new ferry piers in front of Exchange Square. It doesn't matter which village you go to first, since the one-hour walk between them is a Lamma highlight. Plan to visit both in a leisurely afternoon.

Sights to See

26 **Hung Shing Ye Beach.** "Beach" overstates the scale of this small, sandy oceanside strip next to the Hong Kong Electric power plant. Roughly midway between Sok Kwu Wan and Yung Shue Wan, Hung Shing Ye Beach is a pleasant place to enjoy the sun and is sometimes swimmable (don't go in if you see plastic bags or other refuse on the water). You can spend the night at the modest 12-room **Concerto Inn** (☎ 2982–1668, FAX 2982–0022); some rooms have nice views, and the inn has a garden café.

27 **Sok Kwu Wan.** The smaller and grittier of Lamma's two villages, Sok Kwu Wan is notable mainly for the string of cavernous seafood restaurants that line the path leading from the pier. If you arrive on foot from Yung Shue Wan, however, your first glimpse of the bay from the hills will be quite stunning.

NEED A
BREAK? The hub of expat community life (and a great place for vegetarian food) is the **Bookworm Café** (✉ 79 Main St., ☎ 2982–4838), which bills itself as a "health café with net surfing and community happenings."

28 **Yung Shue Wan.** By comparison with Sok Kwu Wan, Yung Shue Wan whirrs with activity. Formerly a farming and fishing village, it has in the past couple of decades become an enclave for expats, especially artists and journalists. Main Street is lined with small shops selling handicrafts and the occasional bohemian outpost, although the lingering smell of the fish markets is a reminder of Lamma's humbler, less cosmopolitan origins. **Lamma Fine Craft** (✉ 61 Main St., ☎ 2982–2120) sells handmade crafts and jewelry from across the region.

Peng Chau

The tiniest of Hong Kong's four major Outer Islands, Peng Chau was once home to a few farmers, fishermen, and a fireworks factory. Although the factory has long since closed and the island has been discovered as a weekend retreat for Hong Kong's cityfolk, the port-side community feeling remains.

Stand on the Peng Chau ferry quay and watch the kaido for Lantau's Trappist monastery sputter toward dark-green hills. Breathe in that stirring ambience of Hong Kong's islands—a mix of salt air, shrimp paste, and dried fish combined with a strong dose of local pride and a sense of independence, both of which have been lost in urban Hong Kong.

The ferry from Central takes an hour each way; alternatively, you can make a short hop from Nim Shue Wan on Lantau in about 15 minutes. Go on a sunny afternoon, if possible, and plan to spend about two hours.

25 **Peng Chau village.** The village is small and charming, and its shopping district is known for its unpretentious little stores selling locally made porcelain at remarkably low prices.

NEED A
BREAK? Peng Chau doesn't have Lamma's lively café scene, but the **Forest** (✉ 38C Wing Hing St., ☎ 2983–8837) is a popular watering hole among locals, with home-style American cooking and live music several nights a week.

Other Islands

If you have extra time or a venturesome spirit, try one of Hong Kong's more out-of-the-way islands, not so easy to reach but all the more rewarding for their isolation.

Ping Chau

This minuscule island, not to be confused with Peng Chau, is 1 square mi (2.6 square km) of land in the far northeast of the New Territories, near the mainland coast. Now almost deserted, it has a checkered history. Guns and opium were smuggled out of China through Ping Chau, and during the Cultural Revolution many mainlanders swam through shark-infested waters in hope of reaching Ping Chau and the freedom of Hong Kong. The island's largest village, **Sha Tau,** is something of a ghost town, with many cottages boarded up, but here and there you'll find old farming families eager to take you in, maybe even for the night.

A large part of the island is country parkland, with footpaths overgrown with orchids, wild mint, and morning glories. Look for the strange rock formations at either end of the island. At the south end are two huge rocks known as the **Drum Rocks,** or Watchman's Tower Rocks. At the north end is a chunk of land that has broken away from the island; the Chinese say it represents the head of a dragon.

Plan your visit for a weekend and be prepared to stay the night, as the ferry to Ping Chau departs only on Saturday at 11:15 AM and returns only on Sunday at 11:15 AM. Bring camping gear, or accept lodging from villagers if they offer. Board the ferry at Ma Liu Shui, near the University KCR stop. Call the **HKTB visitor hot line** (☎ 2508–1234) to confirm departure times before you go.

Po Toi Islands

This chain of three barren little fishing islands, virtually unchanged since medieval times, sits in the extreme southeast of Hong Kong's waters. Only Po Toi Island itself is inhabited (sort of), with a population of fewer than 100. It offers spectacular walks and fine seafood restaurants.

Walk uphill past primitive dwellings, many deserted, to the Tin Hau Temple, or walk east through the hamlet of Wan Tsai, past banana and papaya groves, to Po Toi's famous **rock carvings.** The geometric patterns on these rocks are believed to have been carved during the local Bronze Age, about 2,500 years ago.

Getting to the Po Toi Islands is an all-day affair and takes some planning. The most convenient way to go is by junk—to rent one call **Simpson Marine Ltd.** (☎ 2555–7349; ☞ Junking *in* Chapter 6). **Ferries** leave Aberdeen on Tuesday, Thursday, and Saturday at 9 AM and return from Po Toi at 10:30 AM the following day, so you have to stay overnight. On Sunday and holidays, however, you can get a morning ferry (10 or 11:30 from St. Stephen's Beach in Stanley) and return the same day at 3 or 4. You can make reservations by calling ☎ 2554–4059, but you'll need the help of a Cantonese speaker.

3 DINING

The surroundings may be Chinese, but cuisine in Hong Kong begins with carefully prepared Cantonese feasts and travels around the globe making stops in Thailand, Vietnam, Italy, France, Australia, the United States, and everywhere in between.

Updated by
Denise Cheung

WHEREVER YOU GO IN HONG KONG, you're bound to see a restaurant sign. Establishments that sell prepared food are as old as Chinese culture itself, and because most people live in small apartments and have little space to entertain at home, restaurants are usually the chosen venues for special occasions and family gatherings. Cooking may be more varied in Hong Kong than anywhere else in the world: Cantonese cuisine (long regarded by Chinese gourmands as the most intricate and sophisticated in Asia) is joined by foods from other parts of China and nearly every other culinary region on earth. The deeply rooted Chinese love of good food extends here to French, Italian, Portuguese, British, Spanish, Australian, Japanese, Indian, Thai, Vietnamese, Korean, Mexican, and specialty American fare.

Be advised, however, that Hong Kong's extraordinary culinary vitality is offset by some of Asia's worst restaurants. It's possible to find a hole-in-the-wall with unexpectedly exciting food, but don't expect any old neighborhood restaurant to turn out dreamy dishes.

Don't be shocked when you get your bill. You'll be charged for everything, including tea, rice, and even those side dishes placed automatically on every table, which are often mistaken for complimentary snacks. Tips are generally expected, even if the bill includes a service charge.

Restaurants in Hong Kong tend to change menus as often as people change their clothes, following the season and the clientele's tastes. Don't be surprised if your favorite dish is no longer on the list the second time you visit.

For many kinds of Asian cuisines, in particular Chinese cuisine, food is meant to be shared. Instead of having an entrée for yourself, a table—whether it's two or 12 people—will order several dishes to share. For example, a table of four might order a whole or half chicken, a vegetable, a fish dish, a meat dish, and fried noodles, all of which are placed on a lazy Susan and made available to everyone at the table. The sizes and prices of the dishes can also be altered according to the number of diners. In many sophisticated restaurants, fresh seafood prices vary daily and are determined by the weight (ask the waiter for the market price). In this chapter, the price range given is for an average main dish that is normally shared among two to four diners. Please note that market prices of seafood, and prices of outrageously expensive dishes and specialties—abalone, bird's nest, shark's fin—are not included in the price range to avoid misleading conclusions.

Hong Kongers regularly patronize hotel restaurants, bars, and coffee shops. Service is usually better, and the quality of the food more consistent, than in many independent restaurants.

Reservations are always a good idea; we note only when they're essential, which is often the case at lunchtime (between 1 and 2) or at dinnertime (between 7 and 10) on weekends. Unless otherwise noted, all restaurants listed are open daily for lunch and dinner. We mention dress only when men must wear a jacket or a jacket and tie.

CATEGORY	COST*
$$$$	over HK$280
$$$	HK$180–HK$280
$$	HK$80–HK$180
$	under HK$80

per person, not including 10% service charge

HONG KONG ISLAND

Central and SoHo

One of the busiest sections of Hong Kong, Central is a madhouse at lunchtime, when hungry office workers crowd the streets and eateries. Most restaurants have set lunches with speedy service, making it possible for most customers to get in and out within an hour; these are generally good values. Evening dining is either formal or a quick bite followed by many drinks, especially in Lan Kwai Fong. Another social area is SoHo (the area south of Hollywood Road), spreading mainly along Elgin Street, Staunton Street, and Old Bailey Street, accessible by the long, outdoor Midlevels escalator. Almost every kind of cuisine can be found here including Spanish, Italian, Indian, Argentinian, Cuban, Cajun, French, Portuguese, and Russian. Quality and authenticity of the food varies—but it's worth a visit to experience the SoHo atmosphere. Restaurants in both Lan Kwai Fong and SoHo have a somewhat contrived quality, with highly stylized theme decorating schemes and menus, along with relatively steep prices.

Asian

CANTONESE

$$$$ ✕ **Man Wah.** Even upscale Cantonese restaurants are known for their bustling atmosphere, but this one is a Zen-like haven in the midst of busy Central. Silk paintings of Mandarins hang on the walls, handcarved gold-and-ebony chopsticks polish off each place setting, and rosewood is everywhere you turn. The food is exquisite. Cantonese feasts come in many courses, and it's easy to order a half dozen dishes or more between friends. Steamed crab claws with ginger and rice wine are huge yet light, leaving plenty of room for more. The signature dish of sautéed fillet of sole with chilies in black-bean sauce is close to a work of art. For dessert try the poached pear in tangerine tea—to be savored slowly, while you watch the ships in Victoria Harbour go by. ⊠ *Mandarin Oriental Hotel, 5 Connaught Rd.,* ☎ *2522–0111 ext. 4025. AE, DC, MC, V.*

$$$ ✕ **China Lan Kwai Fong.** This restaurant offers you a culinary journey through China, with regional Chinese delicacies from Guangdong, Chiu Chow, Szechuan, and Beijing and Shanghai. Although it has a posh ambience, there are traditional Chinese touches such as terra-cotta warriors at the door and chirping birds in antique cages. Specialties include panfried Szechuan-style king prawns with chili and spices, Shanghainese crystal river shrimp, and wok-fried diced beef tenderloin with chili and black pepper served in a potato basket—but try the basket before it turns soggy from the juicy filling. Check out the all-you-can-eat dim sum brunch on weekends (HK$128). Reservations are necessary for lunch on weekdays. ⊠ *17-22 Lan Kwai Fong,* ☎ *2536–0968. AE, DC, MC, V.*

$$–$$$ ✕ **Yung Kee.** For more than a half century, this massive eatery has served
★ Cantonese food amid riotous decor featuring writhing gold dragons. Convenient to both hotels and businesses, Yung Kee attracts a varied clientele—from office workers to visiting celebrities—all of whom receive the same cheerful, high-energy service. Roast goose is a specialty, its skin beautifully crisp. Adventurous palates should check out Yung Kee's famous thousand-year-old eggs with ginger. The preserved blackish eggs literally melt in your mouth. Seafood fanciers should try sautéed fillet of pomfret with chili and black-bean sauce or braised *garoupa* (grouper). ⊠ *32–40 Wellington St.,* ☎ *2522–1624. AE, DC, MC, V.*

A CHINESE SAMPLER

GASTRONOMICALLY SPEAK-ING, the words "Chinese cuisine" don't mean much more than the words "European cuisine." The most populous country in the world has dozens of different cooking styles, and five of these are prominent in Hong Kong:

Beijingese. Beijing cuisine, which originated in what was once called Peking, is hearty fare designed for the chilly climate of northern China—noodles, dumplings, and breads are more evident than rice. Peking duck, the perennial favorite, was originally an imperial Mongolian dish and is usually served in two (or three) courses. Mongolian or Manchurian hot pots (a sort of fondue-cum-barbecue) are northern specialties, and firm flavors—such as garlic, ginger, and leek—are popular.

Cantonese. Because 94% of Hong Kong's population comes from the Chinese province of Guangdong (Canton), Cantonese is by far the most popular culinary style. Favoring meats and fresh vegetables, the Cantonese ideal is to bring out the natural taste of each ingredient by cooking them all quickly at very high temperatures. The result is *wok chi*, a fleeting energy that requires food to be served and eaten immediately. If it's properly prepared, you will never taste fresher food.

Chiu Chow. The Chiu Chow people, from around Canton, have a gutsy, hearty cuisine that has never caught on in the West. It begins with Iron Buddha tea and moves on to thick shark's-fin soup, soya goose, whelk (snails), bird's nest, dumplings, and irresistible cold crabs served with vinegar.

Shanghainese. Shanghai is a city of immigrants, not unlike New York and Hong Kong, so it has cosmopolitan cuisine; and because it lies at the confluence of several rivers on the South China Sea, the city has especially good seafood. The rich-flavored Shanghainese hairy crabs are winter favorites. Many Shanghainese dishes are fried in sesame oil or soy sauce and can be a bit greasy. Sautéed freshwater shrimp are also a staple dish. Shanghai is also famous for its great varieties and hearty tastes of buns and dumplings.

Szechuan. Most renowned for its spicy flavors, Szechuan food, also rendered *Sichuan* in English, is beloved around the world. Szechuan rice, bamboo, wheat, river fish, shellfish, chicken, and pork dishes are all prepared with plenty of salt, anise, fennel seed, chili, and coriander. The ingredients are simmered, smoked, stirred, and steamed, and the effect is an integrated flavor—the opposite of Cantonese food, in which each ingredient has its own presence. The cooking style features an eye-watering array of different chili types.

Dining

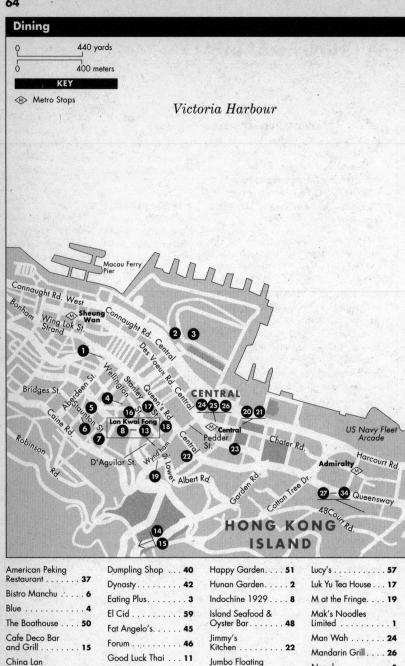

0 ————— 440 yards

0 ————— 400 meters

KEY

Ⓜ Metro Stops

Victoria Harbour

American Peking
Restaurant **37**

Bistro Manchu **6**

Blue **4**

The Boathouse **50**

Cafe Deco Bar
and Grill **15**

China Lan
Kwai Fong **13**

Dan Ryan's **32**

Dim Sum **53**

Dumpling Shop **40**

Dynasty **42**

Eating Plus **3**

El Cid **59**

Fat Angelo's **45**

Forum **46**

Good Luck Thai . . . **11**

Grand Cafe **43**

Grappa's **33**

Grissini **44**

Happy Garden **51**

Hunan Garden **2**

Indochine 1929 . . . **8**

Island Seafood &
Oyster Bar **48**

Jimmy's
Kitchen **22**

Jumbo Floating
Restaurant **52**

Lao Ching Hing . . . **41**

Lobster Bar **30**

Lucy's **57**

Luk Yu Tea House . . . **17**

M at the Fringe . . . **19**

Mak's Noodles
Limited **1**

Man Wah **24**

Mandarin Grill **26**

Nepal **5**

Nice Fragrance
Vegetarian
Kitchen **39**

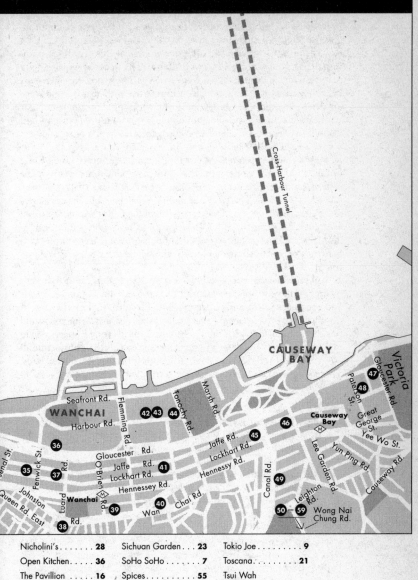

Nicholini's **28**	Sichuan Garden . . . **23**	Tokio Joe **9**
Open Kitchen **36**	SoHo SoHo **7**	Toscana **21**
The Pavillion **16**	Spices **55**	Tsui Wah Restaurant **18**
The Peak Lookout Hong Kong **14**	Stanley's French Restaurant **56**	The Verandah **54**
Petrus **29**	Steam and Stew Inn **38**	Vong **25**
Saigon Beach **37**		W's Entrecote **49**
Shanghai Shanghai **20**	ToTT's Asian Grill & Bar **47**	Ye Shanghai **31**
Shek O Chinese and Thailand Seafood Restaurant **58**	Thai Basil **27**	Yung Kee **10**
	Thai Lemongrass . . . **12**	Zen **34**

$$ ✕ **Luk Yu Tea House.** Food takes a backseat to atmosphere in this institution. Luk is a living museum with extraordinary character—it's been in business for more than 60 years, and as such lets you catch a rare glimpse of old colonial Hong Kong from the Chinese perspective. Don't expect top-notch service and attentive waiters at Luk Yu. It's a traditional and typical noisy Chinese teahouse. The decor is worth a look in itself, with handsome, carved wooden doors, hardwood paneling, marble facings, and spittoons (which customers use with gusto)—and waiters dress in traditional Chinese uniform. Morning dim sum is popular with Chinese businesspeople, though the fare is no more than standard Cantonese. Seats can be hard to come by at peak hours (1 to 2) unless you're a regular. ✉ *24–26 Stanley St.,* ☎ *2523–1970. MC, V.*

$ ✕ **Mak's Noodles Limited.** Mak's looks just like another Hong Kong noodle shop, but it's one of the best-known noodle joints in town. The restaurant takes pride in its reputation, displaying copies of its reviews—including a write-up in *Time* magazine—at every table. The premises are clean, the attentive staff wears smart-looking uniforms, and the menu even includes some inventive dishes, such as tasty pork-chutney noodles. The real test of a good noodle shop, however, is its wontons, and here they're fresh, delicate, and filled with whole shrimp. ✉ *77 Wellington St.,* ☎ *2854–3810. No credit cards.*

$ ✕ **Tsui Wah Restaurant.** Looking for a hearty meal in Central doesn't mean you have to spend a fortune, as is the case here. Join the locals and order a milk tea and coffee mixture. From toasted sandwiches to noodles, fried rice to steak, this joint has almost anything you could possibly want. Although it's not quite what typical Hong Kongers would make at home, it's as close as you can come to Chinese comfort food. Noodles and fried rice are some of the safest bets for foreign palates. There's also a wide range of set meals with very reasonable prices. ✉ *15 Wellington St.,* ☎ *2525–6338. No credit cards.*

HUNAN

$$ ✕ **Hunan Garden.** Escape the fast lane in this serene restaurant serving the cuisine of Hunan, the Chinese province where Mao Tse-tung was born. Both Hunan food and Hunan temperaments are known for being hot. Fried-fish butterflies are a highly recommended appetizer: these carp pieces, thinly sliced and deep-fried with a sweet coating, are crispy and sweet. The spicy fried chicken with chili may well set your lips and throat on fire; if you like things milder, stick with the codfish fillet with fried minced beans—the chewy and nutty bean paste goes perfectly with the fillet's soft texture. Do try the warm Shaoxing wine, served warm in tiny cups. Ask for lemon slices with the wine if you want a zestier aroma. Live Chinese music accompanies your meal. ✉ *The Forum, Exchange Sq., 3rd floor,* ☎ *2868–2880. AE, DC, MC, V.*

JAPANESE

$$$ ✕ **Tokio Joe.** Labeled as a place for "user-friendly Japanese food," this funky, casual Japanese joint serves up delicate Asian fare with finesse yet without any intimidating formality. Creative design elements make the atmosphere fun—beautiful ceramic pots line faux-fur walls. You can watch the chefs at work in a central bar area—they lend a wonderfully contemporary twist to some classic dishes: the house sushi roll, for example, contains a mixture of deep-fried soft-shell crab, avocado, and crab roe. Other options include seafood ramen, nicely battered tempura shrimp, or broiled sea bass. Ask for a recommendation for a sake selection to go with your food. For dessert, try the homemade sesame ice cream. Service is attentive and courteous. ✉ *16 Lan Kwai Fong,* ☎ *2525–1889. Reservations essential. AE, DC, MC, V. Closed Sun. No lunch.*

MANCHURIAN

$$ ✕ **Bistro Manchu.** This smart little bistro serves up warming, sooth-ing, stomach-filling Manchurian cuisine. Noodles, dumplings, veg-etables, meat—you won't be disappointed by this rarely encountered cuisine. The vegetable stew is a large bowl full of eggplant, potato, cab-bage, and green beans in a clear broth. The northeastern-style smoked chicken will surprise you with its delicate texture and subtle smoky fla-vor. If you're a meat lover, don't miss the stir-fried lamb with scallions. To complement the hearty dishes try a selection from the vast array of Chinese teas or a light and sweet Harbin beer. Take the time to read the introduction to Manchurian cuisine on your menu. ⊠ *33 Elgin St.,* ☎ *2536–9218 or 2536–9996. AE, DC, MC, V.*

NEPALI

$$ ✕ **Nepal.** If you thirst for adventure but don't want to risk an assault on Everest, knock back a Yaktail or Yeti Foot cocktail in this tiny Nepalese restaurant. Don't be deceived by its size—it has more to offer than you might expect. Take a look at the Nepalese wood carving, the *manne* (praying tools), and the musical instruments as you enjoy the Indian/Nepalese music in the background. The *hanta tareko* (grilled eggplant) and *kaju sadeko* (fried cashew nuts) are good starters, and the special Nepalese soup, *golveda-ko-rash,* is perfect for vegetarians. The royal chicken, a light Nepalese curry, is a highly recommended en-trée. End the meal with Nepalese ice cream, which is slightly firmer than Western ice cream. Equally impressive is Nepal's younger sibling **Kath+Man+Du** (⊠ 11 Old Bailey St., ☎ 2869–1298) down the road a bit and serving more modern, and lighter, Nepalese dishes. ⊠ *14 Staunton St.,* ☎ *2869–6212. Reservations essential. AE, DC, MC, V.*

SHANGHAINESE

$$$ ✕ **Shanghai Shanghai.** Part of the trend of retro-Chinese restaurants that try to capture the essence of Shanghai in the 1930s, this newcomer is the best of the bunch. Art Deco touches, stained glass, discreet pri-vate rooms, and wooden booths achieve the nostalgic effect. The menu ranges from simple Shanghainese midnight snacks and cold appetiz-ers, such as mock goose and smoked fish, to pricey delicacies such as abalone. After 9 PM the lights dim, a chanteuse comes onstage to croon Mandarin tunes, and a song-request book is placed at every table. It's imperative you make reservations at least a week in advance, as this intimate restaurant has become a hot spot for affluent Chinese remi-niscing about the good old days. ⊠ *Ritz-Carlton Hotel, 3 Connaught Rd., basement,* ☎ *2869–0328. Reservations essential. AE, DC, MC, V. Closed Sun.*

SZECHUAN

$–$$ ✕ **Sichuan Garden.** This spacious restaurant is renowned for its ex-otic Szechuanese delicacies such as the deep-fried bean curd stuffed with mashed shrimp deserves two thumbs up. Fried sliced mutton with spring onion and sesame pockets is another must-try—to eat this del-icacy you stuff the warm sesame pocket with the tender fried meat and make your own Szechuanese-style mutton sandwich. Friendly and at-tentive service adds to the overall score. ⊠ *Gloucester Tower, The Land-mark, 3rd floor,* ☎ *2521–4433. AE, DC, MC, V.*

THAI

$$$ ✕ **Thai Lemongrass.** Regional Thai cuisine served with a modern twist best describes the food at Thai Lemongrass. Large windows provide natural light and the atmosphere is relaxed and comfortable. The menu features dishes from three different regions, marked under the headings of "North and North East," "Central Plains," and "South." Your gourmet tour of Thailand could include grilled whole freshwater fish and herbs cooked in banana leaves with coriander-chili sauce (North and North East); sizzling seafood mousse with light red curry and coconut milk or roast duck in red curry (Central Plains); or Thai barbecued lamb cutlets (South). ✉ *30–32 D'Aguilar St., California Tower, 3rd floor,* ☎ *2905–1688. AE, DC, MC, V. No lunch Sun.*

$ ✕ **Good Luck Thai.** If you're in the area of Lan Kwai Fong but don't feel like spending a fortune, this Thai spot is one of your best options. Tucked in the dead end of Lan Kwai Fong west, this hole-in-the-wall offers hearty and unpretentious Thai food with very friendly prices and service. Pad Thai, grilled chicken, and diced beef wrapped in lettuce are just some of the favorites here. Enjoy the alfresco seating as you watch the world go by. The nearby bars and pubs are great choices for a pre-meal aperitif and after-dinner drinks. ✉ *13 Wing Wah La.,* ☎ *2877–2971. No credit cards. Closed Sun.*

VIETNAMESE

$$$ ✕ **Indochine 1929.** Colonialism in Asia may be history, but many in Hong Kong retain romantic memories thereof. That may help explain the smashing success of Indochine 1929, which looks like a French plantation veranda at the height of the colonial era. The food is equally tasty and authentic; most of the ingredients used are imported twice a week from Vietnam. Highlights include salt-and-pepper soft-shell crab, fried beef and tomato, stir-fried fillet of pork with shallots and lemongrass, and fried fish Hanoi style. This is not the cheapest Vietnamese food in town, but it's arguably the best. The staff's traditional costumes— *ao dais,* straight, elegant silk gowns worn over flowing pants—and the surrounding old maps and antique fans and lamps add to the authentic atmosphere. ✉ *30–32 D'Aguilar St., California Tower, 2nd floor, Lan Kwai Fong,* ☎ *2869–7399. AE, DC, MC, V. No lunch Sun.*

European
BRITISH

$$ ✕ **SoHo SoHo.** True, Britain is not considered a source of inspired cui-
★ sine, but this smart little restaurant is doing its best to change that. Calling its cuisine "Modern British," SoHo SoHo takes traditional dishes, combines them with eclectic ingredients, and transforms them into modern classics. The roast cod with white beans, chorizo, and garlic aioli has a pleasant Mediterranean flavor, while the lamb shank shepherd's pie with parsnip carrot topping successfully evolves this traditional dish into a culinary highlight. If you have a sweet tooth, don't miss the sticky toffee pudding or the bread-and-butter pudding. The crowds here are a testament to the winning formula of high-quality and delicious food, helpful service, and value for money. ✉ *9 Old Bailey St.,* ☎ *2147– 2618. AE, DC, MC, V. Closed Sun.*

CONTINENTAL

$$$$ ✕ **Mandarin Grill.** The Colonial feeling and impeccable service make this a rare find in Hong Kong these days. You can start your day with kippers and kedgeree for breakfast and end with a dinner of duck pressed tableside or top-quality meat such as Angus or Kobe beef, Dutch Veal, or Australian lamb, prepared on the open grill. Live lobsters or the bouillabaisse are highlights for those who favor fruits de mer. A Sunday champagne brunch (HK$350) is popular for its vast selection and is a good choice for families. ✉ *Mandarin Oriental Hotel, 1st floor, 5 Connaught Rd.,* ☎ *2522–0111 ext. 4020. Reservations essential. AE, DC, MC, V.*

$$$ ✕ **Blue.** Renowned for its fusion cuisine and savvy decor, Australian-owned Blue is one of the most stylish restaurants in Hong Kong and at press time one of *the* places to see and be seen around SoHo. High ceilings, soft lighting, glass-and-chrome furnishings set the scene for

fusion dishes such as sliced beef stacked with layers of crisp Parmesan wafers and Stilton mayonnaise. Blue also has a good range of pastas and seafood dishes. ⊠ *43–45 Lyndhurst Terr.,* ☎ *2815–4005. AE, MC, V. No lunch weekends.*

\$\$\$ ✕ **M at the Fringe.** Set above the Fringe Club, M sets itself apart with
★ quirky yet classy decor and a seasonal menu that mixes Continental with Middle Eastern cuisine. Both vegetarians and carnivores are well served here, and it can be hard to choose from the long list of intriguing descriptions on the artistic handwritten menu. Highly recommended are the rich and juicy poached bone marrow with red wine sauce; the soft-shell crabs on cucumber salad; the Turkish vegetable platter that includes *borek* (cheese pastry pie) and *mahshi khodar* (stuffed yellow pepper); and the house-smoked salmon with a potato and leek pancake. The menu changes seasonally, but always lives up to expectations. If you crave sweets, don't miss the Pavlova or tarte Tatin. The set lunch is a good value. ⊠ *South Block, 2 Lower Albert Rd., 1st floor,* ☎ *2877–4000. Reservations essential. AE, MC, V. No lunch Sun.*

\$\$ ✕ **Jimmy's Kitchen.** Probably the most famous—and still one of the best—of Hong Kong's restaurants, Jimmy's first opened for business in 1928 and has been catering to a deeply devoted clientele (in one location or another) ever since. It's nicely decorated with comfortable booths, dark woodwork, lattice partitions, and brass fittings. Take your time studying the directory-like menu. The food is as charmingly old fashioned as the place itself: where else in Hong Kong can you find corned beef and cabbage? Other European specialties, including borscht, Stroganoff, goulash, and bangers and mash, are presented in an old-English style and accompanied by the restaurant's pickled onions. The extensive and diverse menu also includes a selection of Asian delights from curry to fried rice. The rhubarb tart, steamed ginger pudding, and bread-and-butter pudding finish the meal on a high note. Reservations are necessary here for lunch. ⊠ *South China Bldg., 1 Wyndham St., basement,* ☎ *2526–5293. AE, DC, MC, V.*

\$\$ ✕ **The Pavilion.** Located in one of the best-hidden alleys in the hub of the city, The Pavilion is a secret gem. The 17th-century French decor is quite different from anywhere else in Hong Kong. The well-prepared food complements the refined setting—appetizers of seared scallops and beef tenderloin carpaccio share the menu with roast cod fillets and rack of lamb on rosemary polenta. The restaurant's sister, **El Pomposo** (⊠ *4 Tun Wo La.,* ☎ *2973–0642*) next door, offers a mellow ambience for a glass of wine and some delicious tapas. ⊠ *3 Tun Wo La.,* ☎ *2869–7768. AE, DC, MC, V.*

FRENCH-ASIAN

\$\$\$\$ ✕ **Vong.** This is designer dining. With sister establishments in London and New York, Hong Kong's Vong sits glamorously at the top of the Mandarin Oriental Hotel, overlooking Central and the harbor. Black and gold feature heavily in the visuals, creating a sophistication that's only enhanced by such details as curvaceous cutlery and chic crockery. The menu comprises the world-class innovations of celebrated chef-patron Jean-Georges Vongerichten, whose Asian-inspired French cuisine fuses flavors from both worlds. Good examples are foie gras with ginger and caramelized mango, and quail rubbed with Thai spices. Chicken marinated in lemongrass and served with sticky rice in a banana leaf is another favorite. The warm Valrhona chocolate cake with coconut ice cream sends a surprise torrent of molten chocolate cascading onto your plate. If you're having trouble deciding what to order, the Vong tasting menu—five of the restaurant's signature creations at a very reasonable price—is your easiest choice. Don't expect a quiet dinner: the atmosphere here is high octane. ⊠ *Mandarin Oriental Hotel, 5 Con-*

naught Rd., 25th floor, ☎ *2825–4028. Reservations essential. AE, DC, MC, V.*

$$$–$$$$ ✕ **Toscana.** Toscana is classical Italian dining at its finest—sumptuous,
★   elegant, and relaxed. Huge oil paintings depicting scenes from Venice
cover the walls, a high ceiling amplifies the spacious interior, elegant
drapes shroud the high windows, and Italian opera softly fills the air.
The opulent atmosphere is matched by the food and smooth, friendly
service. The saddle of venison with walnut tagliatelle and chocolate
sauce is a classic—the subtle chocolate sauce complements the flavor
of the delicate venison. The coral trout with herb dressing, fennel, and
black olive puree, and the rack of lamb with a morel mushroom and
leek sauce demonstrate the chef's thoughtful use of ingredients. Match
these with a little-known but much sought-after wine from Chef Um-
berto Bombana's list, and you'll know why regulars from around the
world visit whenever they're in town. The roast mango, banana, and
wild berry tart with vanilla ice cream is a perfect finale. ⊠ *Ritz-Carl-
ton, 3 Connaught Rd.,* ☎ *2532–2062. AE, DC, MC, V. Closed Sun.*

Vegetarian

$ ✕ **Eating Plus.** Healthy eating with elegant simplicity is the principle
of this smart restaurant, making it a popular hangout for the health-
conscious crowds. The menu does not suggest heavy meat intake, but
you can easily find chicken, beef, and seafood, prepared and served to
accompany your carbohydrate-rich choices. The menu includes a wide
selection of noodles, ramens, pastas, and rice, as well as an array of
vegetables and side dishes such as eggplant medallions, crispy tofu, and
chicken and vegetable skewers. A glass of freshly squeezed juice from
the fruit bar completes this healthy dining experience. Located next to
the Hong Kong Station, this is an excellent stop for a hearty treat be-
fore you hop on a train for the airport. ⊠ *1009, Southern International
Finance Centre, 1st floor,* ☎ *2868–0599. AE, DC, MC, V.*

Admiralty

Since this is essentially an office area and a series of large shopping
malls, much of the food is aimed at meeting the lunch needs of work-
ers and shoppers. However, with a major cinema and several good restau-
rants in the Pacific Place mall, it's convenient for dinner as well.

Asian

$$–$$$ ✕ **Zen.** This upscale nouveau Cantonese eatery has the same owner
as the ultrachic London restaurants of the same name. The deep-fried
boneless chicken wings stuffed with glutinous rice have crisp, golden
skin and are served with more rice to catch all the flavorful juice from
the meat. Seafood dishes such as deep-fried shrimp with chili and gar-
lic are also popular. The more standard Cantonese dishes are delicately
prepared and presented. Service is flawless, and the decor is contem-
porary, with dramatic hanging lights and a central waterfall. There's
a second location that's quite popular for dim sum in Festival Walk.
⊠ *The Mall, Pacific Place One, 88 Queensway,* ☎ *2845–4555. AE,
DC, MC, V.*

$$$ ✕ **Ye Shanghai.** "Ye" means "night" in Chinese. And those who want
to capture or recapture the spirit of old Shanghai nightlife will find this
a dining experience. The setting is elegantly nostalgic, the lighting subdued, and the ceiling fans move relentlessly. Once the mood is set, start

with some light appetizers such as chicken in spicy sauce or tea-leaf smoked egg. For an entrée, try the fresh and flavorful stir-fried river shrimp, accompanied by strong dark vinegar, or the sautéed minced chicken with pine nuts, served with sesame pockets. Desserts include the Shanghai staple deep-fried egg white stuffed with banana and mashed red-bean paste and the Japanese-inspired black-sesame ice cream. Reserve early for the comfortable booth seats or the window tables with a view of the bustling Queensway. Its shop next door, Xiao Shanghai (Small Shanghai), sells all sorts of snacks, tea, pickles, and sweets. Live music delivers golden oldies every Thursday through Saturday night. ⊠ *Level 3, Pacific Place, 88 Queensway,* ☎ *2918–9833. AE, DC, MC, V.*

THAI

$$ ✕ **Thai Basil.** You won't miss this smart mall restaurant when stepping out from the Admiralty MTR Station and heading toward Pacific Place. Don't be deceived by its mall location: delicious food with reasonable prices make it a popular dining spot. An Australian chef artfully presents his myriad Asian creations with a contemporary twist, creating deliciously innovative dishes such as scampi and banana bud with lime and mint leaves, stingray salad with green mango, and green papaya and crispy fish. Also highly recommended is the braised lamb shank. Those with a sweet tooth will love the homemade ice-cream selection, from ginger to honeycomb. A dedicated exclusive dining area called The Kitchen at the back of the restaurant services well-heeled diners. ⊠ *Shop 005, Pacific Place, lower ground floor,* ☎ *2537–4682. AE, DC, MC, V.*

European

FRENCH

$$$$ ✕ **Petrus.** Fine modern Mediterranean dining matched with glittering views sums up Petrus. From the 56th floor of the high-end Island Shangri-La hotel, Petrus literally looks down on nearly all other Hong Kong restaurants in location and culinary standards. It attracts the finest and most decorated chefs from Europe to its kitchen. Artichoke and truffle terrine melts in your mouth, the flavorsome seared North Sea scallops get a distinct texture and aroma from a combination of salsify, baby spinach, and truffle butter. Braised Ching Yi fish fillet with artichoke *barigoule* (stewed with onion, lemon, and herbs) is delightfully light and juicy, a real treat for seafood lovers. Naturally enough, the extensive wine list is largely French. ⊠ *Island Shangri-La, Pacific Place, Supreme Court Rd., 56th floor,* ☎ *2820–8590. Reservations essential. Jacket required. AE, DC, MC, V.*

ITALIAN

$$$$ ✕ **Nicholini's.** Separated by a lounge from its French cousin, Brasserie on the Eighth, this elegant and florally decorated establishment regularly picks up awards for its fine Italian food. Featuring northern Italian dishes, the menu serves a wide range of pastas, fish, fowl and meat. Homemade black fettuccine with shrimp, clams, and asparagus tips is deliciously dark, while linguine with clams is a delight. The roast rack of lamb with green tomato compote is young enough to be sweet without overpowering the palate. For dessert, try a soufflé. The wine list features wines especially hand-blended for Nicholini's. ⊠ *Conrad Hotel, Pacific Place, 88 Queensway, 8th floor,* ☎ *2521–3838 ext. 8210. AE, DC, MC, V.*

$$–$$$ ✕ **Grappa's.** Don't let the mall location mislead you. Once inside you can turn your back on the mall and let the kindly staff serve you superb Italian food. The endless selection of pastas can prolong your decision, but nothing will disappoint. Panfried foie gras makes an excellent kickoff, and osso buco, smothered in a rich flavorful sauce, is a dish you shouldn't miss. Game hen stuffed with sun-dried tomatoes, garlic, and fresh rosemary tastes as good as it sounds. With excellent coffee and a range of bottled beers, Grappa's is equally useful for a quick pick-me-up or a post-shopping rendezvous. ⊠ *132 Pacific Place, 88 Queensway,* ☎ *2868–0086. AE, DC, MC, V.*

North American

$$ ✕ **Dan Ryan's.** This popular bar is often standing-room only, so call
★ ahead for a table. Apart from beer, the menu offers a smattering of international dishes—pasta and the like—but Dan Ryan's is known for its great burgers—the kind ex-pats dream about when they think of the States. It's simple, rib-sticking stuff, and Dan Ryan's serves it up without fuss or formality. ⊠ *114 Pacific Place, 88 Queensway,* ☎ *2845–4600. Reservations essential. AE, DC, MC, V.*

Seafood

$$$ ✕ **Lobster Bar.** The giant tropical-fish tank at the entrance sets the scene here. As the name suggests, lobster is the feature presentation, whipped into soups, appetizers, and various entrées. The lobster bisque is creamy yet light, with great chunks of meat at the bottom. Lobster tartare, served with cucumber salad and two good-size lobster claws, fills a starter plate with fresh, succulent shredded lobster meat. For a lighter main course, try the angel-hair pasta with *yabbies* (a smaller Australian cousin of the lobster). The seafood selection—half a lobster thermidor, whole grilled langoustine, prawn, baked oyster, creamy scallops, crab cakes, black cod—delivers on its promise. If you must avoid the fruits of the sea, meats are also available. The space is large and elegant, decorated in blue and gold; the atmosphere is at once formal and relaxed. ⊠ *Island Shangri-La, lobby level,* ☎ *2877–3838 ext. 8560. Reservations essential for lunch. AE, DC, MC, V.*

The Peak

On a clear day, even the views en route via tram or taxi will justify a trip to the highest dining points in Hong Kong. (Note that if there are low clouds, you won't be able to see a thing; you'll just hear the city beneath you.) At the time of writing, The Peak Lookout Hong Kong restaurant was slated to open in the historic 1888 café space at the Peak.

PAN-ASIAN

$$$ ✕ **Cafe Deco Bar and Grill.** If you're in Hong Kong on a clear day, take
★ the Peak tram to the top and dine at this spiffy double-decker restaurant overlooking the entire city. The views are stunning, and the decor is Art Deco to the hilt—you can spend an age looking at original period fittings. The menu is international, with Chinese, Indian (the kitchen has a proper tandoor), Italian, Mexican, and Thai dishes. The arugula and Parmesan salad with Parma ham, pear, and balsamic dressing is a harmonious combination. Other good appetizer selections include crab cakes and BBQ duck salad. Pizza and pasta choices are always popular, and the tandoori Himalayan kebab makes you feel as if you're up on the Nepalese mountains instead of the of at the top of Hong Kong. The wine list is very reasonably priced with an extensive selection of wines from around the world. ⊠ *Peak Galleria, 118 Peak Rd,, 1st level,* ☎ *2849–5111. AE, DC, MC, V.*

Wanchai

At lunchtime Wanchai is just another jumble of people, not a particularly invigorating shopping area; but after dark it comes into its own. This is Hong Kong's prime nightlife area, its long roads lined with fluorescent lights and jam-packed with taxis and wide-awake crowds. The range of dining options is extreme—from fail-safe five-star luxury to authentic and welcoming street-level spots with fine food.

Asian

BEIJINGESE

$$ ✕ American Peking Restaurant. Full of red and gold fixtures, this overdecorated restaurant has been a gastronomic Hong Kong entity for more than 40 years. Favorites here include hot-and-sour soup, fried and steamed dumplings, and, in the winter, delicious hot pots; you might also try the excellent beggar's chicken cooked in clay and lotus leaves (order one day in advance), minced pigeon, and, of course, Peking duck. Each meal begins with complimentary peanuts and sliced cucumber in vinegar—perfect for practicing chopstick skills. The name American Peking is fitting: the authenticity of the food is questionable, but it caters well to those unaccustomed to Chinese food. ⊠ *20 Lockhart Rd.,* ☎ *2527–7770. Reservations essential. AE, DC, MC, V.*

$ ✕ Dumpling Shop. If the Marco Polo story is true, you can get a taste of the forerunner of spaghetti Bolognese at this clean and smart Beijingese food shop. Thick, northern-Chinese noodles arrive in a bowl accompanied by a rich minced-pork sauce; it's just a matter of mixing them together before slurping them up. Even a small portion is enough for two, so be careful not to over-order. Buns and dumplings, also Beijingese specialties, appear in abundance, such as the panfried spring-onion cake. The staff is friendly and ready to assist. Leave room for the sweet bean ball—looking for all the world like a donut, it consists of sweet red-bean paste encased in a light dough made of fluffy egg whites. More branches are opening up in other areas, including Mong Kok (⊠ 576 Nathan Road, ☎ 2771–2399). ⊠ *138 Wanchai Rd.,* ☎ *2836–0000. DC, MC, V (for dinner over HK$200).*

CANTONESE

$$$–$$$$ ✕ Dynasty. One of the two entrances to this hotel restaurant takes you past a beautiful, two-story-long chandelier to a typically subdued Cantonese environment: beige tones, mirrors, unobtrusive fixtures. The beautiful crockery—designed especially for Dynasty—combines Art Deco elements with a traditional Asian touch. Palm trees and live traditional Chinese music form a total contrast to the modernity outside the windows: neon signs pushing familiar brand names and the Wanchai Ferry traversing the harbor. The menu is extensive, comprising luxurious abalone and bird's nest along with a variety of high-quality and elegant meat, seafood, and vegetable dishes. To finish things off try the signature dessert of chilled sago cream with mango and grapefruit. ⊠ *Renaissance Harbour View, 1 Harbour Rd., 3rd floor,* ☎ *2802–8888. AE, DC, MC, V.*

$ ✕ Steam and Stew Inn. You can't miss the red lanterns marking the inn's entrance down a short alley. This hole-in-the-wall with simple decoration dishes out healthy, home-style Cantonese cooking—it serves red rice and uses no MSG, both rare in Hong Kong. Go for the steamed fish and eggplant casserole (one of the most popular items) or one of the deep-fried dishes, of which they have a wide variety, including an irresistible deep-fried eel. Another find is the double-boiled chicken and ginseng, which is said to help lower body heat. If you're concerned about cholesterol, you can request preparation with egg whites rather than whole eggs. There's also a seasonal menu, and dim sum at lunchtime.

This gem was opened by a group of young professionals who craved inexpensive, healthy Chinese food, and it draws a young crowd. ⊠ *21–23 Tai Wong St. E, Wanchai,* ☎ *2529–3913. MC, V. No lunch Sun.*

SHANGHAINESE

$$$ ✕ **Lao Ching Hing.** One of the oldest Shanghainese restaurants in Hong Kong (open since 1955), Lao Ching Hing has earned its good name over the years. From simple stuff such as the Shanghainese buns and dumplings to deluxe abalone, you're bound to find something intriguing. Chicken in wine sauce and sautéed river shrimp are popular. Also check out the famous Shanghainese dumplings and buns. For a real adventure, investigate the braised sea cucumber in brown sauce for its distinct texture and strong sauce. Try the freshwater crab if you're here in September or October. ⊠ *Century Hong Kong Hotel, 238 Jaffe Rd., basement,* ☎ *2598–6080. AE, MC, V.*

VEGETARIAN

$ ✕ **Nice Fragrance Vegetarian Kitchen.** Ingredients as simple as bean curd, mushrooms, and taro are whipped into unexpected and delicious forms here. Don't be surprised to see a whole fish on the next table: taro paste molded into a fish shape and deep-fried is one of the most popular dishes in Chinese vegetarian cooking. Crispy on the outside and succulent inside, the "fish" is served with a tangy sweet-and-sour sauce. Assorted vegetables wrapped in a sheet of bean curd form a flavorful combo that might surprise your palate, and a delicious fried rice with both tomato and white sauce will please those who can't make up their mind which way to go. Vegetarian dim sum and a snack counter at the door round out the offerings. ⊠ *105–107 Thomson Rd.,* ☎ *2838–3608 or 2838–3067. AE, DC, MC, V (over HK$200).*

VIETNAMESE

$ ✕ **Saigon Beach.** This tiny place can seat only about 20, so avoid coming here at the lunch rush hour unless you don't mind standing in line. The decor, an amalgam of nautical paraphernalia—cheap plastic fish hung from nets, folding chairs, and Formica tables, isn't likely to impress. Rather, the authentic Vietnamese fare and the opportunity to rub convivial elbows with people who know the place well more than make up for the unprepossessing environs. Soft-shell crab and lemon chicken, washed down with French 33 beer, are always a pleasure. Set meals are a good value for the money. ⊠ *66 Lockhart Rd.,* ☎ *2529–7823. No credit cards.*

European

ITALIAN

$$$$ ✕ **Grissini.** It's named after the Italian bread stick, and you won't miss the aroma of a long one baking visibly in the oven as you walk in. To start, the hot tomato soup is topped with a surprising chilled tomato emulsion. Porcini mushroom and pumpkin risotto is moist and subtly sweet, and roasted quail wrapped in pancetta and stuffed with foie gras is a rich and flavorful mixture of tastes. The Wine Gallery houses 1,000 bottles of mainly Italian wines. The dessert sampler comprises perfect mini-portions of five delectable sweets including sabayon and sherbet, panna cotta with red-wine cherry compote, ricotta mouse and hot chocolate, and gianduja pudding. ⊠ *Grand Hyatt, 1 Harbour Rd., 2nd floor,* ☎ *2588–1234 ext. 7313. Reservations essential. AE, DC, MC, V.*

International

ECLECTIC

$$ ✕ **Grand Cafe.** Grander than you'd expect for a coffee shop, the Grand Cafe has an impressive menu. "Sandwich" is interpreted loosely here—

marinated lamb fillet on naan bread is one option—and you can opt for quesadillas, pastas, and Asian-style noodles and rice in addition to free-range chicken, panfried veal chops, and oven-glazed king prawns. Start with a salad or a creative appetizer such as steamed asparagus with cold-pressed olive oil, poached egg, and shaved Parmesan, a dish that outperforms the fare at far pricier restaurants. The Hainanese chicken rice with soup is as flavorful and ample as this traditional Chinese dish is meant to be. Desserts—sorbets, tarts, and cakes—are heavenly. The café draws both locals and tourists, not to mention a few long-term resident sparrows, who flutter around overhead and enjoy whatever crumbs diners will share with them. ⊠ *Grand Hyatt Hotel, 1 Harbour Rd.,* ☎ *2588–1234 ext. 7273. AE, DC, MC, V.*

$ ✕ **Open Kitchen.** This sit-down cafeteria in the Hong Kong Arts Centre has a large selection of good food and a nice view of the harbor. It's ideal for a pre- or post-performance meal or coffee. Flavors range from Malaysian *laksa*—a rich and flavorsome noodle with bean curd, shrimp, fish ball, and spices—and Indian curries to fresh Italian pasta, Chinese casseroles, and fish-and-chips, not to mention a selection of pastries for dessert or coffee. The spacious and quiet seating areas are always tidy, and you can linger and read here undisturbed. The balcony area offers an excellent view of Victoria Harbour. ⊠ *Hong Kong Arts Centre, 2 Harbour Rd., 6th floor,* ☎ *2827–2923. AE, MC, V (for over HK$150).*

Causeway Bay

Home to a series of large Japanese department stores and a number of shopping malls, Causeway Bay is one of Hong Kong's busiest shopping districts and becomes a real cultural phenomenon on Saturday afternoon. The density of the population can be overwhelming. Several pubs are in the vicinity, but they're not concentrated on one strip; likewise, there are several good restaurants, but they can be hard for the uninitiated to find. Times Square, a huge, modern shopping mall, has four floors of restaurants in one of its towers, serving international cuisines including Korean, French, steak, and regional Chinese.

Asian
CANTONESE

$$$$ ✕ **Forum.** The name of this prestigious restaurant connotes two things: chef Yeung Koon Yat and his special abalone. Yeung has earned an international reputation with his Ah Yat abalone. The price is steep, but if you want to experience this luxurious Asian ingredient, you really must come here. Your beautiful abalone is boiled and braised to perfection and served with a rich brown sauce—one of the most extravagant dishes in Cantonese cooking. If you want to leave with some cash in hand, you can choose from several more affordable Cantonese dishes. ⊠ *485 Lockhart Rd.,* ☎ *2891–2516. AE, DC, MC, V.*

$$ ✕ **Dim Sum.** Most restaurants in Hong Kong serve dim sum only at
★ lunchtime, but this elegant jewel breaks with tradition and serves it from dusk till dawn. The menu goes beyond Cantonese morsels from the essential *har gau* (steamed shrimp dumpling) to northern choices such as chili prawn dumplings, Beijing onion cakes, and steamed buns. The creative lobster bisque and abalone dumplings are popular picks. Lunch reservations are not taken on weekends, so there's always a long line. Arrive early, or admire the antique telephones and posters of old Chinese advertisements while you wait. Happy Valley is near Causeway Bay, but not near the MTR; take a tram or a cab to get here. ⊠ *63 Sing Woo Rd., Happy Valley,* ☎ *2834–8893. AE, DC, MC, V.*

European

CONTEMPORARY

$$–$$$ ✕ **ToTT's Asian Grill & Bar.** Talk of the Town sits atop the Excelsior Hotel, looking down on Causeway Bay and the marina. The funky decor, which includes zebra-stripe chairs, a central oval bar, and designer tableware, is matched by the East-meets-West cuisine. Caesar salad with tandoori chicken is a good example of the culinary collision as is the red-crab bisque served in a baby papaya. The grilled rare tuna steak is another long-standing favorite, and the sampler platter of desserts is a grand finale. Live music kicks in late during the evening, offering a chance to burn a few calories on the dance floor. ⊠ *Excelsior Hotel, 281 Gloucester Rd.,* ☎ *2837–6786. AE, DC, MC, V.*

ITALIAN

$$ ✕ **Fat Angelo's.** Diners cram into this place—partly for the lively atmosphere, but mostly for the huge piles of pasta that weigh down the tables. Fat Angelo's is an Italian-American–style diner, its green-checked tablecloths and wooden chairs watched from the walls by prints of elder Italian common folk. Portions come in "big" (serving five–eight) and "not so big" (serving two–four). Favorites are the mounds of steamed green-lipped mussels in tomato sauce, massive meatballs, roast chicken with rosemary, and pastas of every kind. Linguine with pesto is hearty and fulfilling. Meals come with a salad and a bread basket. Wine is served in water glasses. If you're around the SoHo area or Tsim Sha Tsui, check out the branches at 49 Elgin Street (☎ 2973–6808) and 29–43 Ashley Road (☎ 2730–4788). The atmosphere is just as fun. ⊠ *414 Jaffe Rd.,* ☎ *2574–6263. AE, DC, MC, V.*

Seafood

$$–$$$ ✕ **Island Seafood & Oyster Bar.** Tucked into a Causeway Bay shopping area that was once Hong Kong's Food Street, this laid-back spot is drawing foodies back. The deliciously fresh oysters come in several varieties from around the world. Pick them as creamy or firm as you like from the oyster bar, where the staff will happily make suggestions and serve the sexy mollusk on ice or cooked hot to your taste. (Note that eating raw shellfish can put you at risk for hepatitis.) Read the chalkboard for daily specials, which are bound to include seafood and meat. ⊠ *Shop C, Towning Mansion, 50–56 Paterson St.,* ☎ *2915–7110. AE, DC, MC, V.*

STEAK

$$$ ✕ **W's Entrecote.** W's is a dining dictatorship: you can order steak, steak, or steak. Your only choices have to do with size and cooking time. Some call this the best steak in town, and the price includes a salad and as many fries as you can eat. The wine list is French, as is the interior: red-and-white checked tablecloths and French posters. Service is attentive and friendly, and it's a good place for a family meal. If you come with children and want to share a portion, just ask and the waiters will happily help you. Perched at the top of bustling Times Square, it's ideal for a bout of protein replenishment after battling the crowds. ⊠ *1303 Times Square, 13th floor,* ☎ *2506–0133. AE, DC, MC, V.*

Aberdeen

Seafood

$$–$$$ ✕ **Jumbo Floating Restaurant.** This is it—the floating restaurant you see on postcards. A huge, pagoda-shape building that burns with a thousand lights at night, it floats replete with a throne for all those visiting emperors. It sounds more like a sightseeing outing than a meal, and indeed it's one of the most interesting dining experiences you may have

in Hong Kong. Jumbo comprises three floating outlets—Tai Pat, Sea Palace, and Jumbo Palace, where you eat "on board." Naturally enough, seafood is the draw, and it's made the old-fashioned way: you peer into the fish tank, pick your prey, and it shows up on your table in minutes. You get here by shuttle ferry; ferries depart every two to three minutes from Shum Wan Pier, every 15 minutes from Aberdeen Pier. ⊠ *Shum Wan Pier Path, Wong Chuk Hang,* ☎ *2553–9111. AE, DC, MC, V.*

Repulse Bay

The south side of Hong Kong Island is a string of beaches, rocky coves, and luxury developments, and Repulse Bay, 20 minutes by bus from Central, comprises all three. Popular on weekends and in summer, its beach is one of the best on the island, and The Repulse Bay complex houses a number of quality restaurants and shops along with corporate apartments.

Asian
PAN-ASIAN

$$ ✕ **Spices.** Alfresco dining is something of a rarity in Hong Kong, but at Spices you can dine on classic Asian food surrounded by lawns and patios. (If the weather fails, there's an elegant interior.) The menu here flies from India to Japan and back again. Singaporean satay of beef, chicken, and lamb, and Indonesian *kuwe udang goreng* (deep-fried prawn cakes) make good starters. Main courses include Indian tandoori plates, Vietnamese fried soft-shell crabs, Japanese beef *shogayaki* (pan-fried fillet with sake sauce), and Malaysian *char kwayt teow* (seafood fried noodles). Curry lovers can try different versions, with varying degrees of spice, from India, Vietnam, Singapore, and Indonesia; these involve mutton, duck, chicken, seafood, and even oxtail. Combine them with one of several Indian breads. ⊠ *The Repulse Bay, 109 Repulse Bay Rd.,* ☎ *2812–2711. AE, DC, MC, V.*

European
CONTEMPORARY

$$$ ✕ **The Verandah.** Step into another era here: the walls are white; the
★ doors are dark wood; fans spin silently high overhead; champagne-cocktail trolleys cross the cool, granite-tile floor; palm trees wave through the arched teak windows; and tuxedoed waiters attend to your every whim. A pianist entertains while budding Bogarts and Bergmans act out (or watch) the romance. The Verandah is an unashamed celebration of the halcyon days of colonial rule, and creates popular appeal by serving an excellent Sunday brunch and daily afternoon tea. It comes into its own at night, however, when the chef whips up an impressive array of dishes, from lobster to rack of lamb. For dessert, Verandah's soufflé is a classic. ⊠ *109 Repulse Bay Rd.,* ☎ *2812–2722. AE, DC, MC, V.*

Stanley Village

A visit to Stanley Village reveals another side of Hong Kong: a much slower pace of life than in the city. After exploring the market, historical sights, and beaches, take a leisurely meal at one of the top-notch but laid-back restaurants scattered around, some of which have harbor views.

European
CONTEMPORARY

$$–$$$ ✕ **The Boathouse.** With a lovely view of the seafront and a cozy decor, The Boathouse is a perfect spot to hang out with friends and family. A bucket of mussels, served with nicely toasted garlic bread, goes down well with a glass of chilled white wine. Sandwiches and pastas are good bets for casual dining. The cobbler, a crumble with wild berries, will send you home happy. ⊠ *86–88 Stanley Main St.,* ☎ *2813–4467. DC, MC, V.*

FRENCH

$$$
★ ✕ **Lucy's.** There's something incredibly comforting about Lucy's. The lighting is low, the decor is warm, and the waiters are friendly and casual, creating a generally laid-back atmosphere. This intimate restaurant draws regulars back again and again. A colorful chalkboard lists the chef's recommendations for the day as well as a list of wines from around the globe. The food is fresh and lovingly presented with familiar tastes combined in dishes that lack any pretentiousness but deliver full flavor and satisfaction. The phyllo pastry filled with a combination of Stilton, spinach, and walnuts is a perfect starter. The veal fillet with polenta and crispy Parma ham is delicate in texture but powerful in taste, while the sea bass with pumpkin mash and Italian parsley is delightfully light and clean. Leave room for desserts such as a quintessential chocolate cake that guarantee to end the meal on high note. ⊠ *64 Stanley Main St.,* ☎ *2813–9055. MC, V.*

$$–$$$
★ ✕ **Stanley's French Restaurant.** Both floors here have beautiful harbor views from balconies, adding to the romantic quasi-Mediterranean atmosphere. The colors are soft; wood blends nicely with eye-catching tiles, and the curtains match the pretty cushions on the wrought-iron chairs. Mardi Gras parade posters in French and sketches of Parisian ladies of the night look down from the walls. The warm lobster salad with artichoke hearts is a favorite. Seasonal items are featured on a daily chalkboard and tend to be in great demand. The prix fixe meal options, which include meat and fish options, are a great bargain. Finish the evening off with a light soufflé or a selection of cheeses from the Swiss Alps. ⊠ *90B Stanley Main St., 1st–2nd floors,* ☎ *2813–8873. Reservations essential. AE, DC, MC, V.*

SPANISH

$$–$$$ ✕ **El Cid.** It sounds a bit weird to eat Spanish food and fiesta at the former British Army Officers' quarters; however, the historical building is now a permanent fixture in Stanley, with a museum and restaurants, and it's definitely worth a visit. Enjoy a few tapas and a sangria or Rioja as you admire the beautiful sea view and ponder how much the architecture has been through since it was built in 1848. Garlic prawns and stuffed mushrooms are some of the best choices here. Ask for a table with a view. ⊠ *1st floor, Murray House, Stanley Plaza,* ☎ *2899–0858. AE, DC, MC, V.*

Shek O

Shek O is a tiny seaside village, but it has a few decent open-air restaurants. And once you've made the trek—the longest overland trip possible from Central—you'll need some sustenance.

Asian

PAN-ASIAN

$$ ✕ **Shek O Chinese and Thailand Seafood Restaurant.** Nothing particularly stands out about the food or aesthetics here, but this place is a legend—it's just such *fun*. On summer weekends, people arrive en masse and sit for hours despite the relentless heat. The curious hybrid cuisine ensures plenty of rice, noodle, and fish dishes. The *tom yung kung* (spicy prawn and coconut soup) is guaranteed to bring color to your cheeks; the green curry is a safe chicken choice; and the honey-fried squid is amazing. The festive ambience is a real experience, and you'll eat heartily without breaking the bank. ⊠ *303 Shek O Village* *(main intersection, next to the bus stop),* ☏ *2809–4426. Reservations essential. AE, DC, MC, V (for over HK$300).*

THAI

$$ ✕ **Happy Garden.** It picked the right name—you can tell from the diners' faces. There's nothing gimmicky or fancy here, just simple Thai treats with reasonable prices, huge portions, and swift service. The appetizer sampler—prawn cakes, fish cakes, chicken in vine leaves, and spring rolls—is the house specialty. Soups are hearty and satisfying, served over a burner to keep them sizzling hot. Steamed fish in sour soup finds its way to almost every table and is one of the most popular choices here. Thai fried rice and fried Chinese broccoli with salty fish are both down-to-earth goodies. The restaurant often has a queue of people awaiting tables with eager and hungry looks in their eyes. ✉ *786 Shek O Village,* ☏ *2809–4165 or 2809–2770. No credit cards.*

KOWLOON

Parts of Kowloon are among the most densely populated areas on the planet, and support a corresponding abundance of restaurants. Many hotels, planted here for the view of Hong Kong Island (spectacular at night), also have excellent restaurants, though they're uniformly expensive. You may have just as much luck walking into places on a whim, though of course you'll take your chances. Some of the best food in Kowloon is served in the backstreets, where immigrants from Vietnam, Thailand, and all over Asia keep their native cooking skills sharp.

Kowloon City

Locals flock to Kowloon City for casual, authentic, tasty meals at affordable prices.

Asian

CANTONESE

$ ✕ **Tso Choi Koon.** If you're of delicate constitution, or insist on fine food, pass on this home-style Cantonese restaurant. Tso Choi (Rough Dishes) is not everyone's cup of tea. Tripe lovers and haggis fans, however, might like to try the Chinese versions of some of their favorites: fried pig tripe, fried pig brain (served as an omelet), double-boiled pig brain . . . you get the idea. The older Hong Kong generation still likes this stuff; younger folks may demur. The wary can opt for creamy congee, fried chicken, or a fish fillet. ✉ *17–19A Nga Tsin Wai Rd.,* ☏ *2383–7170. No credit cards.*

THAI

$–$$ ✕ **Golden Orchid Thai Restaurant.** Golden Orchid serves some of the best and most innovative Thai cuisine in the territory. The curried crab and the seafood curry in pumpkin are excellent. Proactive eaters should not miss *mein come,* a kind of Thai leaf served with little bowls of spices and fixings such as fried coconut, peanuts, garlic, chili, lime, and dried shrimp. Wrap your choices in the leaf and delve in. The steamed seafood cakes, served in Thai stone pots, are also delicious. Try the roasted pork-neck slices, prawn cakes, and rice with olives. Unlike most restaurants, the Golden Orchid neither levies a service charge nor accepts tips, making this already cheap place a major bargain. ✉ *12 Lung Kong Rd.,* ☏ *2383–3076. MC, V.*

Sai Kung

Renowned for its seafood restaurants and neighborhood hill-walking tracks, Sai Kung is a town worth investigating. Many restaurants run

80

The Best Noodle
Restaurant **7**

Chung Thai Food
Restaurant and
Seafood **1**

Felix **17**

Gaddi's **17**

Golden Orchid Thai
Restaurant **2**

Great Shanghai
Restaurant **9**

Happy Garden
Noodle and
Congee Kitchen **20**

Jaspa's **5**

Kung Tak Lam **8**

Lo Chiu Vietnamese
Restaurant **6**

Mistral **10**

The Northern
Noodle **13**

Oyster & Wine
Bar **15**

Planet Hollywood . . . **18**

Sabatini **11**

Spring Moon **17**

T'ang Court **19**

Tso Choi Koon **3**

Tung Kee Seafood
Restaurant **4**

Wu Kong **14**

Yü **16**

Kowloon Dining

Bute St.

Mongkok St.   Fife St.

Mong Kok

Argyle St.

Sai Yee St.

Guanzhou-Kowloon R.R.

Argyle St.

Waterloo Rd.

Fat Kong St.

Shantung St.

Yim Po Fong St.

Portland St.

Reclamation St.

Shanghai St.

Nathan Rd.

Ferry St.

Dundas St.

Wylie Rd.

Waterloo Rd.   **Yau Ma Tei**

Market St.

Kings Park

Wylie Rd.

Chung Hau St.

Hong Chong Rd.

Kansu St.

Ferry St.

Canton Rd.

Temple St.

Gascoigne Rd.

TO HUNGHOM

Jordan Rd.

Bowring St.

Jordan

Cox's Rd.

Austin Rd.

Nathan Rd.

Cheong Wan Rd.

Kowloon Park

Kimberley Rd.

Granville Rd.

Cameron Rd.

Chatham Rd. South

Mody Rd.

Haiphong Rd.

Kowloon Park Dr.

Canton Rd.

Tsim Sha Tsui

Mody Rd.

Cross-Harbour Tunnel

Middle Rd.

Salisbury Rd.

Victoria Harbour

| 0 | 220 yards |
| 0 | 200 meters |

KEY

◇ Metro Stops

adjoining seafood shops, so you can select a fresh catch from tanks and have it cooked to order—steamed, fried, sautéed, or deep-fried with salt and pepper. You'll also find a good selection of Western restaurants serving delicious food with an easy, intimate, and laid-back ambience.

International

$$ ✕ **Jaspa's.** What could be better than heading straight to a cozy restaurant after a day out in the countryside? Here the food is always deliciously fulfilling, perfect after a day walking in the hills or fun-seeking in the water. Whether sitting out on the terrace or indoors, an enjoyable dining experience is guaranteed. The goat cheese parcel makes a delectable starter, and tasty chicken fajitas arrives on your table sizzling hot. Pasta with bay bugs and lamb chops never disappoint. The hearty food and friendly service makes Jaspa's a key culinary attraction in Sai Kung. ✉ *13 Sha Tsui Path,* ☎ *2792–6388. AE, MC, V.*

Seafood

$$-$$$ ✕ **Tung Kee Seafood Restaurant.** Here you can order whatever you want from the deep blue sea. Lobsters, slipper lobsters, clams, abalone, crabs, prawns, and fish of all kind are here for the tasting. Crustaceans and fish are quickly cooked by steaming and wok-frying, and are presented whole, leaving no illusions as to the freshness of your food. A quick look inside the tank is better than a marine biology lesson. Pick your favorites, and leave the rest for the chef. From lobster sashimi to steamed fish, this well-established eatery will impress you with a feast *de la mer.* ✉ *96–102 Man Nin St.,* ☎ *2792–7453. AE, DC, MC, V.*

$-$$ ✕ **Chung Thai Food Restaurant and Sea Food.** As its name suggests, this seafood corner is best known for both Chinese and Thai cooking, prepared separately by chefs of both nationalities. Those with a taste for spice can try the Thai fried crabs with curry or fried prawns with chili; otherwise, pick any seafood you like from the store next door, and the chef will prepare it to order. Steaming is highly recommended for fresh fish, as it retains the fresh taste and tender texture. Prices depend on the type and weight of the seafood you choose. ✉ *93 Man Nin St.,* ☎ *2792–1481;* ✉ *Seafood shop, 5 Siu Yat Bldg., Hoi Pong Sq.,* ☎ *2792–8172. MC, V.*

Tsim Sha Tsui

Tsim Sha Tsui, on the tip of Kowloon, is crammed with shops and with dining options, from five-star hotels to holes-in-the-wall.

Asian

CANTONESE

$$$-$$$$ ✕ **Spring Moon.** Yes, it's like old Shanghai—antique-style teak floors with Oriental rugs, oak paneling, stained glass, elm chairs and tables, dim lighting, a traditional tea-leaf cabinet displaying some 200 miniature clay teapots, and a showcase of porcelain and old silverware. Everything at Spring Moon is très Shanghai except, funnily enough, the cuisine. This prestigious restaurant at the Peninsula has adopted a northern setting, but the kitchen still turns out first-rate Cantonese food. Start with typical Cantonese barbecued meat such as succulent chicken marinated in dark soya sauce and delicious sliced barbecued pork, then gradually move on to sample the other culinary treats. Waiters prepare drunken prawns right at your table, subtly infusing them with Shaoxing wine. Braised abalone in oyster sauce, with freshly cooked vegetables, is rich in flavor and melts in your mouth. The popular roast pigeon flavored with cinnamon is another winner. A team of tea masters (tea sommeliers, if you will) can help you flatter your meal with one of 20 different teas. ✉ *The Peninsula, Salisbury Rd.,* ☎ *2315–3160. AE, DC, MC, V.*

THE DIM SUM EXPERIENCE

A VISIT TO HONG KONG is not complete without a visit to a dim sum restaurant. Dim sum is the staple food in Hong Kong and is always accompanied by Chinese tea. Served from before dawn to around 5 or 6 PM, these traditional Cantonese daytime tidbits are miniature works of art. More than 2,000 kinds of dim sum are in the Cantonese repertoire, and most dim sum restaurants prepare 100 varieties daily. Many are filled with such ingredients as pork, prawns, rice, and flour, and can efficiently fill up your stomach before you even notice it.

In the old days, dim sum restaurants were always associated with noise. Trolleys filled with steaming dishes were pushed around in restaurants while dim sum ladies shouted the names of the dishes. Today, in many of Hong Kong's hundreds of dim sum restaurants, a dim sum order form awaits you at the table and is subsequently stamped as your dishes arrive, creating a much quieter dining experience.

Generally steamed in bamboo steamers, panfried, baked, or deep-fried, the buns, crepes, and cakes are among the world's finest hors d'oeuvres. Many are minor culinary achievements—such as a soup with prawns served in a translucent rice-pastry shell, or a thousand-layer cake, or the ubiquitous spring roll. Most items come in a serving for three or four, allowing diners to share a good variety of delicacies around a table. Although every restaurant has its own dim sum menu, certain traditional items can be found in almost all dim sum outlets.

Popular dim sum items you need to know before a fun and fulfilling dim sum hunting meal include:

Cha siu bao: barbecued pork buns

Cha siu so: baked barbecued pork pastry

Cheong fun: steamed rice rolls (with various fillings such as prawns, beef, barbecued pork, and more)

Chun kuen: spring rolls

Dan tart: baked egg tarts

Har gau: steamed prawn dumplings with a light translucent wrap

Har kok: deep-fried prawn dumplings

Lou mei gai: glutinous rice wrapped in lotus leaf

Ngau yuk: steamed beef balls

Siu mai: steamed pork dumplings

Don't be surprised, however, if you discover some novelty items that you, or even your Hong Kong friends, have never heard of. Dim sum chefs in Hong Kong like to come up with innovative ideas and introduce creative elements to make a dim sum meal satisfying.

$$$ ✕ **T'ang Court.** Bedecked with golden silk drapes and contemporary sculptures, T'ang Court is one of the most elegant Chinese restaurants on the Kowloon peninsula. Spread over two floors connected by a spiral staircase, its distinctly modern look is offset by its foundation of traditional Chinese cuisine—the home-style Cantonese soups will make you feel like you're dining with a Chinese family. After covering its bases, however, the menu gets creative: baked blue-point oysters with port wine are an unfamiliar but tasty appetizer. The baked salty chicken (half or whole) has delicately flavored meat and a gorgeously crispy skin. Desserts are just as irresistible: try the steamed pumpkin dumplings with egg-yolk cream. Lunchtime dim sum, from steamed shrimp dumplings to barbecue-pork buns, are real delicacies. ✉ *Great Eagle Hotel, 8 Peking Rd.,* ☎ *2375–1133 ext. 2250. AE, DC, MC, V.*

$ ✕ **Happy Garden Noodle & Congee Kitchen.** For a taste of down-to-earth Hong Kong fare without the intimidation of trespassing in Chinese-only local joints, Happy Garden is the place to go. Bright and clean, with helpful waitresses and an English menu, this small place works for a typical local breakfast, an easy lunch, and even a big dinner. A popular morning combination is Cantonese congee and a glutinous rice dumpling wrapped in lotus leaf. A bowl of wonton soup or a plate of fried rice or noodles makes a simple but satisfying lunch. For dinner, the diced chicken with cashew nuts and sweet-and-sour pork are delicious Cantonese staples. ✉ *76 Canton Rd.,* ☎ *2377–2603 or 2377–2604. No credit cards.*

SEAFOOD

$$$$ ✕ **Yü.** You're welcomed by denizens of the deep, peering out from a huge, curving aquarium. Yü is a seafood lover's dream—look elsewhere for food of terrestrial origin. Start things off with some oysters—served on ice, glazed with champagne sauce, or prepared a variety of other ways. Lobster bisque and sautéed jumping shrimp with chili and pepper are perfect hot appetizers. Moving over to the fish tank, a dozen or so fresh catches of the day are cooked to suit either Asian or Western tastes, and some specialties combine the two, such as sautéed Boston lobster with black beans and fine noodles. The atmosphere is laid-back, making this a great place to enjoy the unobstructed view of the harbor and, at night, the stunning light show on the island side. ✉ *Inter-Continental Hong Kong, 18 Salisbury Rd.,* ☎ *2721–1211. Reservations essential. AE, DC, MC, V. No lunch.*

$$$ ✕ **Oyster & Wine Bar.** Lovers of that sensuous slippery mollusk the oyster should definitely consider a trip to the top of Sheraton Hotel & Towers. On its 18th floor, set against a romantic backdrop of Hong Kong's twinkling harbor, diners can slurp their way through more than 30 types of oysters flown in fresh from around the world and kept alive on ice at the huge oyster bar, ready for shucking. The staff behind the oyster bar will cheerfully explain the characteristics of each kind and can help you pick one to suite your tastes. The current record for oysters consumed in one sitting stands at nearly 60. On the hot dish menu, the San Francisco Fisherman's stew, with cherrystone clams, mussels, crab, and cod fish, is a definite winner. The oven-baked black cod with garden vegetables and boiled potatoes is another ace. A selection of wine from around the world is stored in wine cellars that line the walls. ✉ *Sheraton Hotel & Towers, 20 Nathan Rd.,* ☎ *2369–1111. AE, DC, MC, V. No lunch.*

SHANGHAINESE

$$ ✕ **Great Shanghai Restaurant.** Great Shanghai is not esteemed for its decor (which is old and dingy), but it's perfect for those who prefer the bold flavors of Shanghainese food to the more delicate tastes of local

Cantonese fare. You may not be ready for the sea blubber or braised turtle with sugar candy, but do try one of the boneless eel dishes, the Shanghai-style yellow fish soup, the beggar's chicken (order before noon for dinner), or the excellent spiced soy duck. For less adventurous palates there are more fundamental Shanghainese goodies such as sautéed river shrimp, Chinese cabbage with Yunnan ham, tasty fried noodles, or juicy dumplings. ⊠ *26–36 Prat Ave.,* ☎ *2366–8158. AE, DC, MC, V.*

$$ ✕ **Wu Kong.** You won't miss the big sign hanging out in the air just at the intersection of Nathan Road and Peking Road, but you can easily miss the tiny entrance that leads down to this unpretentious restaurant. Nevertheless, the small entrance belies the big basement dining room where first-rate Shanghainese fare is offered at a reasonable price. The pigeon in wine sauce is an excellent appetizer to share. The subtle sauce prepared with Chinese wine adds a delicate aroma to the meat pieces arranged in the shape of the bird. Vegetarian goose with vegetables wrapped in crispy bean curd skin is delicious and authentic. A whole fish smothered in a piquant sweet and vinegary sauce will leave you wanting more. Save some space for the deep-fried sweet ball whipped up with fluffy egg white stuffed with red bean and banana—a very good alternative to a doughnut. ⊠ *Alpha House, 23–33 Nathan Rd., basement (entrance on Peking Rd.),* ☎ *2366–7244. AE, DC, MC, V.*

$ ✕ **The Best Noodle Restaurant.** Tucked on a side street away from Nathan Road, near the Jordan MTR station, this humble place is a popular choice among locals who want a quick bowl of noodles or a simple yet tasty Shanghainese dish. English and Japanese menus are available on request, and the staff will happily make recommendations. The Shanghainese rice cooked with vegetables and topped with your choice of meats and vegetables is full of flavor, making a good change from ordinary steamed or fried rice. Fried noodles and soup noodles always live up to high expectations. The sweet spareribs are remarkably flavorsome. Leave room for the deep-fried pastry with red bean filling. ⊠ *105 Austin Rd.,* ☎ *2369–0086 or 2736–2786. No credit cards.*

$ ✕ **The Northern Noodle.** Conveniently located near the Tsim Sha Tsui metro and shopping area, this smart little joint has a great variety of northern dishes and makes a nice spot for a quick lunch or snack. Chow down on a bowl of noodles or dumplings accompanied with a chilled soya drink, or sample the typical northern specialties such as braised bean curd or spicy diced chicken. It's cramped and crowded, but the staff offers friendly and cheerful service. ⊠ *44 Hankow Rd.,* ☎ *2367–9011. No credit cards.*

VEGETARIAN

$–$$ ✕ **Kung Tak Lam.** Health-conscious diners will appreciate this simple Shanghainese vegetarian food. Don't turn your back when you see the no-frills decor; it's the food that makes this place so popular. Try the cold noodle plates, which come with an array of sauces to mix and match for as sweet or sour a flavor as you want. The bean curd ravioli also gets a big thumbs up. Set-price meals are incredibly cheap. Also check out its sibling in Causeway Bay, which is more elegantly decorated with paintings and high-back chairs but serves a very similar menu (⊠ Lok Sing Centre, 31 Yee Wo Street, ☎ 2890–3127). ⊠ *45–47 Carnarvon Rd., 1st floor,* ☎ *2367–7881. AE, DC, V.*

VIETNAMESE

$–$$ ✕ **Lo Chiu Vietnamese Restaurant.** The spartan interior may not impress you at the first glance, but pay no heed, what you're here for is the hearty, authentic food. Take your time and try not to burn your tongue on the sizzling hot and wonderfully flavorsome lemon grass chicken wings. Deep-fried sugarcane with minced shrimp is sweet and juicy. There's also a good variety of noodles and vermicelli served in soup or with fish sauce. A bottle of imported French beer is just the thing to wash it all down. ⊠ *17–19 Hillwood Rd.*, ☎ *2314–7983 or 2314–9211. MC, V.*

European

FRENCH

$$$$ ✕ **Gaddi's.** Gaddi's is a world unto itself. A private elevator takes you to the lobby overlooking the spacious restaurant, designed to evoke the hotel's original 1928 neoclassical elegance. The crystal chandeliers and sparkling silverware create a classical look. It's also one of the few places left where well-trained waiters carry out full service, such as carving a whole braised veal shank at your table. Although Gaddi's is moving forward, it retains its exceptional quality and gracious style. The menu has eased slightly from its former classical French style, relying less on heavy sauces and concentrating more on perfecting nature's finest flavors. Poached salmon ravioli with Osetra caviar is both stimulating and delicate; while the potato and foie gras soup with foie gras royal, black truffles, and crispy smoked bacon impresses with its distinct consistency and rich flavor. Sweetbread and crayfish strudel with young leeks comes in a flavor-filled, creamy Madeira sauce. The Barbary duck in a five-spice sauce set on a puree of haricots verts demonstrates the chef's creative fusion of French style and local ingredients—and it works remarkably well. End with the cheese board or Gaddi's famous soufflé. ⊠ *Peninsula Hotel, Salisbury Rd.*, ☎ *2315–3171 or 2366–6251 ext. 3989. Reservations essential. Jacket and tie required. AE, DC, MC, V.*

International

CONTEMPORARY

$$$–$$$$ ✕ **Felix.** Felix sits on the 28th floor of The Peninsula and should be
★ on every traveler's list of places to go, even if only for an overpriced drink at the bar. Love it or hate it, you can't deny that both the interior and the views are stunning. Every nook and cranny in this ultramodern space was designed by the French designer Philippe Starck, from chairs bearing the faces of Starck's friends to the most celebrated bathrooms in Asia. After dark, Hong Kong Island glitters from across the harbor through a floor-to-ceiling glass wall. On busy nights there's a buzz that's hard to find anywhere else. Some find the high-tech look unsettling, but its fans hail it as a "brasserie for the 21st century." The menu is no less adventurous—goose liver is stuffed with shredded duck meat, onions, and mushrooms and served with fresh fig puree; a ragout of escargots comes with Chinese sausage and chicken broth; miso-grilled butter fish rests on a shrimp-and-ginger risotto; and seared big-eye tuna is served with carrot gnocchi and curried carrot jus. Service is top-notch. ⊠ *Peninsula Hotel, Salisbury Rd., 28th floor,* ☎ *2366–6251 or 2315–3188. AE, DC, MC, V.*

North American

$$ ✕ **Planet Hollywood.** Come see Jackie Chan and Sylvester Stallone's handprints, grab a souvenir T-shirt, and enjoy a hilarious movie-museum tour. The food, with choices for both Eastern and Western palates, is satisfying, but it's the outrageous decor (movie pictures, props, and costumes) that packs a bigger punch. ⊠ *3 Canton Rd., Harbour City,* ☎ *2377–7888. AE, DC, MC, V.*

Tsim Sha Tsui East

European
ITALIAN

$$$–$$$$ ✗ **Mistral.** You know you're on to a good thing when the clientele is
★   largely Italian nationals and expatriates in search of a true taste of home.
The restaurant is packed every night with diners obviously enjoying
themselves. The cozy, candlelit interior buzzes with conversation. The
large open kitchen serves a selection of exquisitely prepared delicacies.
The chef is extremely creative and artistic—and it's well demonstrated
in his cooking and presentation. Carpaccio served with Parmesan
flakes and olive oil is a strict Italian classic. Pastas are first-rate at Mis-
tral—linguine with vegetables scented with truffle oil and the home-
made tagliolini with porcini mushrooms, Tyrolian speck ham, and
deep-fried parsley will make you feel as if you're in Italy. Fresh turbot
grilled with seasonal herbs and vegetables impresses as much with its
colorful presentation as its delicate flavor. If you want something
unique, ask the chef to prepare a special menu according to your taste.
⊠ *Grand Stanford Inter-Continental Harbour View, 70 Mody Rd.,* ☏
2731–2870. AE, DC, MC, V. Closed Sun.

$$$ ✗ **Sabatini.** Run by the Sabatini family, who also have eponymous restau-
rants in Rome, Japan, and Singapore, this Italian spot, with warm,
sponge-painted walls, wooden furnishings, and windows that look
onto the trees and shrubbery of the Royal Garden's atrium, attracts a
large local following who crave a taste of Italy. Linguine Sabatini, the
house specialty, is prepared according to the original Roman recipe—
cooked in a marvelous fresh tomato and garlic marinara sauce and served
with an array of luscious seafood. Try to avoid the classic mistake of
being too stuffed from the first two courses to have room for the terrific tiramisu or refreshing wild-berry pudding. ⊠ *Royal Garden, 69
Mody Rd., 3rd floor,* ☏ *2733–2000. Reservations essential. AE, DC,
MC, V.*

OUTER ISLANDS

Lamma Island

Lamma Island is relatively easy to get to, with ferries leaving Central's
pier almost hourly. Yung Shue Wan, where you disembark, has a collection of local seafood restaurants, one or two Western ones, and an
odd assortment of shops.

Asian
CANTONESE

$ ✗ **Han Lok Yuen.** Roast pigeon is the biggest star at Han Lok Yuen.
Arrive early so you don't miss it—the pigeon can be sold out by 8 PM
on busy days. For seafood lovers, fresh fish needs to be ordered one
day in advance. The restaurant will get the seafood you want on the
day you're dining to ensure its freshness. When you call to make your
request, tell them how you'd like your catch to be cooked—then leave
the rest to the professionals in the kitchen. The kitchen also turns out
a good array of typical Chinese dishes if you haven't called ahead. The
beautiful sea view here plays a role in making it a popular dining place
for both locals and visitors. The restaurant has an early kitchen closing, so be sure to arrive before 8:30 weekdays and Saturday (7 on Sunday). ⊠ *16–17 Hung Shing Ye, Lamma,* ☏ *2982–0680. AE, DC, MC,
V. Closed Mon.*

$ ✗ **Lancombe.** This Cantonese seafood restaurant is Lamma's best
source for no-nonsense food at no-nonsense prices. The huge En-
glish/Cantonese menu features seafood, seafood, and more seafood.

Try deep-fried squid, garoupa in sweet corn sauce, broccoli in garlic, and beef with black beans. Dishes come in three sizes; the small one is generally sufficient for four people. Seafood prices depend on the type and weight of the seafood you choose. Take a seat on the terrace out back where you'll have a view of the sea and distant Peng Chau Island. ⊠ *47 Main St., Yung Shue Wan,* ☎ *2982–0881. AE, MC, V.*

International

$$ ✕ **Toochka.** After exploring Lamma Island, a chilled beer and a beautiful curry dish at Toochka will end your day on high note. Choose from the extensive menu: salads, pastas, steaks, and the all-time-favorite curries (vegetables, meat, fish—you name it). The patio seats give a good location for you to watch island life drift by. ⊠ *44 Main St., Yung Shue Wan, Lamma Island,* ☎ *2982–0159. AE, MC, V. Closed Mon.*

4 LODGING

From breathtaking views, the finest service, and some of the world's top hotels to cheap and cheerful guest houses in neon-lit neighborhoods, Hong Kong has something to suit every budget and taste.

Updated by
Toby Parker

SINCE HONG KONG'S CELEBRATED RETURN to the Motherland, its status as an international financial and business center, as well as gateway to the rest of China, remains a strong attraction. The region's return to economic growth has, once again, been bringing in crowds of tourists and businesspeople.

Accommodations can be expensive here, but almost no one pays the quoted rate. Travel agents both in Hong Kong and abroad frequently offer huge discounts or package deals that allow you to stay at a fine hotel for a fraction of its full rate. Inquire about bargains before you reserve. Hotels do their part, too, with such features as discounts and credits for use in their restaurants and bars. Considering its size, Hong Kong has more than its fair share of five-star hotels, and more often than not these provide magnificent views over Victoria Harbour from either the Hong Kong or the Kowloon side. As they focus increasingly on the business traveler with an expense account, hotels can charge at least US$150 a night for rooms of a normal international standard. These may not be in prime locations, but they offer basic and reliable facilities—color TV, radio, telephone, same-day valet laundry service, room service, safe-deposit box, refrigerator and minibars, air-conditioning, and business services. Most hotels also have at least one restaurant and bar, a travel desk, and limousine or car rental. If you pay the full rate, many hotels will offer perks such as limousine pickup at the airport.

Of course, it's the business services that set Hong Kong apart. Most major hotels have business centers that provide secretarial, translation, courier, telex, fax, Internet, and printing services. Some provide PCs in-room, while others offer support for guests' own plug-in hardware. Executive floors or clubs have become standard in well-established hotels; these floors typically have extra concierge services, complimentary breakfast and cocktails, express check-in, personalized stationery, and an area where guests can meet with their business contacts. Executive rooms also have enhanced business features, such as in-room fax machines, Internet TV, and twin phone lines, though some charge extra for their use. Many hotels have large ballrooms, and most have smaller meeting and conference rooms.

For an overview of Hong Kong meeting, convention, and incentive facilities, contact the **Convention and Incentive Department** (✉ Hong Kong Tourist Bureau, 10/F, Citicorp Centre, 18 Whitfield Rd., North Point, Hong Kong Island, ☎ 2807–6543).

Book your room well in advance for a trip to Hong Kong, especially in March and from September through early December, the high seasons for conventions and conferences. Some hotels offer attractive seasonal packages.

The **Hong Kong Tourist Board** (HKTB, www.discoverhongkong.com) publishes the *Hotel Guide,* which lists rates, services, and facilities for all of its members. The HKTB does not make hotel reservations. The Hong Kong Hotel Association (HKHA) does, and at no extra charge, but only through its reservations office at Hong Kong International Airport.

Where to stay in Hong Kong depends on the nature of your trip. Thanks to the three tunnels that run underneath the harbor, the Star Ferry, and the Mass Transit Railway (MTR, or subway), it no longer matters whether you stay "Hong Kong side" or "Kowloon side"; the other side is only minutes away. The new airport rail link will whisk you over the Tsing Ma Suspension Bridge through Kowloon to Central in around 25 minutes.

If you want to avoid the main tourist accommodation areas, the New Territories and Outer Islands offer a few quieter and cheaper alternatives to Hong Kong Island and Kowloon.

For price ranges, *see* the lodging chart *in* Smart Travel Tips A to Z. Our categories for hotel rates are based on the average price for a standard double room in high season for two people; a single person in a double room will get a slightly lower rate. Prices are higher for a larger room or for a room with a view. All rates are subject to a 10% service charge and a 3% government tax, which is used to fund the activities of the Hong Kong Tourist Board (HKTB). Accommodations are grouped by geographical area—Hong Kong Island, Kowloon, and New Territories and the Outer Islands—and neighborhood, and are alphabetical within each price category.

HONG KONG ISLAND

If you need to be near the city's financial hub, you'll prefer the Central or Admiralty districts, on Hong Kong Island, but will pay for the convenience and views. Central is as busy as New York on weekdays, but, except for the Lan Kwai Fong area, it's quiet at night and on weekends. Nearby, Hong Kong's very own SoHo (South of Hollywood Road) boasts an eclectic mix of restaurants serving everything from Nepalese to modern European cuisine. Wanchai, east of Central, was once a sailor's dream of booze and Suzie Wong types. It still has plenty of nightlife, but new office high-rises and the Hong Kong Convention & Exhibition Centre—the territory's most popular venue for large-scale exhibitions and conferences—now draw businesspeople. Causeway Bay, farther east, is a brightly lit shopping district with restaurants, cinemas, and permanent crowds. Happy Valley is near the racetrack and Hong Kong Stadium, the territory's largest sports facility. Hotels and restaurants have also sprung up farther east along the MTR line, in residential North Point and Taikoo Shing.

Central

$$$$ 🏨 **Mandarin Oriental.** Long acclaimed as one of the world's great ho-
★   tels, the Mandarin Oriental represents Hong Kong's high end, serving the well-heeled and the business elite since 1963. While there are arguably more modern, luxurious hotels in Hong Kong, what sets the Mandarin apart is the extremely efficient service from the highly professional staff. Take the opportunity to greet Robert Chan, who has been guarding the prestigious entranceway for more than two decades. The hotel has a distinctly timeless elegance: the vast lobby is decorated with Asian antiques, and the comfortable guest rooms have antique maps and prints, traditional wooden furnishings, Eastern knickknacks, and glamorous black-and-gold accents. Bucking the current trend, the rooms are designed for luxury rather than mere efficiency. The top floor houses Vong (☞ Chapter 3), a French-Asian fusion restaurant run by world-renowned chef Jean-Georges Vongerichten. Man Wah, on the 25th floor (☞ Chapter 3), serves Cantonese cuisine in a genteel atmosphere. Centrally located beside the

Star Ferry concourse, the Mandarin is the lodging of choice for many a celebrity and VIP. A live band performs in the mezzanine Clipper Lounge early in the evening. ⊠ *5 Connaught Rd.,* ☎ *2522–0111,* FAX *2810–6190,* WEB *www.mandarin-oriental.com/hongkong. 502 rooms, 40 suites. 4 restaurants, 3 bars, in-room data ports, in-room safes, minibars, room service, indoor pool, barbershop, hair salon, health club, dry cleaning, laundry service, concierge, business services. AE, DC, MC, V.*

$$$$ 🏨 **Ritz-Carlton.** A rare gem of a hotel, the Ritz-Carlton couples an air
★ of refinement with superb hospitality. European antiques and reproductions mix with Asian accents, and everything from the Chippendale-style furniture to the gilt-frame mirrors is spotless and shining. The staff is exceptionally friendly and helpful, and the attention to detail is nonpareil. Complimentary homemade cookies and mineral water in the reception area hint at the level of customer care, and twin bathroom sinks, shoe polish, a beautiful tea and coffee cabinet, and fresh flowers help make you feel welcome in your own quarters. The rooms have an elegant yet comfortable feel, with calming colors emanating from the plush carpets, draperies, and furniture. Rooms overlook either Victoria Harbour or Chater Garden. Bath menus are available through room service for ladies, gentlemen, romantics, and kids while enjoying a hot soak. The main restaurant, Toscana (☞ Chapter 3), serves northern Italian cuisine. The Executive Business Center has Internet and e-mail access as well as computer workstations and color printers. ⊠ *3 Connaught Rd.,* ☎ *2877–6666; 800/241–3333 in the U.S.,* FAX *2877–6778,* WEB *www.ritzcarlton.com. 187 rooms, 29 suites. 5 restaurants, bar, lounge, in-room data ports, in-room safes, minibars, 13 no-smoking floors, room service, pool, health club, shop, dry cleaning, laundry service, concierge, business services. AE, DC, MC, V.*

Admiralty

$$$$ 🏨 **Conrad International.** This luxurious business hotel occupies part of a gleaming-white, oval-shape tower rising from Pacific Place, an upscale complex with a multistory mall on the edge of Central. Looking down from the top 21 floors of this 61-story building, the rooms are among the most spacious in Hong Kong and have dramatic views of the harbor and city. On-staff masseurs can massage you in the comfort of your own room on request. The four floors of executive rooms have in-room Internet and e-mail access, fax machines, and even personal step machines. The restaurant Brasserie on the Eighth is popular for its French fare and views of the park; Nicholini's (☞ Chapter 3) is one of the city's top spots for Italian cuisine. ⊠ *Pacific Place, 88 Queensway,* ☎ *2521–3838,* FAX *2521–3888,* WEB *www.conrad.com.hk. 467 rooms, 46 suites. 4 restaurants, bar, in-room data ports, in-room safes, minibars, room service, pool, health club, dry cleaning, laundry service, concierge, business services. AE, DC, MC, V.*

$$$$ 🏨 **Island Shangri-La.** From the moment you walk into the spacious lobby
★ this deluxe hotel sparkles. With more than 780 dazzling Austrian crystal chandeliers, high ceilings, and huge windows allowing in the sun, there's a sense of space and light. A 16-story glass-topped atrium houses

Lodging

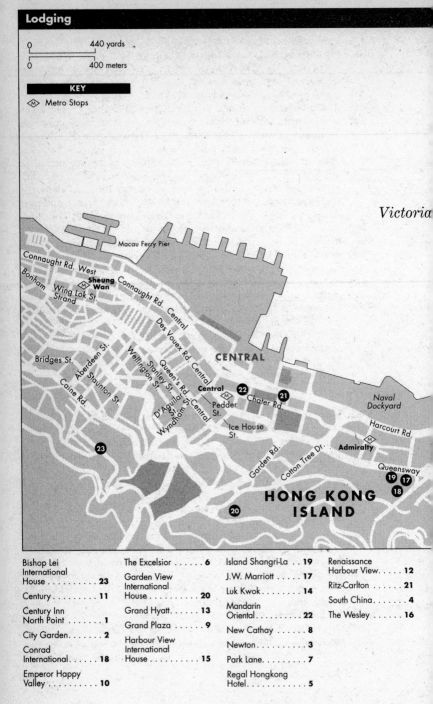

KEY

◈ Metro Stops

Victoria

Macau Ferry Pier

Connaught Rd. West

Bonham

Wing Lok St.

Strand

Sheung Wan

Connaught Rd. Central

Des Voeux Rd. Central

Bridges St.

Aberdeen St.

Staunton St.

Caine Rd.

Wellington St.

Stanley St.

Queen's Rd. Central

D'Aguilar St.

Wyndham St.

CENTRAL

Central

Pedder St.

Chater Rd.

Ice House St.

Garden Rd.

Cotton Tree Dr.

Naval Dockyard

Harcourt Rd.

Admiralty

Queensway

HONG KONG ISLAND

Bishop Lei International House 23

Century 11

Century Inn North Point 1

City Garden 2

Conrad International 18

Emperor Happy Valley 10

The Excelsior 6

Garden View International House 20

Grand Hyatt 13

Grand Plaza 9

Harbour View International House 15

Island Shangri-La . . 19

J.W. Marriott 17

Luk Kwok 14

Mandarin Oriental 22

New Cathay 8

Newton 3

Park Lane 7

Regal Hongkong Hotel 5

Renaissance Harbour View 12

Ritz-Carlton 21

South China 4

The Wesley 16

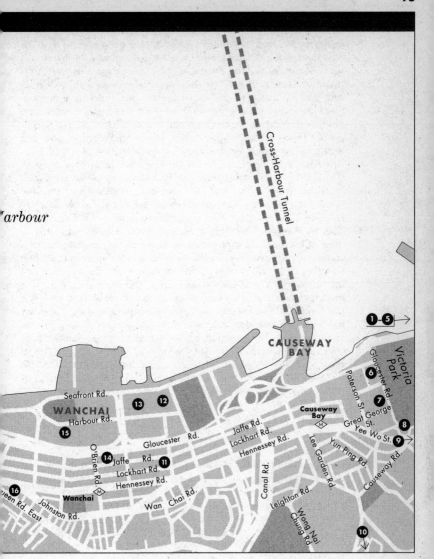

the world's largest Chinese landscape painting, *The Great Motherland of China* hanging from the 39th through the 55th floors. It took the 40 artists from Beijing six months to paint it. Take a trip upward from the 39th floor by the elevator for the experience of watching the mainland's misty mountains drift by. Priding itself on Asian hospitality, the staff is friendly and efficient. All rooms have extra-large desks with modem access that are handy for business travelers, and suites have in-room DVD players and a host of movies. You can eat very well at the renowned French eatery Petrus, the classy Lobster Bar (☞ Chapter 3), and the imperial Chinese outlet Summer Palace. The tranquil outdoor pool and health club overlook Hong Kong Park. ⊠ *Supreme Court Rd., 2 Pacific Place, 88 Queensway,* ☎ *2877–3838; 800/942–5050 in the U.S.,* FAX *2521–8742,* WEB *www.shangri-la.com. 531 rooms, 34 suites. 4 restaurants, bar, in-room data ports, in-room safes, minibars, 4 no-smoking floors, room service, pool, barbershop, hair salon, health club, dry cleaning, laundry service, concierge, business services. AE, DC, MC, V.*

$$$$ 🏨 **J. W. Marriott.** This elegant American-style hotel was the first to open at Pacific Place catering to the tastes of the traveling business community. Its extravagant, glass-wall atrium lobby has a cascading waterfall and is filled with plants. Modern rooms have harbor and mountain views and endless amenities, including data ports for modems or fax machines, coffeemakers, and ample work space. JW's California Grill serves popular California cuisine, and the Cigar Bar has a walk-in humidor with more than 100 types of stogies. Fitness facilities include a well-equipped 24-hour gym and an outdoor pool complete with an instant spin-dryer for your bathing togs. ⊠ *Pacific Place, 88 Queensway,* ☎ *2810–8366; 800/228–9290 in the U.S.,* FAX *2845–0737,* WEB *www.marriotthotels.com. 602 rooms, 25 suites. 4 restaurants, 3 bars, in-room data ports, in-room safes, minibars, 14 no-smoking floors, room service, pool, health club, dry cleaning, laundry service, concierge, business services. AE, DC, MC, V.*

Midlevels

$$ 🏨 **Bishop Lei International House.** Owned and operated by the Catholic diocese, this guest house is in a residential area of the Midlevels. Rooms are clean and functional, and half have harbor views. There's a fully equipped business center, a workout room, a pool, and a restaurant serving Chinese and Western meals. ⊠ *4 Robinson Rd.,* ☎ *2868–0828,* FAX *2868–1551,* WEB *www.asiatravel.com/hongkong/bishoplei. 122 rooms, 81 suites. Restaurant, in-room data ports, minibars, pool, gym, laundry service, business services. AE, DC, MC, V.*

$ 🏨 **Garden View International House.** This attractive, cylindrical guest
★ house on a hill overlooking the botanical gardens and harbor is run by the YWCA. Its well-designed rooms make excellent use of small, irregular shapes and emphasize the picture windows. If you want to do your own cooking, ask for a suite with a kitchenette (which will include a microwave oven); if not, the coffee shop serves European and Asian dishes. You can also use the swimming pool and gymnasium in the adjoining YWCA. Garden View is a five-minute drive (Bus 12A or Minibus 1A) from Central and just a few minutes from the Peak tram station. ⊠ *1 MacDonnell Rd.,* ☎ *2877–3737,* FAX *2845–6263,* WEB *www.ywca.org.hk. 130 rooms and suites. Coffee shop, pool, in-room data ports, minibars, laundry service, business services. AE, DC, MC, V.*

Wanchai

$$$$ 🏨 **Grand Hyatt.** "Grand" is the key word here. The Hyatt's Art Deco-
★ style lobby is topped by a ceiling hand-painted by Italian artist Paola Dindo. Artful black-and-white photographs of classic Chinese scenes

lend interest to the modern backdrop of corridors and rooms. A black-and-tan color scheme and light-wood paneling in the rooms and suites resemble the airy modern apartments you might see featured in an interior-design magazine. Work space has been subtly maximized, with twin phone lines and hidden fax machines in every room. A huge Internet TV on a rotating plinth with a cordless keyboard provides entertainment. The business center features an IBM room with IBM's latest technology and software, and access to Reuters Business Briefing. The Italian Grissini restaurant (☞ Chapter 3) and the Cantonese One Harbour Road are notable—as is JJ's nightclub—and the ground-floor breakfast buffet is a decadent feast. The Grand Hyatt is close to the Wanchai Star Ferry, yet its slight removal from the main walkways assures less foot traffic than other high-profile hotels. The hotel shares extensive outdoor facilities with the Renaissance Harbor View hotel. ⊠ *1 Harbour Rd.,* ☏ *2588–1234,* FAX *2802–0677,* WEB *www.hongkong.hyatt.com. 519 rooms, 51 suites. 4 restaurants, bar, in-room data ports, in-room safes, minibars, room service, pool, hair salon, driving range, 2 tennis courts, gym, nightclub, dry cleaning, laundry service, concierge. AE, DC, MC, V.*

$$$ 🏨 **Century.** This 23-story hotel is ideal for conventioneers—it's a five-minute walk by covered overpass (a lifesaver in the steamy summer heat) from the convention center and the MTR. The hotel caters to business travelers, offering a well-equipped business center and executive floors. Rooms are modern, with wooden furniture and a color scheme of blue, green, and gray. The health club has an outdoor pool, a gymnasium, and a golf driving bay. Within the complex are a popular, independently run Shanghainese restaurant, a 24-hr coffee shop (in keeping with Wanchai's reputation for nightlife), and a karaoke lounge. ⊠ *238 Jaffe Rd.,* ☏ *2598–8888,* FAX *2598–8866,* WEB *www.century-hongkong-hotel.com. 497 rooms, 19 suites. 2 restaurants, 2 bars, in-room data ports, in-room safes, minibars, no-smoking floor, room service, pool, health club, shop, dry cleaning, laundry service, concierge, business services. AE, DC, MC, V.*

$$$ 🏨 **Luk Kwok.** This contemporary hotel and office tower designed by Hong Kong's leading architect, Remo Riva, has replaced the Wanchai landmark of the same name immortalized in Richard Mason's novel *The World of Suzie Wong.* Luk Kwok's appeal is its proximity to the Hong Kong Convention & Exhibition Centre, the Academy for Performing Arts, and the Arts Centre. Guest rooms, located between the building's 19th and the 29th floors, are clean and simple, with contemporary furniture; higher floors afford mountain or city views. It has a good Chinese restaurant. ⊠ *72 Gloucester Rd.,* ☏ *2866–2166,* FAX *2866–2622,* WEB *www.lukkwokhotel.com. 191 rooms, 5 suites. 2 restaurants, lounge, in-room data ports, in-room safes, minibars, no-smoking floor, room service, laundry service, business services. AE, DC, MC, V.*

$$$ 🏨 **Renaissance Harbour View.** Sharing the Hong Kong Convention & Exhibition Centre complex with the Grand Hyatt is this more modest but equally attractive hotel. Guest rooms are medium size and modern, with plenty of beveled-glass mirrors. Rooms on the executive floors are done in sophisticated dark colors and have large, no-nonsense desks. More than half of the rooms have superb views overlooking the harbor. Every room has a fax machine. Amenities include the Dynasty (☞ Chapter 3) and Scala restaurants, a cozy bar, the largest hotel outdoor pool in town, gardens, jogging trails, tennis courts, and health-club facilities on the recreation deck between the two hotels. The lobby lounge has one of the best easy-listening jazz bands in town, and is a popular rendezvous spot for local and visiting businesspeople. ⊠ *1 Harbour Rd.,* ☏ *2802–8888,* FAX *2802–8833,* WEB *www.renaissancehotels.com/HKGHV. 807 rooms, 53 suites. 4 restaurants, 2 bars, in-room data ports, in-room* *safes, minibars, 16 no-smoking floors, room service, pool, barbershop, hair salon, health club, 4 tennis courts, dry cleaning, laundry service, concierge, business services. AE, DC, MC, V.*

$–$$ ⚃ **Harbour View International House.** This waterfront YMCA property offers small but clean and relatively inexpensive accommodations near the Wanchai Star Ferry pier. The best rooms face the harbor. It's well placed for travelers who want to attend cultural events in the evening: both the Arts Centre and Academy for Performing Arts are next door. Opposite Harbour View is the Hong Kong Convention & Exhibition Centre. The 16-story hostel provides free shuttle service to Causeway Bay and the Central Star Ferry. Guests can use the superb YMCA Kowloon facilities, just a short ferry ride away, for a small fee. ✉ *4 Harbour Rd.,* ☎ *2802–0111,* FAX *2802–9063. 320 rooms. Restaurant, no-smoking floor, laundry service. AE, DC, MC, V.*

$–$$ ⚃ **The Wesley.** Opened in 1992 on the site of the old Soldiers and Sailors Home, this 21-story, moderately (for Hong Kong) priced hotel is a short walk from the Hong Kong Convention & Exhibition Centre, the Academy for Performing Arts, and the MTR. Rooms are small but pleasantly furnished, and the more spacious corner "suites" have alcove work areas. No health center or pool is on the premises, but you can use the facilities in Wesley's sister Grand Plaza Hotel, in Quarry Bay, for a discounted fee. A tram stop is right outside the door, and Pacific Place and the bars of Wanchai are close by. ✉ *22 Hennessy Rd.,* ☎ *2866–6688,* FAX *2866–6613,* WEB *www.grandhotel.com.hk/wesley. 251 rooms. Restaurant, no-smoking floor, laundry service, business services. AE, DC, MC, V.*

Causeway Bay

$$$$ ⚃ **Regal Hongkong Hotel.** The slightly over-the-top decor in this 33-story hotel leans toward European, with marble floors and a dramatic lobby with high windows, Louis XIV furniture, and a huge mural depicting a Mediterranean scene. The reception area is small, but that doesn't affect the efficient service. Gilded elevators lead to guest rooms with maple-inlay furniture crafted by local artisans, walls and carpets in muted earth tones, brightly colored bedspreads, and spacious bathrooms with triangular tubs. The hotel has four executive floors and sumptuous dining rooms, especially the top-floor Mediterranean restaurant Zeffirino's, which has great views of Victoria Park. The rooftop pool and terrace allow escape from the surrounding chaos. Close to the Hong Kong Stadium and the Happy Valley racecourse, as well as the city's most popular shopping area, this deluxe hotel is one of the most convenient in town. ✉ *88 Yee Wo St.,* ☎ *2890–6633; 800/222–8888 in the U.S.,* FAX *2881–0777,* WEB *www.regalhongkong.com. 393 rooms, 32 suites. 6 restaurants, bar, in-room data ports, in-room safes, minibars, no-smoking floor, room service, pool, health club, shops, dry cleaning, laundry service, concierge, business services. AE, DC, MC, V.*

$$$ ⚃ **The Excelsior.** The Excelsior opened in 1974 and remains one of Hong
★   Kong's most popular hotels. Though a veteran, it readily adapts to the changing demands of the group and business markets. Eighty percent of the rooms enjoy splendid sea views, including the Hong Kong Yacht Club's neatly aligned yachts and boats. The spacious and clean rooms have large beds, long desks, and, according to the hotel, the cheapest minibars in town. The location is ideal for shopping and dining. At ToTT's (Talk of The Town) Asian Grill & Bar (☞ Chapter 3), the top-floor restaurant-bar-nightclub, you can sample a creative East-meets-West cuisine while listening to live music. The fitness-minded will appreciate the rooftop tennis courts, the well-equipped gym, and the jogging track in adjacent Victoria Park. A business center provides a plethora of services including fax machines, computer terminals, and

Internet access. On a historical note, the hotel sits on the first plot of land auctioned by the British government when Hong Kong became a colony in 1841. ✉ *281 Gloucester Rd.,* ☎ *2894–8888,* FAX *2895–6459,* WEB *www.mandarin-oriental.com/excelsior. 866 rooms, 21 suites. 6 restaurants, 2 bars, in-room data ports, in-room safes, minibars, no-smoking floor, room service, hair salon, 2 tennis courts, health club, shop, dry cleaning, laundry service, concierge, business services. AE, DC, MC, V.*

$$–$$$ 🏨 **Park Lane.** With an imposing facade reminiscent of London's Knightsbridge area, this elegant hotel overlooks Victoria Park and backs onto one of Hong Kong Island's busiest shopping, entertainment, and business areas, Causeway Bay. The lobby is extraordinarily spacious, and all rooms have luxurious marble bathrooms, elegant handcrafted furniture, and marvelous views of the harbor and Victoria Park or the city. The rooftop restaurant has a panoramic view and serves international cuisine with a touch of Asian flavor. Those who can't resist retail temptations may never find time to use the well-equipped fitness center, but they'll probably get enough exercise walking the two-floor shopping arcade, whose 17 stores include such designer boutiques as agnes b, Enrico Coveri, and Perry Ellis. ✉ *310 Gloucester Rd.,* ☎ *2293–8888,* FAX *2576–7853,* WEB *www.parklane.com.hk. 759 rooms, 33 suites. 2 restaurants, bar, in-room data ports, in-room safes, minibars, no-smoking floor, room service, hair salon, health club, shop, dry cleaning, laundry service, concierge, business services. AE, DC, MC, V.*

$ 🏨 **New Cathay.** Close to Victoria Park, this Chinese-managed hotel is fairly basic and is favored by tour groups from China. The small rooms have basic amenities, such as air-conditioning and TV, and an independently run Chinese seafood restaurant is on the top floor. The hotel is just a few minutes from the bustling shopping center in Causeway Bay. ✉ *17 Tung Lo Wan Rd.,* ☎ *2577–8211,* FAX *2576–9365,* WEB *newcathay.gdhotels.net. 219 rooms, 3 suites. 2 restaurants, in-room safes, minibars, room service, laundry service. AE, DC, MC, V.*

Happy Valley

$$ 🏨 **Emperor Happy Valley.** Catering mainly to business and corporate travelers, this reasonably priced hotel is one of few places to stay in the predominantly residential Happy Valley area. The Emperor is also the best deal in town for horse-racing fans, as it's just a few minutes' walk from the Happy Valley racetrack. It's also 5–10 minutes by taxi from the Causeway Bay shopping area. Corridors are narrow, but rooms are clean and functional. ✉ *1A Wang Tak St.,* ☎ *2893–3693,* FAX *2834–6700,* WEB *www.emperor-hv-hotel.com.hk. 157 rooms, 1 suite. 2 restaurants, bar, in-room safes, minibars, no-smoking floor, room service, laundry service. AE, DC, MC, V.*

North Point

$$ 🏨 **Century Inn North Point.** One of the newest hotels in the increasingly developed eastern harborfront area, Century Inn is well located for business travelers centered around Quarry Bay but somewhat out of the way for vacationers. However, it is targeted for the budget minded who want to stay Hong Kong side. Many rooms have harbor views, compensating for their small size, and a full range of functional amenities. ✉ *136–142 Java Rd.,* ☎ *2204–6618,* FAX *2204–6677,* WEB *www.centuryhotels.com. 202 rooms, 1 suite. 2 restaurants, lounge, in-room data ports, minibars, room service, pool, laundry service, business services. AE, DC, MC, V.*

$$ 🏨 **City Garden.** Although not as close to the MTR as its brochure suggests, this hotel has the advantage of being easily accessible to the East-

ern Corridor Expressway, which links Causeway Bay to Taikoo Shing and the Eastern Harbour crossing. Rooms are basic and rather small. The hotel caters to Asian tour groups and has a good Cantonese restaurant. ⊠ *9 City Garden Rd.,* ☎ *2887–2888,* ℻ *2887–1111,* WEB *www.citygarden.com.hk. 613 rooms, 2 suites. 2 restaurants, bar, in-room data ports, minibars, room service, pool, sauna, health club, laundry service, business services. AE, DC, MC, V.*

$$ 🏨 **Newton.** Housed in a boxy high-rise that is functional but largely featureless, this hotel has the advantages of proximity to the Fortress Hill MTR station and surrounding office blocks and a pleasant on-site restaurant-bar with live entertainment. Many claim that the Old Hong Kong Restaurant, located in the basement, is one of the better Shanghainese restaurants in town. Rooms are small but adequate. ⊠ *218 Electric Rd.,* ☎ *2807–2333,* ℻ *2807–1221,* WEB *www.newtonhk.com. 362 rooms, 9 suites. 2 restaurants, bar, coffee shop, in-room data ports, minibars, room service, pool, sauna, laundry service, business services. AE, DC, MC, V.*

$$ 🏨 **South China.** Managed by a mainland Chinese company and thus naturally attracting groups from mainland China, this hotel is small and functional, though it has a large Chinese restaurant and bar. It's some distance from the North Point MTR. ⊠ *67 Java Rd.,* ☎ *2503–1168,* ℻ *2512–8698,* WEB *www.gdihml.com/schina/. 202 rooms, 1 suite. 2 restaurants, minibars, room service, laundry service, business services. AE, DC, MC, V.*

Quarry Bay

$$ 🏨 **Grand Plaza.** Part of a large residential-commercial-entertainment complex, the boxy rooms here are a little out of the way, but the hotel connects to the Taikoo MTR station and has a vast recreational club with a huge pool, squash courts, a billiard room, a gymnasium, an aerobics hall, a miniature-golf course, a playground, and a jogging track that guests can use for a small fee. It also has an upmarket coffee shop, and plenty of shopping in the adjoining Jusco department store. ⊠ *2 Kornhill Rd.,* ☎ *2886–0011,* ℻ *2886–1738,* WEB *www.grandhotel.com.hk/grandplaza. 208 rooms, 40 suites. 2 restaurants, in-room data ports, minibars, room service, indoor pool, miniature golf, tennis court, health club, badminton, squash, billiards, laundry service, business services. AE, DC, MC, V.*

KOWLOON

Most of Hong Kong's hotels are on the Kowloon Peninsula, which includes Tsim Sha Tsui, Tsim Sha Tsui East, Harbour City, and the Yau Ma Tei and Mong Kok districts, just north of Tsim Sha Tsui. The fabled Golden Mile of shopping, on Nathan Road, runs through Tsim Sha Tsui, and restaurants, stores, and hotels fill the surrounding backstreets.

Tsim Sha Tsui East is a grid of modern office blocks—many with restaurants or nightclubs—and luxury hotels. This area was created on land reclaimed from the harbor in the last decade, so all of the hotels are reasonably new. Hung Hom includes a noisy old residential area and a private-housing complex with cinemas and shops.

North of Tsim Sha Tsui are Yau Ma Tei and Mong Kok, which have more older, smaller, more moderately priced hotels. Most of these are on or near Nathan Road and are probably the best bets for travelers on budgets. Excellent bus service and the MTR connect these areas to the center of Tsim Sha Tsui.

Kowloon Lodging

Booth Lodge 5

BP International . . . 13

Caritas Bianchi
Lodge 7

Concourse 1

Dodsett Seaview 6

Eaton 8

Grand Stanford
Inter-Continental . . . 30

Grand Tower 4

Great Eagle 17

Holiday Inn
Golden Mile 23

Inter-Continental
Hong Kong 35

Kimberley 27

Kowloon Hotel 21

Kowloon
Shangri-La 33

Majestic 10

Marco Polo
Hong Kong 18

Marco Polo
Gateway 16

Marco Polo Prince . 15

Metropole 3

Miramar 25

Nathan 9

New Astor 24

New World
Renaissance 34

Nikko 29

Peninsula 20

Pruton Prudential . . . 11

Ramada Hotel
Kowloon 28

Regal Kowloon 31

Royal Garden 32

Royal Pacific
Hotel & Towers . . . 14

Royal Plaza 2

Salisbury YMCA . . . 19

Shamrock 12

Sheraton Hong
Kong Hotel and
Towers 22

Windsor 26

Bute St.

Mong Kok St.

Fife St.

Mong Kok

Sai Yee St.

Argyle St.

Argyle St.

Waterloo Rd.

Guangzhou-Kowloon R.R.

Yim Po Fong St.

Fat Kong St.

Shantung St.

Dundas St.

Wylie Rd.

Portland St.

Shanghai St.

Nathan Rd.

Reclamation St.

Ferry St.

Waterloo Rd.

Yau Ma Tei

Kings Park

Chung Hau St.

Hong Chong Rd.

Market St.

Kansu St.

Ferry St.

Canton Rd.

Temple St.

Wylie Rd.

Gascoigne Rd.

TO HUNGHOM

Jordan Rd.

Jordan

Cox's Rd.

Bowring St.

Austin Rd.

Cheong Wan Rd.

Kowloon Park

Nathan Rd.

Kimberley Rd.

Granville Rd.

Cameron Rd.

Chatham Rd. South

Mody Rd.

Haiphong Rd.

Tsim Sha Tsui

Mody Rd.

Cross-Harbour Tunnel

Canton Rd.

Kowloon Park Dr.

Middle Rd.

Salisbury Rd.

Victoria Harbour

0   220 yards

0   200 meters

KEY

Metro Stops

Hung Hom

$$$ 🏨 **Harbour Plaza.** The opulent Harbour Plaza's slightly out-of-the-way location allows a unique perspective on the harbor—from Wanchai out to the South China Sea. Hotel buses shuttle to and from Tsim Sha Tsui all day long; the Kowloon–Canton Railway station, from which trains leave for China, is five minutes away; and ferries ply the choppy waters between Hong Kong Island and the nearby ferry terminal. The atrium lobby is spacious and well designed, with good views from lounges on two levels. Rooms are large, comfortable, and contemporary. Dining options include a Japanese *robatayaki* barbecue, a Cantonese restaurant, a grill, and a fun pub called the Pit Stop, which features actual racing cars. A scenic rooftop pool, a fitness center, and health spa are also available. ⊠ *20 Tak Fung St.,* ☎ *2621–3188,* 🅵🅰🆇 *2621–3311,* 🆆🅴🅱 *www.harbour-plaza.com/hphk/. 381 rooms, 30 suites. 4 restaurants, pub, in-room data ports, in-room safes, minibars, room service, pool, hair salon, spa, health club, shop, dry cleaning, laundry service, concierge, business services. AE, DC, MC, V.*

$ 🏨 **Holy Carpenter Guest House.** Occupying the fifth and sixth floors of a community center that also houses a church, this small hostel is a 10-minute walk from the Kowloon–Canton Railway station. Don't expect more than a humble room and very small bathroom; lodgings here are very cheap by Hong Kong standards, and are used mainly by budget travelers who just want a place to sleep *and* can reserve at least a month in advance. Those staying for more than two weeks may get a further discount on the room rate. ⊠ *1 Dyer Ave.,* ☎ *2362–0301,* 🅵🅰🆇 *2362–2193. 14 rooms. MC, V.*

Tsim Sha Tsui

$$$$ 🏨 **Hyatt Regency.** The Hyatt Regency's modern facade, top-end shopping arcade, and dramatic, marble-and-teak lobby exude glamour. The Buddhist gods of hospitality guarding the spacious lobby's reception area are meant to give travelers warm blessings and ensure a nice stay. To that end the hotel even has its own feng shui expert. Rooms are recently refurbished, well equipped, and comfortable. Next door to the Tsim Sha Tsui MTR station and five minutes from the Star Ferry, the hotel also has a gallery of Asian antiques and an authentic Chinese restaurant. ⊠ *67 Nathan Rd.,* ☎ *2311–1234,* 🅵🅰🆇 *2739–8701,* 🆆🅴🅱 *hongkong.hyatt.com. 723 rooms, 4 suites. 4 restaurants, 2 bars, coffee shop, in-room data ports, in-room safes, minibars, 5 no-smoking floors, room service, shop, dry cleaning, laundry service, concierge, business services. AE, DC, MC, V.*

$$$$ 🏨 **Inter-Continental Hong Kong.** This hotel, formerly known as the Regent, is modern luxury at its most opulent. Its world-class style and ★ innovation are coupled with what may well be the best views in Hong Kong. All this has a price, but management is constantly coming up with packages that allow you to stay here without robbing a bank. The spacious, bright, and sophisticated rooms all have huge desks. Browse the Web through the TV, or plug in your own laptop and get a local high-speed connection. All rooms have sunken baths in Italian marble, and most suites have a separate steam shower. The health spa, also open to the public, is highly recommended for those who wouldn't mind feeling five years younger. The hotel's five restaurants include the high-profile Yü, serving spectacular seafood (☞ Chapter 3); Plume, with contemporary European cuisine; and The Steak House. ⊠ *18 Salisbury Rd.,* ☎ *2721–1211; 800/545–4000 in the U.S.,* 🅵🅰🆇 *2739–4546,* 🆆🅴🅱 *www.interconti.com. 510 rooms, 92 suites. 5 restaurants, pool, spa, health club, shop, dry cleaning, laundry service, concierge, business services. AE, DC, MC, V.*

$$$$
★

Peninsula. Established in 1928, the Pen is a legend worldwide and a must-visit on most Hong Kong visitors' lists. Its impeccable taste and old-world style are evident throughout: colonial architecture, a columned and gilt-corniced lobby where high tea is served, a fleet of Rolls-Royces, attentive room valets, and luxurious bath accessories. The Pen is also one of the few hotels in Asia that offers helicopter sightseeing tours that take off from the hotel's own helicopter pad, located on the roof. Classically European deep blue, gold, and ivory fabrics adorn the spacious guest rooms and decadent suites; Chinese prints and furniture lend a subtle Eastern accent. Service is marvelously professional and always discreet. All rooms have silent fax machines, deluxe bedside remotes that operate everything from the overhead lights to the curtains on the windows, and the Pen's famous shoe box (staff retrieve your shoes through an opening in the corridor). Huge corner suites allow you to wallow in your private hot tub while you look out over the glorious city skyline. The superb spa treats you like royalty, with a pool, sundeck, hot tub, sauna, and steam room. For some retail therapy head to the swanky shops—including a branch of Shanghai Tang—located in the Pen's exclusive shopping arcade or stop off at the in-house Clarin's beauty spa where you'll be buffed and polished into a blissful state. Restaurants include Gaddi's, one of the finest eateries in town; Chinese Spring Moon; and the hippest of the hip rooftop restaurants, Felix (☞ Chapter 3 for all). ⊠ *Salisbury Rd.,* ☎ *2366–6251,* FAX *2722–4170,* WEB *www.peninsula.com. 246 rooms, 54 suites. 7 restaurants, bar, in-room data ports, in-room safes, minibars, room service, pool, hair salon, spa, health club, shops, dry cleaning, laundry service, concierge, business services, helipad. AE, DC, MC, V.*

$$$$

Sheraton Hong Kong Hotel and Towers. Across the street from the Space Museum at the southern end of the fabled Golden Mile, the Sheraton is contemporary, even avant-garde, its spacious, modern lobby full of arty knickknacks and paintings. Guest rooms are standard Sheraton and have a choice of harbor, city, or courtyard views. Make your way to the rooftop pool and terrace via the exterior glass elevator. The sky lounge has a terrific harbor view, Someplace Else is a popular hangout at happy hour, and those needing an aphrodisiacal pick-me-up should head up to the delightful Oyster & Wine Bar (☞ Chapter 3) on the top floor. ⊠ *20 Nathan Rd.,* ☎ *2369–1111,* FAX *2739–8707,* WEB *www.sheraton.com. 686 rooms, 94 suites. 5 restaurants, 3 lounges, in-room data ports, in-room safes, minibars, 2 no-smoking floors, room service, pool, health club, shop, dry cleaning, laundry service, concierge, business services. AE, DC, MC, V.*

$$$–$$$$

Great Eagle. What Great Eagle lacks in exterior presence it makes up in understated comfort. The lobby ceiling is painted with beautiful murals, and glowing backlit onyx pillars create a comfortable yet sophisticated atmosphere. Once inside, you'll find a selection of beautifully appointed rooms as well as bars, restaurants, and business services. Guest rooms are comfortable yet elegant, and all rooms on the Renaissance Club executive floors have fax machines and data ports. The Bostonian restaurant offers a great variety of seafood dishes, meats, and wines; Asian-attuned palates will love the innovative and delicately presented Chinese dishes at T'ang Court (☞ Chapter 3). ⊠ *8 Peking Rd.,* ☎ *2375–1133,* FAX *2375–6611,* WEB *www.gehotel.com. 473 rooms, 27 suites. 3 restaurants, 2 bars, lounge, in-room data ports, in-room safes, minibars, 4 no-smoking floors, room service, pool, health club, shop, dry cleaning, laundry service, concierge, business services. AE, DC, MC, V.*

$$$–$$$$

Holiday Inn Golden Mile. Right on the Golden Mile of Nathan Road, the hub of Kowloon's business and shopping area, this business-style hotel has been popular for more than 20 years. Rooms here are relatively small and nondescript but windows on the facade have sweeping views of Nathan Road and the Avenue restaurant serves delicious contemporary European cuisine in a fashionably decorated third-floor setting overlooking the neon sights and sounds of Tsim Sha Tsui's main artery. ⊠ *50 Nathan Rd.,* ☎ *2369–3111,* FAX *2369–8016,* WEB *www.goldenmile.com. 592 rooms, 8 suites. 3 restaurants, bar, lounge, in-room data ports, in-room safes, minibars, 7 no-smoking floors, room service, pool, health club, shop, dry cleaning, laundry service, business services. AE, DC, MC, V.*

$$$–$$$$ 🏨 **Marco Polo Hongkong.** Lovers of things German might raise a glass to this hotel's prominent and outrageous Oktoberfest. The Marco Polo Hongkong, the largest of three Marco Polo hotels along the same street, holds the record for hosting the largest such gathering in the territory— up to 1,000 participants attend each night through the month for thigh-slapping, beer-swilling fun. Next to the Star Ferry, the hotel is part of the wharf-side Harbour City complex, along with its sister hotels Marco Polo Gateway and Prince. The complex houses offices, shopping malls, movie theaters, and restaurants, and is near the pop-culture landmarks Hard Rock Cafe and Planet Hollywood. It has a somewhat dated feel, with key drops and coattailed waiters, but personal comfort gets plenty of attention. Rip Van Winkles can choose from 11 kinds of pillows, and parents are provided miniature bathrobes, mild shampoos, and rubber ducks for their tots. Rooms on the executive floor have Internet TVs with remote keyboards. ⊠ *Harbour City, Canton Rd.,* ☎ *2113–0088,* FAX *2113– 0011,* WEB *www.marcopolohotels.com/thehongkonghotel/index.html. 621 rooms, 44 suites. 6 restaurants, lounge, in-room data ports, in-room safes, minibars, 2 no-smoking floors, room service, pool, barbershop, hair salon, dry cleaning, laundry service, concierge, business services. AE, DC, MC, V.*

$$$ 🏨 **Marco Polo Gateway.** This 16-story hotel, popular with Japanese tour groups, is in the shopping and commercial area along Canton Road and close to the MTR station. The brightly colored rooms and suites have large windows and comfortable beds. The most notable restaurant is La Brasserie, serving provincial French cuisine in a typical brasserie setting (long bar, dark wood, leather seats, red-checkered tablecloths). The business center is well supplied, and the staff is helpful and well trained. Guests may use the pool at the nearby Marco Polo Hongkong. ⊠ *Harbour City, Canton Rd.,* ☎ *2113–0888,* FAX *2113– 0022,* WEB *www.marcopolohotels.com/marco-frame.html. 384 rooms, 56 suites. 3 restaurants, bar, in-room data ports, in-room safes, minibars, 3 no-smoking floors, room service, barbershop, dry cleaning, laundry service, business services. AE, DC, MC, V.*

$$$ 🏨 **Marco Polo Prince.** Like its neighboring Marco Polo namesakes in the Harbour City complex (the Hongkong and Gateway), the Marco Polo Prince is very convenient to upscale shops and cinemas and to the restaurants and shops of Tsim Sha Tsui. It's also near the China Hong Kong Terminal, where ferries, boats, and buses depart for China. Most small, comfortable rooms overlook expansive Kowloon Park, and some suites have views of Victoria Harbour. The Spice Market restaurant serves Southeast Asian buffets and an international menu. Guests can use the pool at the Marco Polo Hongkong, a five-minute walk away. ⊠ *Harbour City, Canton Rd.,* ☎ *2113–1888,* FAX *2113–0066,* WEB *www.marcopolohotels.com/prince. 345 rooms, 51 suites. Restaurant, bar, deli, in-room data ports, in-room safes, minibars, no-smoking floor, room service, shop, dry cleaning, laundry service, business services. AE, DC, MC, V.*

$$$ 🏨 **New World Renaissance.** This popular lodging is part of a large shopping complex. On the Tsim Sha Tsui waterfront, its perfect views of Hong Kong Island are rivaled only by the adjacent Regent Hotel, part of the same complex. Long escalators lead from the shopping area to the hotel's large second-floor lobby. The comfortable guest rooms with pleasantly modern decor feel homey—plenty of space for working and relaxing. Greenery surrounds the outdoor pool, which stays open throughout the year. Among the three restaurants, the Panorama has one of the best harbor views in town. ⊠ *22 Salisbury Rd.,* ☎ *2369–4111,* FAX *2369–9387,* WEB *www.renaissancehotels.com. 501 rooms, 42 suites. 3 restaurants, lounge, in-room data ports, in-room safes, minibars, 4 no-smoking floors, room service, pool, hair salon, health club, dry cleaning, laundry service, business services. AE, DC, MC, V.*

\$\$–\$\$\$ 🏨 **Miramar.** Opened in 1948, Miramar was Hong Kong's first post–World War II hotel. It was originally owned by the Spanish Catholic Mission, which intended to use the structure as a shelter for missionaries expelled from China; as tourism blossomed here, the priests changed their plan and turned the premises into a hotel. At the top of the Golden Mile and across from Kowloon Park, the Miramar has a vast lobby with a dramatic stained-glass ceiling, functional rooms, and smiling service. The adjacent Miramar Shopping Centre has two Chinese restaurants (run by the hotel) and a microbrewery. You're close to both the Jordan and Tsim Sha Tsui MTR stations. ⊠ *130 Nathan Rd.,* ☎ *2368–1111,* FAX *2369–1788. 512 rooms, 13 suites. 3 restaurants, bar, no-smoking floor, indoor pool, shop, dry cleaning, laundry service, business services, meeting rooms. AE, DC, MC, V.*

\$\$ 🏨 **BP International House.** Built by the Boy Scouts Association, this hotel next to Kowloon Park offers excellent value. A portrait of BP himself, association founder Baron Robert Baden-Powell, hangs in the spacious modern lobby. The small hostel-like rooms justify their hotel-like costs with amenities such as TVs, telephones, and electronic key cards. Most rooms have panoramic views of Victoria Harbour and clear views of the busiest part of Kowloon. A multipurpose hall hosts exhibitions, conventions, and concerts, and the health club is one of the biggest in town. A major attraction for budget travelers is a self-service coin laundry. Note that you can park in the hotel's own garages—finding a parking space in Hong Kong is far more difficult than getting a room. ⊠ *8 Austin Rd.,* ☎ *2376–1111,* FAX *2376–1333,* WEB *www.megahotels.com.hk/hotel/bp_int_house. 524 rooms, 11 suites. 2 restaurants, health club, coin laundry, business services, parking (fee). AE, DC, MC, V.*

\$\$ 🏨 **Kimberley.** On one of the colorfully busy streets between Nathan Road and Tsim Sha Tsui East, this hotel offers plenty of bright, clean rooms. Its health spa includes masseurs to ease away the aches and pains of shopping. Golf driving nets are available for those who can't kick the habit. The two main restaurants serve Cantonese and Japanese cuisines. ⊠ *28 Kimberley Rd.,* ☎ *2723–3888,* FAX *2723–1318,* WEB *www.kimberley.com.hk. 497 rooms, 49 suites. 3 restaurants, bar, in-room data ports, minibars, room service, spa, health club, laundry service, business services. AE, DC, MC, V.*

\$\$ 🏨 **Kowloon.** A shimmering, mirrored exterior and a chrome, glass, and
★ marble lobby reflect the Kowloon's efficient, high-tech orientation. Kowloon—Chinese for "nine dragons"—is the design theme here. The triangular windows and pointed lobby ceiling, made from hundreds of hand-blown Venetian-glass pyramids, represent dragons' teeth. Lesser sibling to the adjacent Peninsula hotel, guests at the Kowloon can sign for services at the Pen and charge it to their room account. Although the clean and functional guest rooms are small, each is equipped with a "work and entertainment center" that includes Web and e-mail access, on-line news, and a CD-ROM drive, as well as a fax machine. Airline information is displayed in the lobby *and* in each guest room. Located on the southern tip of Nathan Road's Golden Mile, the Kowloon is next door to the Tsim Sha Tsui MTR and minutes from

the Star Ferry. ⊠ *19–21 Nathan Rd.,* ☎ *2929–2888,* FAX *2739–9811,* WEB *www.peninsula.com/hotels/kowloon/kowloon.html. 719 rooms, 17 suites. 3 restaurants, in-room data ports, minibars, 5 no-smoking floors, room service, hair salon, shop, dry cleaning, laundry service, business services. AE, DC, MC, V.*

$$ 🏨 **Ramada Hotel Kowloon.** The Ramada is relatively small and tries for a home-away-from-home ambience. A decorative fireplace in the lobby and comfortable rooms furnished with natural wood create a cozy atmosphere. The bar attracts many young locals for drinks and karaoke. ⊠ *73–75 Chatham Rd., South Tsim Sha Tsui,* ☎ *2311–1100,* FAX *2311–6000,* WEB *www.ramadahotels.com. 203 rooms, 2 suites. Restaurant, bar, in-room safes, minibars, room service, laundry service, business services. AE, DC, MC, V.*

$–$$ 🏨 **New Astor.** This small, inviting, triangular hotel is on a busy corner of Old Tsim Sha Tsui across the road from the MTR. Rooms have standard dark-wood furniture and basic amenities such as minibars, hair dryers, and refrigerators. Guests tend to be groups from China and more affluent backpackers. Just a short walk away is Granville Road, where factory outlets cluster. ⊠ *11 Carnarvon Rd.,* ☎ *2366–7261,* FAX *2722–7122,* WEB *www.newastor.com.hk. 147 rooms, 1 suite. Restaurant, in-room safes, minibars, room service, shop, laundry service, business services. AE, DC, MC, V.*

$–$$ 🏨 **Royal Pacific Hotel & Towers.** Right on the Tsim Sha Tsui waterfront, the Royal Pacific is part of the Hong Kong China City complex, which includes the terminal for ferries to China. Guest rooms—which are arranged in two blocks, the hotel and tower wings—are small but attractive and equipped with tea- and coffeemakers. The hotel connects to Kowloon Park by a footbridge and is close to shops and cinemas. ⊠ *33 Canton Rd.,* ☎ *2736–1188,* FAX *2736–1212,* WEB *www.royalpacific.com.hk. 641 rooms, 32 suites. 3 restaurants, bar, in-room data ports, in-room safes, minibars, room service, health club, squash, dry cleaning, laundry service, business services. AE, DC, MC, V.*

$–$$ 🏨 **Windsor.** This humble but smart little hotel offers clean, functional accommodations just east of the Golden Mile on Nathan Road. It has a coffee shop, a bar, and business services ranging from secretarial support to Internet access. When taking a cab here, specify your destination as the hotel, as both the Windsor Cinema and, in Causeway Bay, the Windsor House are more widely known. ⊠ *39–43A Kimberley Rd.,* ☎ *2739–5665,* FAX *2311–5101,* WEB *www.windsorhotel.com.hk. 165 rooms, 1 suite. 2 restaurants, bar, in-room data ports, minibars, room service, laundry service, business services. AE, DC, MC, V.*

$ 🏨 **Salisbury YMCA.** If you can't afford the Pen, settle at this five-star ★ Y, where you can enjoy the same magnificent harbor view at a fraction of the price. The YMCAs in Hong Kong far surpass most Ys in other parts of the world in terms of either price tag or amenities. The Salisbury YMCA, Hong Kong's most popular, sits on a huge, sterile-looking block opposite the Cultural Centre, Space Museum, and Art Museum—an excellent location for theater, art, and concert crawls. The clean rooms are polished up in pastels and equipped with data ports. The superb health facilities include a fitness center, sauna, hot tub, dance studio, and even an indoor climbing wall. The Y also has a chapel, a beautiful garden, lecture rooms, a conference room with a built-in stage, and a children's library. Enjoy the free in-house movie if you have spare time. The restaurants serve good, cheap Chinese food, and the shops are very affordable. ⊠ *41 Salisbury Rd.,* ☎ *2369–2211,* FAX *2739–9315,* WEB *www.ymcahk.org.hk. 303 rooms, 62 suites. 2 restaurants, lounge, in-room data ports, in-room safes, room service, indoor pool, hair salon, health club, squash, shop, coin laundry, meeting room. AE, DC, MC, V.*

Tsim Sha Tsui East

$$$$ 🏨 **Kowloon Shangri-La.** This upscale hotel caters mainly to business trav-
★   elers. The business center is open 24 hours; each room has a fax machine and modem line; and global-vision teleconferencing is available on
request. Remarkably, the elevator carpets are changed nightly at midnight to indicate the day of the week, to remind you of your schedule
from the moment you approach the lift. The modern, pastel rooms are
large by Hong Kong standards, and daily business newspapers are de-
livered to your room free of charge. On-site restaurants include the Japanese restaurant Nadaman and the California-inspired Napa, with
magnificent harbor views. The sumptuous lounge and Blue Note bar provide live entertainment, with international jazz acts keeping the tunes
going past midnight most nights. Guest rooms look out on the city or
Victoria Harbour. The owners' attention to detail, the expert, highly professional staff, and the regular fine-tuning of all facilities ensure repeat
business. ⊠ *64 Mody Rd.,* ☎ *2721–2111; 800/942–5050 in the U.S.,*
FAX *2723–8686,* WEB *www.shangri-la.com/eng/hotel/index.asp?id=20. 705
rooms, 25 suites. 5 restaurants, bar, lounge, in-room data ports, in-
room safes, minibars, no-smoking floor, room service, indoor pool, barbershop, health club, dry cleaning, laundry service, concierge, business
services. AE, DC, MC, V.*

$$$ 🏨 **Grand Stanford Inter-Continental.** More than half the rooms in this
luxury hotel, at the east end of Tsim Sha Tsui East, have an unobstructed
harbor view. The elegant lobby is spacious, the staff is helpful and
friendly, and the modern, comfortable rooms are decorated in warm
earth tones, with fine wood fittings and expansive desks. Each room
on the executive floors has a direct-line fax machine and a trouser
press. The restaurants are well known locally, including Mistral (Ital-
ian; ☞ Chapter 3), Belvedere (regional French), and, particularly,
Tiffany's New York Bar, which celebrates the Roaring '20s with antique
furniture, Tiffany-style glass ceilings, and entertainers singing popular
American songs. ⊠ *70 Mody Rd.,* ☎ *2721–5161,* FAX *2732–2233,* WEB
*www.grandstanford.com. 554 rooms, 25 suites. 4 restaurants, bar, in-
room data ports, in-room safes, minibars, room service, pool, health club,
shop, dry cleaning, laundry service, business services. AE, DC, MC, V.*

$$$ 🏨 **Nikko.** Part of the Japanese Nikko chain, this luxury harbor-front
hotel at the far end of Tsim Sha Tsui East attracts mostly Japanese tourists.
Here you can brush up on your Japanese and learn the gracious national greeting: a smile and a bow. The spacious premises are clean but
a little dated. Nearly 200 rooms enjoy harbor views, and rooms on
the executive floors are equipped with additional facilities such as tea-
and coffeemakers and in-room data ports. The popular restaurant
Sagano cooks with freshly imported ingredients from Japan. ⊠ *72 Mody
Rd.,* ☎ *2739–1111,* FAX *2311–3122,* WEB *www.hotelnikko.com.hk. 444
rooms, 17 suites. 4 restaurants, 3 bars, in-room data ports, in-room
safes, minibars, room service, pool, health club, shop, business services.
AE, DC, MC, V.*

$$$ 🏨 **Royal Garden.** A garden atrium with lush greenery and whispering
running water rises from the ground floor to the Royal Garden's rooftop.
Glass elevators, live classical music, trailing greenery, and trickling
streams create a sense of serenity. All the soft, spacious, and comfort-
able rooms surround the atrium. Guests and locals alike appreciate Saba-
tini (☞ Chapter 3), sister to the famous Roman restaurant, and the rooftop
state-of-the-art health club complete with tennis court, indoor-outdoor
pool, and spa services. Fashioned after an ancient Roman bath with foun-
tains, a colorful sun mosaic, and underwater music, the pool is heated
and covered in winter by a huge bubble top. ⊠ *69 Mody Rd.,* ☎ *2721–
5215,* FAX *2369–9976,* WEB *www.theroyalgardenhotel.com.hk. 374 rooms,*

48 suites. 4 restaurants, bar, in-room data ports, in-room safes, mini-bars, no-smoking floor, room service, indoor-outdoor pool, hair salon, spa, tennis court, health club, shop, dance club, dry cleaning, laundry service, concierge, business services. AE, DC, MC, V.

$$ 🏨 **Regal Kowloon.** If you're in the mood for a French environment, check in at the Regal. The lobby has an impressive tapestry, and Louis XVI–style furniture graces the guest rooms and one of the lounges. Rooms on the club floors have a more minimalist modern two-tone appeal than the rest of the hotel would suggest. The French restaurant Maman serves home-style French cooking in a relaxed setting. ✉ *71 Mody Rd.,* ☎ *2722–1818,* FAX *2369–6950,* WEB *www.regalkowloon.com. 564 rooms, 34 suites. 4 restaurants, 2 bars, in-room data ports, in-room safes, minibars, no-smoking floor, room service, hair salon, health club, shop, dry cleaning, laundry service, concierge, business services. AE, DC, MC, V.*

Yau Ma Tei and Mong Kok

$$ 🏨 **Concourse.** One of Hong Kong's nicer budget hotels, the Concourse is run by the China Travel Service. It's tucked away from Nathan Road but only a minute's walk from the Prince Edward MTR station, in Mong Kok. Rooms are basic and functional, and business services are available. The hotel is well placed for a glimpse of real, day-to-day life in Hong Kong—sip coffee (or a strong mixture of tea and coffee) at a local coffee house or slurp a bowl of noodles at a neighborhood hole-in-the-wall. Loads of simple eateries dot the area, and nearby is an active nightlife scene. The hotel has both a Chinese and a pan-Asian restaurant. ✉ *22 Lai Chi Kok Rd., Mong Kok,* ☎ *2397–6683,* FAX *2381–3768,* WEB *www.hotelconcourse.com.hk. 425 rooms, 5 suites. 2 restaurants, bar, coffee shop, in-room data ports, minibars, room service, laundry service, business services. AE, DC, MC, V.*

$$ 🏨 **Eaton.** Housed in a brick-red shopping and cinema complex in the middle of Nathan Road, Eaton provides quick access to Hong Kong's down-to-earth street scene after dark: it's a stone's throw from Temple Street, the busy night market that bustles with vendors, fortune-tellers, and Chinese opera singers. The clean, modern rooms have all the necessities including fast Internet access, and business services are available. The top floor has a swimming pool and a gym. ✉ *380 Nathan Rd., Yau Ma Tei,* ☎ *2782–1818,* FAX *2782–5563,* WEB *www.eaton-hotel.com. 458 rooms, 30 suites. 6 restaurants, bar, in-room data ports, minibars, no-smoking floor, room service, pool, gym, laundry service, business services. AE, DC, MC, V.*

$$ 🏨 **Grand Tower.** Above a shopping mall in the busiest part of Kowloon, the Grand Tower puts travelers near the real Hong Kong. The mall does not sell designer goods but rather ordinary consumer needs from cushion covers and knickknacks to watches, clothes, and shoes. A short walk away are Bird Street (where many Chinese walk and talk, together with their caged birds), the Women's Market, and the Mong Kok MTR. Rooms are adequately clean and functional, with facilities including modem ports with fast Internet access. ✉ *627–641 Nathan Rd., Mong Kok,* ☎ *2789–0011,* FAX *2789–0945,* WEB *www.grandhotel.com.hk/grandtower. 539 rooms, 10 suites. 3 restaurants, in-room data ports, minibars, room service, barbershop, hair salon, laundry service, business services. AE, DC, MC, V.*

$$ 🏨 **Majestic.** This hotel is on the site of the old Majestic Cinema on upper Nathan Road. The lobby is clean and plain, and the sparsely furnished rooms have contemporary furniture, minibars, TVs, and refrigerators. All suites are equipped with fax machines. Facilities are minimal—no pool or gym, and only a coffee shop and a bar for dining and imbibing. But the complex holds shops and a cinema, and plenty of restaurants—running the gamut from Chinese food to Malaysian cuisine—are nearby, as well as the Jordan MTR. ✉ *348 Nathan Rd., Yau Ma Tei,* ☎ *2781–1333,* FAX *2781–1773,* WEB *www.majestichotel.com.hk. 387 rooms, 9 suites. Bar, coffee shop, in-room data ports, minibars, no-smoking floor, room service, shop, cinema, laundry service, business services. AE, DC, MC, V.*

$$ 🏨 **Pruton Prudential.** Rising from a busy corner on upper Nathan Road, above the Jordan MTR station, this hotel is a find if you're on a modest budget. The spacious rooms have views of bustling Nathan Road, with the neon-lit shop signs and banners. The hotel shares a building with a lively shopping mall and has its own pool. Rooms on the five executive floors have tea- and coffeemakers. ✉ *222 Nathan Rd., Yau Ma Tei,* ☎ *2311–8222,* FAX *2311–1304. 415 rooms, 17 suites. Bar, coffee shop, in-room data ports, minibars, room service, pool, shop, laundry service, business services. AE, DC, MC, V.*

$–$$ 🏨 **Dorsett Seaview.** Reclamation of the harbor front and the subsequent construction have taken away most of this slender hotel's sea view, but it has compensatory features. Convenient to the Yau Ma Tei MTR, it's located on Shanghai Street, where traditional Hong Kong lives on, with shops selling handmade kitchenware, temple offerings, and wedding dresses. Temple Street, a must-see for Hong Kong's street nightlife, is nearby, as is the territory's art house cinema, Broadway Cinematheque (☞ Chapter 5). The restaurant has bargain-priced buffets, especially for lunch. Guest rooms are very small. The hotel attracts mainly tour groups from Europe and Asia. ✉ *268 Shanghai St., Yau Ma Tei,* ☎ *2782–0882,* FAX *2388–1803,* WEB *www.dorsettseaview.com.hk. 254 rooms, 3 suites. Restaurant, bar, lounge, minibars, room service, laundry service. AE, DC, MC, V.*

$–$$ 🏨 **Metropole.** Just north of Nathan Road's major shopping area, the Metropole is a diner's delight. The on-site Chinese restaurant, House of Tang, is locally renowned for its Szechuanese resident master chefs, who serve authentic Szechuan and Cantonese food. The modern, clean rooms have simple decor, a harmonious mélange of East and West. The rooftop pool and health club offer a relaxing atmosphere. ✉ *75 Waterloo Rd., Yau Ma Tei,* ☎ *2761–1711,* FAX *2761–0769,* WEB *www.metropole.com.hk. 479 rooms, 8 suites. 3 restaurants, bar, in-room data ports, minibars, room service, pool, health club, laundry service, business services. AE, DC, MC, V.*

$–$$ 🏨 **Nathan.** Popular with tour groups from both the East and the West, this busy hotel is near the Jordan MTR and just a stone's throw away from the street-market attractions of Mong Kok and Yau Ma Tei. Rooms are moderately sized and colorful, and include all the basic necessities. ✉ *378 Nathan Rd., Yau Ma Tei,* ☎ *2388–5141,* FAX *2770–4262. 185 rooms. Restaurant, bar, in-room data ports, minibars, room service, shop, laundry service, business services. AE, DC, MC, V.*

$–$$ 🏨 **Royal Plaza.** One of the newer additions to Hong Kong's long list of lodgings, the Royal Plaza is easily accessible from either the adjacent Kowloon–Canton Railway station or the nearby Mong Kok MTR station. As part of the massive New Century Place shopping complex, it's a consumer's paradise. The hotel itself offers a mix of restaurants, bars, and leisure facilities, including a ballroom and a 40-m pool with underwater music. The garden allows seekers of solitude to contemplate the true meaning of Mong Kok in peace and quiet. ✉ *193 Prince Edward Rd. W, Mong Kok,* ☎ *2928–8822,* FAX *2628–3383,* WEB *www.royalplaza.com.hk. 419 rooms, 50 suites. 3 restaurants, bar, in-room data ports, in-room safes, minibars, room service, indoor pool, spa, health club, laundry service, business services. AE, DC, MC, V.*

$ ⊞ **Booth Lodge.** This pleasant contemporary retreat, located down a dead-end side street near the Jade Market, is operated by the Salvation Army. But contrary to the image that might conjure up, everything in this renovated lodge is clean, bright, and new, from freshly painted walls to starched sheets on the double beds. The lobby is a study in minimalism and has an officelike atmosphere, but the Booth is a good value. The coffee shop serves mainly buffets, with a small outdoor balcony offering nice views. The Yau Ma Tei MTR is nearby. ⊠ *11 Wing Sing La., Yau Ma Tei,* ☎ *2771–9266,* FAX *2385–1140. 54 rooms. Coffee shop, laundry service. AE, MC, V.*

$ ⊞ **Caritas Bianchi Lodge.** This clean and friendly hostel with simple, modern decor has basic facilities including TVs, minibars, air-conditioning, and private bathrooms. Just around the corner from busy Nathan Road, it's also close to the Jade Market and the nightly Temple Street Market, but offers peace and quiet due to its no-through-road location. ⊠ *4 Cliff Rd., Yau Ma Tei,* ☎ *2388–1111,* FAX *2770–6669. 88 rooms, 2 suites. Restaurant, minibars, laundry service. AE, DC, MC, V.*

$ ⊞ **Shamrock.** One of the oldest budget hotels on Nathan Road (it's more than 40 years old), the hotel has spruced itself up with refurbished rooms, lobby, and facade. It's just north of Kowloon Park and steps from the Jordan MTR, putting it in the middle of all the 24-hour-a-day Yau Ma Tei action. Rooms are a decent size for the price, and the hotel offers buffet-style dining from its in-house restaurant. ⊠ *223 Nathan Rd., Yau Ma Tei,* ☎ *2735–2271,* FAX *2736–7354,* WEB *www.asiatravel.com/shamrock. 128 rooms, 19 suites. Restaurant, in-room data ports, minibars, room service, laundry service. AE, DC, MC, V.*

THE NEW TERRITORIES AND THE OUTER ISLANDS

Although lodging options are limited outside the cities of Hong Kong and Kowloon, some are worth considering, especially if you're traveling to or from China on the Kowloon–Canton Railway. You're also closer to the airport out here. Some islands, such as Cheung Chau, do a booming business in rooms for rent, with agents displaying photographs of available rentals on placards along the waterfront opposite the ferry pier.

The New Territories

$$–$$$ ⊞ **Panda.** You can't miss the huge panda mural on the side of the largest hotel in the western New Territories; its 30 stories dominate the skyline of bustling Tsuen Wan. Decor in this hotel recalls hotels in Tokyo's Ginza district, with lots of open-plan lounges and ultramodern rooms in warm and natural tones. Some rooms have harbor views. On the premises are a pool, a health club, business and meeting facilities, a variety of restaurants, and a department store. Executive guests in the Mega Club also get in-room Nintendo and Internet access. Complimentary bus service runs to and from Tsim Sha Tsui and Mong Kok, and the MTR is nearby. The Panda is one of the closest hotels to Hong Kong International Airport. ⊠ *3 Tsuen Wan St., Tsuen Wan,* ☎ *2409–1111,* FAX *2409–1818,* WEB *www.megahotels.com.hk. 971 rooms, 55 suites. 4 restaurants, 2 bars, in-room data ports, minibars, no-smoking floor, room service, pool, health club, shop, laundry service, business services, meeting room. AE, DC, MC, V.*

$$ ⊞ **Gold Coast.** The Gold Coast is Hong Kong's only conference resort. Its vast complex on Kowloon's western harbor front is well connected to the city center by public bus, and the hotel runs shuttle buses to the MTR and the airport. Inside, the decor is extravagant, with acres of marble, miles of wrought-iron balustrades, a grand ballroom, and palm-court atriums. Facilities include a large marina, a water-sports area, tennis courts, volleyball and soccer fields, pitch-and-putt golf, a full-service spa, and even an archery range. The resort is known among conference planners for facilities that can accommodate over 1,000 people. All guest rooms face the sea over a beautiful beach. Last, but not necessarily least, this is the only hotel in Hong Kong with equipment for outdoor training-style courses. ⊠ *1 Castle Peak Rd., Tuen Mun, New Territories,* ☎ *2452–8888,* ℻ *2440–7368,* WEB *www.goldcoasthotel.com.hk/. 440 rooms, 10 suites. 4 restaurants, bar, in-room data ports, minibars, room service, pool, hair salon, spa, putting green, 2 tennis courts, archery, health club, soccer, volleyball, boating, laundry service, business services. AE, DC, MC, V.*

$$ 🏨 **Regal Riverside.** This large, modern hotel in the foothills of Shatin overlooks the Shing Mun River. Rooms have river and garden views. The 8,000-square-ft health club has a full range of facilities, from an aerobics room to a hot tub to Hong Kong's only float capsule—purported to soothe away the day's pressures. You can also join the healthy horde of people jogging or cycling along the river, or just watch rowers at practice. Guest rooms, however, seem a little dated and in need of an overhaul. The hotel is a few minutes from the busiest shopping center in Hong Kong, the New Town Plaza; shuttle service leaves every hour for the plaza and every half hour for Tsim Sha Tsui. ⊠ *Tai Chung Kiu Rd., Shatin,* ☎ *2649–7878,* ℻ *2637–4748,* WEB *www.regalriverside.com. 789 rooms, 41 suites. 5 restaurants, bar, in-room data ports, minibars, no-smoking floor, room service, pool, barbershop, hair salon, health club, dance club, laundry service, business services. AE, DC, MC, V.*

$–$$ 🏨 **Royal Park.** Next to New Town Plaza, the busiest shopping mall in the territory, this 16-story hotel is far from the city yet easily accessed by train and buses. It's also the nearest hotel to the Shatin Racecourse. The lobby is decorated in deep colors, and rooms have bay windows with panoramic views of Shatin. ⊠ *8 Pak Hok Ting St., Shatin,* ☎ *2601–2111,* ℻ *2601–3666,* WEB *www.royalpark.com.hk. 436 rooms, 12 suites. 4 restaurants, lounge, in-room data ports, minibars, no-smoking floor, room service, pool, tennis court, gym, jogging, laundry service, business services. AE, DC, MC, V.*

Cheung Chau Island

$ 🏨 **Cheung Chau Warwick.** Miles from the fast-paced city, this six-story beachfront nook aims to assure you have a carefree and relaxed stay—a nice pool and a sandy beach take the place of business services and executive floors. An hour by ferry from Hong Kong Island, it's a popular getaway for Hong Kong families. There are no cars on the leisurely island, but the hotel is just a 10-minute walk from the pier. ⊠ *East Bay, Cheung Chau,* ☎ *2981–0081,* ℻ *2981–9174. 71 rooms. 2 restaurants, pool, beach. AE, DC, MC, V.*

Lantau Island

$ 🏨 **Silvermine Beach Hotel.** This bay-side resort in Mui Wo steers entirely clear of Hong Kong's sound and fury. It's an hour by ferry from Hong Kong Island, then a five-minute walk from the pier. A pool is open in summer, and a tennis court, gym, and sauna are open year-round. Guest rooms are spacious and have tea- and coffee-making facilities. The island of Lantau has plenty of sights of its own, including the bronze statue Tin Tan Buddha, the Po Lin Monastery, and Tai O fishing village; and you'll thank yourself for hiking a section of the Lantau Island trail—the scenery is unexpectedly beautiful. ⊠ *D.D. 2, Lot*

648 Silvermine Bay, Mui Wo, Lantau Island, ☎ *2984–8295,* FAX *2984–1907,* WEB *www.resort.com.hk. 128 rooms, 2 suites. 2 restaurants, pool, gym. AE, DC, MC, V.*

Hong Kong International Airport

$$$ ⊡ **Regal Airport.** Ideal for transit passengers, or those who want to visit Hong Kong without staying near the city, this modern hotel does not suffer from the size restrictions found elsewhere in the territories. It's some distance from the city itself, but the efficient high-speed rail system can have you on Hong Kong Island in around 25 minutes. Connected directly to the passenger terminal by an air-conditioned moving walkway, the modern hotel is aimed at leisure and business travelers alike. It's Hong Kong's largest hotel and one of the largest airport hotels in the world. Some rooms have terrific views of planes landing from afar. For a more resortlike feel, rooms with balconies and outdoor furniture overlook the hotel's two swimming pools. The Grand Ballroom is the largest hotel ballroom in Hong Kong, with space for up to 1,000 people and simultaneous translation, video-conferencing capability, and a built-in stage. ⊠ *Chek Lap Kok,* ☎ *2286–8888,* FAX *2286–8686,* WEB *www.regalairporthotel.com. 1,100 rooms, 25 suites. 7 restaurants, bar, 2 lounges, in-room data ports, in-room safes, minibars, 2 no-smoking floors, room service, indoor-outdoor pool, gym, shop, dry cleaning, laundry service, business services. AE, DC, MC, V.*

5 NIGHTLIFE AND THE ARTS

Hong Kongers play as hard as they work. With cabaret and wine bars giving way to dance clubs and avant-garde theater, the work-weary have no shortage of diversions to choose from.

NIGHTLIFE

Updated by
Eva Chui

A RIOT OF NEON, heralding frenetic after-hours action announces Hong Kong's nightlife districts. Hectic workdays make way for an even busier night scene. Clubs and bars fill to capacity nightly, evening markets pack in shoppers looking for bargains, restaurants welcome hearty diners, cinemas pop corn as fast as they can, and theaters and concert halls prepare for full houses. Hong Kong has sophisticated piano bars, elegant lounges, superstrobe discos, rowdy pubs, smoky jazz dens, hostess clubs, and classy bars.

All premises licensed to serve alcohol are supposedly subject to stringent fire, safety, and sanitary controls, although at times this is hard to believe, given the overcrowding at the hippest places. Wise travelers should think twice before succumbing to the city's raunchier hideaways. If you stumble into one, check out cover and hostess charges *before* you get too comfortable. Pay for each round of drinks as it's served (by cash rather than credit card), and never sign any blank checks. Hong Kong is a surprisingly safe place, but as in every tourist destination the art of the tourist rip-off has been perfected. If you're unsure, visit places signposted as members of the Hong Kong Tourist Board (HKTB). You can pick up the association's free membership listing (that is, approved restaurants and nightspots) at any HKTB information office.

Take note, too, of Hong Kong's laws. You must be over 18 to buy alcohol. Drugs, obscene publications, and unlicensed gambling are ostensibly illegal. There is some consumer protection, but the generally helpful police, many of whom speak English, expect everyone to know the meaning of *caveat emptor* (let the buyer beware).

Note that many of Hong Kong's smarter nightspots are in hotels. Fast-paced, competitive Hong Kong is a world of change where buildings seem to vanish overnight and new fads emerge weekly; don't be surprised if some places have changed their decor, changed their name, or closed altogether since this book went to press. Also, many clubs have a "members only" policy, but don't let this deter you. Usually this just means a visitor must pay a cover charge, while members do not.

Bars

Hong Kong has its share of licensed designer bars that provide some diversion from the staid pubs. Whether it's because of the transient nature of the city or hardworking lifestyles that leave little time for relationships, there's a rampant singles scene here, with lots of people out looking for that special someone or even that special someone just for the night.

Many Westerners and "chuppies," or Chinese yuppies, meet in crowded comfort in the Lan Kwai Fong area, a hillside section around Central's D'Aguilar Street, with many appetizing bistros and bars.

Singles mix happily at the ultramodern **California** (⌧ 32–34 D'Aguilar St., Lan Kwai Fong, Central, ☎ 2521–1345), which has a late-night disco most nights and after several years as a trendsetter is still one of the hottest places to be seen. The tiny bar **La Dolce Vita** (⌧ 9 Lan Kwai Fong, Central, ☎ 2810–9333)—beneath its sister restaurant **Post 97** and next to its other sibling **Club 97**—often spills onto the pavement. With sleek decor and a crowd to match, this chic, name-dropping, mass of people is a place to be seen. **Insomnia** (⌧ 38–44 D'Aguilar St., Lan Kwai Fong, Central, ☎ 2525–0957) is so crowded with perfumed

LAN KWAI FONG

A **CURIOUSLY L-SHAPE** cobblestone lane in Central is the centerpoint of nightlife and dining in Hong Kong. Lan Kwai Fong, or just "the Fong," is a must-go-to spot that really shines after the sun sets. You can have a pre-dinner drink at any number of bars, enjoy some of the territory's finest dining, and then pop into a nightclub to boogie the night away.

For such a small warren, Lan Kwai Fong has an incredibly broad range of nightlife to offer, with more than 20 bars, restaurants, and clubs within just a few blocks. Since most of the ground-floor establishments spill out onto the pavement, there's an audible buzz about the place, an atmosphere not matched elsewhere in Hong Kong. Whether its corporate financiers celebrating their latest million-dollar deals at California, La Dolce Vita, or Oscars, or more humble office workers having drinks with their buddies at Le Jardin or Insomnia, there's quite literally something here for everyone.

The same something for everyone motto extends to the plethora of upmarket eateries in the Fong. For Asian taste buds there are Chinese, Thai, Japanese, and Vietnamese restaurants, while European flavors are on offer at French and Italian establishments. If your wallet's feeling a little light from your latest shopping expedition, take heed of the excited waiters waving to potential customers along nearby Wing Wah Lane. Here you'll find rowdy Indian, Thai, and Malaysian restaurants that serve piping-hot dishes at reasonable prices.

Lan Kwai Fong used to be a hawkers' place before the Second World War. Its modern success is largely due to Canadian expatriate Allan Zeman, an eccentric figure who has been dubbed the "King of Lan Kwai Fong" by the local media. He opened his first North American–style restaurant here 20 years ago; today he not only owns dozens of other restaurants and bars, but also the buildings they're in. He claims to have about 100 restaurants, and although he doesn't actually own them all, he acts as the landlord for most of them. The Fong is now simply a hobby for Zeman, whose business empire includes everything from property development to fashion.

New Year's Eve on December 31 is undoubtedly the busiest time for Lan Kwai Fong. Thousands of people line the tiny area to celebrate and party. You'll notice a strong police presence moving the human traffic through the streets and keeping an eye out for any troublemakers. While it's reassuring to have a watchful eye over the festivities, the police presence is actually to prevent another tragedy like the one that occurred here in 1993. On New Year's Day that year, as a massive throng ushered in the new year, 21 people were crushed to death when the huge crowds went out of control. The accident shocked the territory and left a black mark on the authorities. Now when large crowds are anticipated—usually New Year's Eve, Christmas Eve, and, interestingly, Halloween—the police carefully monitor the number of people entering the area.

Call it progress or a type of survival-of-the-strongest evolution, but the trendy area has opened as many establishments as it has closed. New spots are constantly in development, or old places are under refurbishment. Regardless of the changes, Lan Kwai Fong is always alive with scores of people and places to be merry.

— Eva Chui

women and suited men on weekend nights you have to fight your way to the back to the bathrooms. If you stay up at the front bar, by the arched windows, you might have some breathing room.

The arts-minded mingle at the **Fringe Club** (✉ 2 Lower Albert Rd., Lan Kwai Fong, Central, ☎ 2521–7251), in a historic redbrick building that also houses the members-only Foreign Correspondents Club. The Club is the headquarters for Hong Kong's alternative arts scene and normally stages live music twice a week. Writers, artists, travelers, and the occasional banker gravitate toward the unpretentious environs of **Club 64** (✉ 12–14 Wing Wah La., Lan Kwai Fong, Central, ☎ 2523–2801), where you can get a reasonably priced drink in a humble and cozy, if a little run-down setting. For a gregariously cosmopolitan ambience, the trendy **Le Jardin** (✉ 10 Wing Wah La., Lan Kwai Fong, Central, ☎ 2526–2717) has a lovely outdoor terrace overlooking a not-so-lovely alley.

When people tire of Lan Kwai Fong, there are plenty of more bars just around the corner. Straddling "the Fong" (as locals call it) and SoHo is **Petticoat Lane** (✉ 2 Tun Wo La., Central, ☎ 2973–0642), with rich red walls and large gilt-framed oil paintings. Tucked discreetly away in an alley near the Midlevels escalator between Lyndhurst Terrace and Hollywood Road, it's a little hard to find, but definitely worth the wander. **Drop** (✉ Basement, On Lok Mansion, 39–43 Hollywood Rd., entrance off Cochrine St., Central, ☎ 2543–8856) may take some effort to find, but it adds an air of exclusivity to the speakeasy-like location. A favorite with the hip crowd, Drop has killer martinis and the best DJ in town on weekends. Although it claims to be members only, a little confidence and a lot of dazzle goes a long way. Sophisticated guys and dolls flock to **Alibi** (✉ 73 Wyndham St., Central, ☎ 2167–1676), a cool bar (with fine dining upstairs) that's wall to wall with bodies most nights. For the more laid-back set, the tiny **Phibi** (✉ Basement, 79 Wyndham St., entrance off Pottinger St., Central, ☎ 2869–4469) is a great bar that plays dance music. It really gets going around 11 PM. **Après** (✉ Upper basement, 79 Wyndham St., entrance off Pottinger St., Central, ☎ 2524–7722) is so named because management says the steep street the bar opens onto could double as a ski slope. Although it's highly unlikely that the sticky Hong Kong weather will ever allow for snow, you can still enjoy a drink alfresco style here.

Hong Kong is proud of its own *très* chic SoHo, a small warren of streets between Central and Midlevels. This area is filled with commensurately priced cosmopolitan restaurants ranging from Middle Eastern and Portuguese to Vietnamese and Cajun, as well as a handful of bars. **Club Cubana** (✉ 47B Elgin St., Central, ☎ 2869–1218) stays open until late and has a smallish dance floor and small courtyard in back. Adjacent to Hong Kong's famous outdoor escalator is the hip bistro-style **Staunton's Wine Bar & Cafe** (✉ 10–12 Staunton St., Central, ☎ 2973–6611). Partly alfresco, it's the perfect place to people-watch and attracts crowds at night to drink and by day to sip coffee or take in a meal. It's a Sunday-morning favorite for nursing hangovers over brunch. **Barco** (✉ 42 Staunton St., Central, ☎ 2858–1487) is one of many small drinking holes popping up in Soho. It's cozy with a small lounge area and a courtyard in the back. Affectionately known by locals as the Vodka Bar, the **V 13** (✉ 13 Old Baily St., SoHo, ☎ 8208–1313) teems with locals and expats who enjoy hearty libations. Once the bartenders start pouring the vodka, they don't stop until they reach the rim. Then they add the tonic.

Over in Wanchai, shaken or stirred is what **Tango Martini** (✉ 3/F, Empire Land Commercial Centre, 81–85 Lockhart Rd., Wanchai, ☎

2528–0855) is all about. A stylish and sophisticated lounge, this joint also has an adjoining restaurant. Much like a New York neighborhood bar, **Brown** (⊠ 18 Sing Woo Rd., Happy Valley, ☎ 2891–8558; ⊠ 30 Robinson Rd., Midlevels, ☎ 2971–0012) has a comfy, homey feeling for those who need to wind down from a hectic day (either working or shopping). Spacious high ceilings give an airy atmosphere to the bar, which has sink-down-and-chill sofas at the back. Solo businessmen can always find someone to talk to in hotel bars, frequented by both locals and expats. The **Mandarin Oriental** (⊠ 5 Connaught Rd., Central, ☎ 2522–0111) is home to the **Chinnery Bar** and **Captain's Bar**, where the smart, Cohiba-cigar set meets to discuss the day's business or to enjoy a post-meeting drink. The **Hyatt Regency's Chin Chin** and **Nathan's** (⊠ 67 Nathan Rd., Tsim Sha Tsui, ☎ 2311–1234) both appeal to the executive set.

Cabarets and Nightclubs

Club 97 (⊠ 9–11 Lan Kwai Fong, Central, ☎ 2810–9333 or 2186–1819) is a small, glitzy, often crowded nightclub that draws mobs of beautiful people. It started out as a members-only club; a rule that has been selectively enforced, seemingly depending upon how busy business is that night. If any foreign celebrities are in town, from rock stars to supermodels, this is where they'll be partying. The club is open from 9 PM to 4 AM or later, as long as there are customers. The nightly entrance fee is appropriately HK$97.

Ocean Centre's **Ocean Palace Restaurant & Night Club** (⊠ Harbour City, Canton Rd., Tsim Sha Tsui, ☎ 2730–7111) is a favorite for Hong Kong family and wedding parties, which can be shows in themselves.

Propaganda (⊠ 1 Hollywood Rd., lower ground floor, Central, ☎ 2868–1316), off a quaint but steep cobblestone street, is one of the most popular gay clubs in the territory. (It's known as PP to the locals, Props to the expatriate lot.) The Art Deco bar area is stylish, with elegant booths and tables surrounded by soft lighting; at the other end of the aesthetic spectrum, the dance floor has lap poles on either side for go-go boys who willingly flaunt their wares. Crowds don't arrive until well after midnight, and the entrance fee varies from HK$70 to HK$160 depending on the time and day.

Cocktail and Piano Bars

Sophisticated and elegant cocktail bars are the norm at Hong Kong's luxury hotels. They offer live music (usually Filipino trios with a female singer; occasionally international acts) in a gleaming setting. Some venues have a small dance floor. Hong Kong's happy hours typically run from late afternoon to early evening, with two drinks for the price of one.

In all the following hotels, request a window seat when making reservations. High-altitude harbor gazing is the main attraction at the Island Shangri-La's 56th-floor music lounge **Cyrano** (⊠ 2 Pacific Place, Supreme Court Rd., 88 Queensway, Hong Kong, ☎ 2820–8591), which draws a chic, hip, young crowd. The Peninsula's **Felix** (⊠ Salisbury Rd., Tsim Sha Tsui, ☎ 2366–6251) is a must for visitors; it not only has a brilliant view of the island, but the impressive bar and disco were designed by the visionary Philippe Starck. Don't forget to check out the padded disco room. Ride the bubble elevator to the Sheraton's **Sky Lounge** (⊠ 20 Nathan Rd., 18th floor, Tsim Sha Tsui, ☎ 2369–1111) in time for sunset, and you won't be disappointed. At the Excelsior's **Talk of the Town** (⊠ 281 Gloucester Rd., Causeway Bay, ☎

2837–6786), or ToTT's, you're treated to a 270° vista of Hong Kong Harbour.

With spectacular harbor views from the ocean-liner level and a central bar modeled after a high-class London pub, **Gripps** (⊠ Harbour City, Tsim Sha Tsui, ☏ 2113–0088), in the Marco Polo Hong Kong hotel, draws the executive set with its nightly entertainment by visiting pianists and touring cover bands. The Renaissance Harbour View's **Oasis Bar** (⊠ 1 Harbour Rd., Wanchai, ☏ 2802–8888) has a unique glass roof and harbor scenery, albeit slightly obstructed by the Convention & Exhibition Centre's extension.

Feeling pampered is your pleasure at **The Bar** in the Peninsula hotel (⊠ Salisbury Rd., Tsim Sha Tsui, ☏ 2366–6251). Society watchers linger in the Peninsula's lobby; sit to the right of the hotel entrance to better observe the crème de la crème. The lobby lounge at **The Regent** (⊠ 18 Salisbury Rd., Tsim Sha Tsui, ☏ 2721–1211) is a place to see and be seen; be ready to chat about the fashion industry with a parade of Armani-clad and Chanel-scented men and women. The Regent's **Club Shanghai** is an elegant after-dinner spot, decorated in 1930s Chinese style. You won't be out of place if you don your newly purchased, tight-fitting *cheongsam* dress here. Before 9:30 the resident band performs love songs, but later you can hear jazzier, more upbeat tunes.

Discos

Hong Kong's discos are diverse in style and clientele, not to mention price, so there's something to suit everyone. The thriving youth culture is best exemplified in these houses of dance, where young folks prance about in the latest fashions. Cover charges are high by U.S. standards; entrance to the smarter spots is usually HK$100 or more (much more on the eves of major holidays), though this usually entitles you to two drinks. If you prefer dance parties to discos, look for posters in Lan Kwai Fong and Wanchai that scream about the latest international DJ (usually very well known) arriving in town to play for one night only. Some bars and restaurants also hold weekly or monthly club nights, where music ranges from drum-and-bass to happy house.

The dance floor at the **Big Apple Pub and Disco** (⊠ Basement, 20 Luard Rd., Wanchai, ☏ 2529–3461) gets going in the wee hours—and keeps going. There is a sleaze factor here, but when it's late late, who cares?

As its name suggests, **Club Ing** (⊠ Renaissance Harbour View Hotel, 1 Harbour Rd., Wanchai, ☏ 2824–0523) is about slipping into a pair of dancing shoes and hitting the floor.

The perennial favorite is **JJ's** (⊠ Grand Hyatt, 1 Harbour Rd., Hong Kong, ☏ 2588–1234), the Grand Hyatt's entertainment center. The comfortable upstairs lounge area has a dartboard and a bar that screens major sporting events, but JJ's is most revered for its flashy disco lights and resident band in the music room, where wall-to-wall businessmen and their escorts lounge.

Joe Bananas (⊠ 23 Luard Rd., Wanchai, ☏ 2529–1811) is the mainstay of Wanchai nightlife, its reputation for all-night partying and general good times unchallenged. This disco-cum-bar strictly excludes the military and people dressed too casually: no shorts, sneakers, or T-shirts. Arrive before 11 PM to avoid the queue.

Neptune Disco II (⊠ 98–108 Jaffe Rd., Wanchai, ☏ 2865–2238) is another late-night haunt for the dance-till-you-drop set.

Rick's Cafe (✉ 53–59 Kimberly Rd., Luna Court, Tsim Sha Tsui, ☎ 2311–2255) is practically a disco institution, and despite being one of the oldest, remains popular. If you arrive after midnight on a weekend, be prepared to stand in line.

In the basement of the Park Lane Hotel is **Stix** (✉ 310 Gloucester Rd., Causeway Bay, ☎ 2839–3397), which has a large dance floor that fills up with groovers enjoying the house band's latest pop covers.

Hostess Clubs

These are clubs in name only. Hong Kong's better ones are multimillion-dollar operations with hundreds of presentable hostess-companions of many races. Computerized time clocks on each table tabulate companionship charges in timed units; the costs are clearly detailed on table cards, as are standard drink tabs. The clubs' dance floors are often larger than those at discos, and they have one or more live bands and a scheduled lineup of both pop and cabaret singers. They also have dozens of luxuriously furnished private rooms, with partitioned lounges and the ubiquitous karaoke setup. Local and visiting businessmen adore these rooms—and the multilingual hostesses; business is so good that the clubs are willing to allow visitors *not* to ask for companionship. The better clubs are on a par with music lounges in deluxe hotels, though they cost a little more. Their happy hours start in the afternoon, when many have a sort of tea-dance ambience, and continue through to mid-evening. Peak hours are 10 PM–4 AM. Be aware that many hostess-oriented clubs, whether modest or posh, are also prostitution fronts.

Club BBoss, in Tsim Sha Tsui East's Mandarin Plaza (☎ 2369–2883), is the grandest and most boisterous hostess club, tended by a staff of more than 1,000. Executives, mostly locals, provide the entertainment. If your VIP room is too far from the entrance, you can hire an electrified vintage Rolls-Royce and purr around an indoor roadway. Be warned that this is tycoon territory—a bottle of brandy can cost HK$18,000. Along the harbor, in New World Centre, is **Club Deluxe** (☎ 2721–0277), a large, luxurious dance lounge.

Club Kokusai (✉ 81 Nathan Rd., Tsim Sha Tsui, ☎ 2367–6969), as its name applies, appeals to visitors from the Land of the Rising Yen. Karaoke dominates.

Mandarin Palace (✉ 24 Marsh Rd., ☎ 2575–6551) is a grand yet comfortable Wanchai nightclub where clients can indulge their singing aspirations in karaoke duets with hostesses until the wee hours.

Jazz and Folk Clubs

The appropriately named **Jazz Club** (✉ 2/F, California Entertainment Bldg., 34–36 D'Aguilar St., Central, ☎ 2845–8477) offers a wide selection of excellent local jazz, R&B, and soul acts as well as top-notch international acts every month, including harmonica player extraordinaire Carey Bell and bluesmen Georgie Fame and Joe Louis Walker.

Ned Kelly's Last Stand (☞ Pubs, *above*) is an Aussie-managed haven for pub meals and, oddly enough, Dixieland, courtesy of Ken Bennett's Kowloon Honkers. Get here before 10 PM to get a comfortable seat.

Wanchai's unpretentious alternative to the topless bar scene is **The Wanch** (✉ 54 Jaffe Rd., ☎ 2861–1621), which features live local folk and rock performances. The Hong Kong–theme decor (remember *Love Is a Many Splendored Thing?*) is worth a visit in itself.

Late-Night Bite

When the late-night pub-crawl rumbles strike, go to **Al's Diner** (✉ 39 D'Aguilar St., Lan Kwai Fong, ☎ 2869–1869), which is open until 3 AM, serving up hamburgers and fry-ups, along with good bagels and coffee, all to the tunes of '50s bebop in a neon-lit, chrome-plated diner atmosphere. For those who have a bit of a frat-boy spirit, try a vodka-spiked Jell-O shot at HK$46 a go; or for the ultra-insane: a tequila worm Jell-O, with the worm, at a mere HK$62 a round.

Pubs

Lively pubs proliferate in Hong Kong. Some serve cheap drinks in a modest setting, while others are pricier and more elegant. They help ease homesickness for the expats by serving up fish-and-chips while airing rugby and football matches. As is the rage in the United Kingdom these days, the trivia quiz games have taken many of the Hong Kong pubs by storm.

In Central, the business folk flock to the British-managed, oak-beam **Bull & Bear** (✉ 10 Harcourt Rd., Hutchison House, Central, ☎ 2525–7436), which attracts all types—a large share of them British—serves standard pub fare, and is known to get a little rowdy on weekends. Several connecting walkways lead to one of the island's most popular shopping malls, Pacific Place, which houses **Madison's** (✉ The Mall, Pacific Place, Level 3, Admiralty, ☎ 2523–4772). Crowds gather in this congenial, if rather noisy, spot, especially at happy hour.

Cheery Western crowds gather at the wood-paneled pubber's pub **Mad Dogs** (✉ Basement, Century Sq., 1 D'Aguilar St., Central, ☎ 2810–1000), in the Lan Kwai Fong area. This drinking establishment has been open since 1985, albeit in different locations; current theme nights include Trivial Pursuit. Knock back a beer or two with down-to-earth folks at the **Globe** (✉ 39 Hollywood Rd., Central, ☎ 2543–1941).

Both branches of the pioneer of Hong Kong Irish pubs **Delaney's** (✉ Basement, 71–77 Peking Rd., Tsim Sha Tsui, ☎ 2301–3980; ✉ 2/F, 1 Capital Place, 18 Luard Rd., Wanchai, ☎ 2804–2880) have interiors that were made in Ireland and shipped to Hong Kong, and the atmosphere is as authentic as the furnishings. There are Guinness and Delaney's ale (a specialty microbrew) on tap, corner snugs (small private rooms), and a menu of Irish specialties, plus a happy hour that runs from 3 to 8 PM daily. **Dublin Jack** (✉ 37 Cochrine St., Central, ☎ 2543–0081) serves Guinness and Irish ales while airing the latest football games. This pub just off the Midlevels outdoor escalators stands out with a fetching, bright-red exterior.

Pub-hopping in Wanchai is best enjoyed by the energetic and the easy-to-please or those trying to immortalize Suzie Wong. The **Horse & Groom** (✉ 161 Lockhart Rd., ☎ 2507–2517) is down-at-the-heels but certainly a true pub. The **Old China Hand Hand** (✉ 104 Lockhart Rd., ☎ 2893–5980) has been here since time immemorial and the decor suffers accordingly, but the pub atmosphere is intact. It's something of an institution for those wishing to sober up with greasy grub after a long night out. The **Flying Pig** (✉ 2/F, Empire Land Commercial Bldg., 81–85 Lockhart Rd., ☎ 2865–3730) has amusing and original decor. For a reasonably priced hotel drinking hole, try the Excelsior's **Dickens Bar** (✉ 281 Gloucester Rd., ☎ 2837–6782), which offers live music most nights.

If it's not too hot, relax at an outdoor table at Causeway Bay's **King's Arms** (✉ Sunning Plaza, 1 Sunning Rd., ☎ 2895–6557), one of Hong

Kong's few city-center beer gardens. The convivial outdoor area is a great place to meet fellow travelers.

Over in Tsim Sha Tsui a diverse, happy crowd frequents the Aussie-style **Kangaroo Pub** (⊠ 35 Haiphong Rd., ☎ 2376–0083), which has good pub food and interesting views of Kowloon Park.

Rick's Cafe (⊠ 53–59 Kimberly Rd., Luna Court, Tsim Sha Tsui, ☎ 2311–2255), a local hangout, is a restaurant-pub decorated à la *Casablanca,* with potted palms, ceiling fans, and posters of Bogie and Bergman. We guess the curiously named **Just "M"** (⊠ Shop 5, Podium Plaza, 5 Hanoi Rd., Tsim Sha Tsui, ☎ 2311–9188) stands for either "men" (but don't mistake it for a gay bar) or "money," but the owners playfully refuse to give up the goods. The minimalist industrial design gives it a laid-back feel, and the small mezzanine level has large black couches to sink into. **Ned Kelly's Last Stand** (⊠ 11A Ashley Rd., Tsim Sha Tsui, ☎ 2376–0562) is an institution, with Aussie-style beer tucker (pub grub), and rollicking live jazz in the evening.

A trendy place in Tsim Sha Tsui is an out-of-the-way strip called Knutsford Terrace. You'll find tropical rhythms at the Caribbean-inspired **Bahama Mama's** (⊠ 4–5 Knutsford Terr., ☎ 2368–2121), where world music plays and the kitsch props include a surfboard over the bar and the silhouette of a curvaceous woman showering behind a screen over the rest room entrance. You wouldn't think that **Chasers** (⊠ 2–3 Knutsford Terr., ☎ 2367–9487), fitted with genuine English antiques including chairs, lamps, and prints, would be as groovy as it is, but with live pop music most evenings it draws a regular and bustling crowd.

Wine Bars

Tiny, classy **Juliette's** (⊠ 6 Hoi Ping Rd., Causeway Bay, ☎ 2882–5460) provides a cozy ambience for chuppie (Hong Kong's Chinese yuppies) couples and corporate types.

For an intimate encounter, try **Le Tire Bouchon** (⊠ 45A Graham St., Central, ☎ 2523–5459), where fine wines by the glass accompany tasty bistro meals.

THE ARTS

The most comprehensive calendar of cultural events is *HK Magazine,* a free weekly newspaper distributed each Friday to many restaurants, stores, and bars. You can also read daily reviews in the Features section of the *South China Morning Post,* which also has an entertainment pullout every Friday called *24/7.* The other English-language newspaper, *iMail,* also has a weekend guide on Friday called *iMag.*

City Hall (⊠ 5 Edinburgh Pl., by Star Ferry, Hong Kong Island, ☎ 2921–2840) has posters and huge bulletin boards listing events and ticket availability. You can buy tickets for cultural events held in government centers from booths on the ground floor by the main entrance. **URBTIX** (☎ 2734–9009) outlets are the easiest places to buy tickets for most performances; you'll find a branch at the **Hong Kong Arts Centre** (☎ 2582–0232) in addition to the one at City Hall. The free monthly newspaper *City News* lists City Hall events.

Chinese Opera

Cantonese Opera. There are 10 Cantonese opera troupes in Hong Kong, as well as many amateur singing groups. These groups perform "street opera" in, for example, the Temple Street Night Market almost every night, while others perform at temple fairs, in City Hall, or in playgrounds under the auspices of the Urban Council (☎ 2922–8008). Visitors unfamiliar with the form are sometimes alienated by the strange sounds of this highly complex and extremely sophisticated art form. Every gesture has its own meaning; in fact, there are 50 gestures for the hand alone. Props attached to the costumes are similarly intricate and are used in exceptional ways. For example, the principal female often has 5-ft-long pheasant-feather tails attached to her headdress; she shows anger by dropping the head and shaking it in a circular fashion so that the feathers move in a perfect circle. Surprise is shown by what's called "nodding the feathers." One can also "dance with the feathers" to show a mixture of anger and determination. Orchestral music punctuates the singing. It's best to have a local acquaintance translate the gestures, since the stories are so complex that Wagner and Verdi librettos begin to seem basic in comparison.

Peking Opera. This highly stylized variety of opera employs higher-pitched voices than Cantonese opera. Peking opera is an older form, more respected for its classical traditions; the meticulous training of the several troupes visiting Hong Kong from the People's Republic of China each year is well regarded. They perform in City Hall or at special temple ceremonies. Call the Urban Council (☎ 2922–8008) for further information.

Dance

City Contemporary Dance Company. Dedicated to contemporary dance, this group presents innovative programs with Hong Kong themes at various venues both indoors and outdoors. ☎ 2326–8597.

Hong Kong Ballet. This is Hong Kong's first professional ballet company and vocational ballet school. Western oriented in both its classical and its contemporary repertoires, it performs at schools, auditoriums, and festivals. ☎ 2573–7398.

Hong Kong Dance Company. Since 1981, this ensemble has been promoting the art of Chinese dance and choreographing new works with historical themes. The 30-odd members are experts in folk and classical dance. Sponsored by the Urban Council, they perform about three times a month throughout the territory. ☎ 2853–2642.

Drama

Chung Ying Theatre Company. This professional company of Chinese actors stages plays—most of them original and written by local playwrights—mainly in Cantonese. The group also organizes exchanges with theater companies from overseas, often inviting international directors to head productions. Sites vary. ☎ 2521–6628.

Fringe Club. The Fringe presents an enormous amount of alternative theater, ranging from one-person shows to full dramatic performances. It's the only club of its kind to offer facilities to amateur drama, music, and dance groups. Short-run contemporary plays by American and English writers are also presented, as well as shows by independent local groups. ⊠ 2 Lower Albert Rd., Central, ☎ 2521–7251.

Zuni Icosahedron. The best-known avant-garde group in Hong Kong stages multimedia drama and dance, usually in Cantonese, at various locations. ☎ 2893–8419.

Film

Hong Kong reigns as the film capital of Asian martial-arts/Triad-theme movies. Unlike Western shoot-'em-ups, the camera work in martial-arts flicks emphasizes the ricochet choreography of physical combat. The international success of critically acclaimed *Crouching Tiger, Hidden Dragon* is testament to the industry's emerging importance in world cinema.

If you want to experience a true Hong Kong Canto-flick, you'll have plenty to choose from. If a Jackie Chan or Chow Yun-Fat film is in release, you can be sure nearly every cinema in town will be showing it. Other movies are mostly B-grade, centering on the cops-and-robbers and slapstick genres; locals love these because they star popular (and very attractive) Hong Kong actors. Wong Kar Wai, Ann Hui, John Woo, and Ang Lee, all international award–winning filmmakers, have helped draw attention to Hong Kong film with their visionary and dynamic direction. For show times and theaters, check the listings in *HK* magazine, the *South China Morning Post,* and the *iMail*.

If you're looking for more than just a visual feast (that is, you want to see an art-house feature), visit **Broadway Cinematheque** (⊠ Prosperous Garden, 3 Public Square St., Yau Ma Tei, ☎ 2388–3188; 2384–6281 for ticket reservations). The train-station design of this art house has won awards; the departure board displays foreign and independent films (local films are rare). Here you can read the latest reel-world magazines from around the globe in a minilibrary. A shop sells new and vintage film paraphernalia, and there's a coffee bar as well. To get here, use the Temple Street exit at the Yau Ma Tei MTR.

Before the Broadway Cinematheque, cinephiles in search of alternative and independent films from Japan and the West had only two options. The **Cine-Art House** (⊠ Ground floor, Sun Hung Kai Centre, Wanchai, ☎ 2827–4778) is a quaint two-theater complex. **The Hong Kong Arts Centre** (☞ *below*) screens some of the best independent, classic, documentary, and short films from around the world as well as local products, often with themes focusing on a particular country, period, or director.

Orchestras

Hong Kong Chinese Orchestra. Created in 1977 by the Urban Council, this group performs only Chinese works. The orchestra consists of bowed strings, plucked instruments, wind, and percussion. Each work is specially arranged for each concert. ☎ *2853–2622*.

Hong Kong Philharmonic Orchestra. Almost 100 musicians from Hong Kong, the United States, Australia, and Europe perform everything from classical to avant-garde to contemporary music by Chinese composers. Past soloists have included Vladimir Ashkenazy, Rudolf Firkusny, and Maureen Forrester. Performances are usually held Friday and Saturday at 8 PM in City Hall or in recital halls in the New Territories. ☎ *2721–2030*.

Performance Halls

Hong Kong Island

City Hall (☞ *above*). Classical music, theatrical performances, films, and art exhibitions are presented in this complex's large auditorium, recital hall, and theater.

Hong Kong Academy for Performing Arts. This arts school has two major theaters, each seating 1,600 people, plus a 200-seat studio theater and

MARTIAL ARTS GOES HOLLYWOOD

ALTHOUGH A CULT FAVORITE around the globe, martial-arts films in Hong Kong are no less than a phenomenon—their actors no less than superstars. Walk into a Hong Kong shop, visit a tourist office, step into an office atrium, and who do you see? Jackie Chan. Not the man, but his image. A life-size, cut-out figure of the humorous martial-arts superstar with a thousand-watt smile.

Chan has been called a "physical genius" and "the world's greatest action star." After years of international fame and accolades, this ultraflexible stuntman extraordinaire finally broke into the American market with 1996's *Rumble in the Bronx*. Two years later, Chan solidified his fame in the West with his first exclusively U.S. production, *Rush Hour*.

But in Hong Kong he's been a god, a crutch during economic hard times, when he was routinely asked to step in, support, sing praise, and bring up the people. He's the man who's guaranteed to draw the crowds every time a new movie is released. When he's on the silver screen, Hong Kongers know they can kick back and forget about their troubles for a while.

Of course Chan is not the first, or only, martial-arts golden son of Hong Kong. Recent heroes include John Woo, who created such bullet-ridden cult classics as *A Better Tomorrow*, *The Killer*, and *Hard-Boiled*. He was also responsible for launching Chow Yun-Fat's movie career. Chow Yun-Fat, who was born on the small island of Lamma and moved to Hong Kong in 1965, is the ultratough, muscular martial artist who worked with Woo on *A Better Tomorrow*, which propelled both men into the limelight of the action-movie genre. Both men

are also known for the slick Hollywood flick *The Replacement Killers*, which Woo produced and Chow Yun-Fat starred in; but Yun-Fat's name is now most associated with his graceful fighting prowess in the international hit *Crouching Tiger, Hidden Dragon*.

While their Hollywood films do well in the United States, both Chow Yun-Fat and Jackie Chan are equally famous in the Hong Kong film industry for their locally filmed slapstick and heroic bloodshed films. Like the godfather of the genre, Bruce Lee, both are more than just hometown boys made good—they're international stars.

But it was Lee who broke the ground and still shines as the martial artist to live up to in life and on the screen. Martial artists still talk about Lee and his muscular physique and Lee and his style.

Just after moving to America in the 1960s, Lee was challenged to a fight by Cantonese experts in Oakland's Chinatown because he was teaching Chinese "secrets" to non-Chinese individuals. This was perceived as treason among some members of the martial-arts community. Lee won the challenge, and nowadays students around the world study such techniques. In part they can thank Lee for their schooling.

Unlike other areas in the region, Hong Kong isn't a city where you're likely to get into a bar fight with a local who thinks he is Jackie Chan or Bruce Lee. But you are likely to see some of the cheesiest, funniest, most artistically and athletically amazing movies here if you just pop into a local movie theater. It's a Hong Kong experience without parallel.

a 500-seat outdoor theater. Performances include local and international theater, modern and classical dance, and concerts. ✉ *1 Gloucester Rd., Wanchai,* ☎ *2584–8500.*

Hong Kong Arts Centre. Several floors of auditoriums, rehearsal halls, and recital rooms spotlight both local and visiting groups. ✉ *2 Harbour Rd., Wanchai,* ☎ *2582–0232.*

Hong Kong Fringe Club. Some of Hong Kong's most innovative entertainment and art exhibits play here. Shows range from the blatantly amateur to the dazzlingly professional. Entertainment also includes good jazz, avant-garde drama, and many other events. ✉ *2 Lower Albert Rd., Central,* ☎ *2521–7251.*

Queen Elizabeth Stadium. Though it's basically a sports stadium, this 3,500-seat venue frequently presents ballets and orchestral and pop concerts. ✉ *18 Oi Kwan Rd., Wanchai,* ☎ *2591–1346.*

Kowloon

Hong Kong Coliseum. A 12,000-plus-seat stadium that presents everything from basketball to ballet, from skating polar bears to local and international pop stars. ✉ *9 Cheong Wan Rd., Hung Hom railway station, Hung Hom,* ☎ *2355–7234.*

Hong Kong Cultural Centre. This conference and performance facility contains the Grand Theatre, seating 1,750, and a concert hall seating 2,100. The center is used by both local and visiting artists for operas, ballets, and orchestral concerts. ✉ *10 Salisbury Rd.,* ☎ *2734–2009.*

University Hall. Baptist University owns this modern auditorium, which usually hosts pop concerts but also offers dance and symphony concerts. The odd headline act plays here, such as the legendary Tom Jones, but the space usually caters to local talent, which is worth checking out. ✉ *224 Waterloo Rd.,* ☎ *2339–5182.*

The New Territories

Shatin Town Hall. Attached to New Town Plaza, an enormous shopping arcade, this impressive building is a five-minute walk from the KCR station at Shatin. Its cultural events include dance, drama, and concert performances. ✉ *1 Yuen Wo Rd., Shatin,* ☎ *2694–2511.*

Tsuen Wan Town Hall. It's off the beaten path, but this auditorium gets a constant stream of local and international performers. Acts include everything from the Warsaw Philharmonic to Chinese acrobats. The hall seats 1,424 and probably has the best acoustics of any performance hall in Hong Kong. ✉ *72 Tai Ho Rd., Tsuen Wan,* ☎ *2414–0144. MTR: Tsuen Wan.*

6 SPORTS AND OUTDOOR ACTIVITIES

Hong Kong's international reputation as a fast-paced metropolis doesn't prepare most travelers for its athletic and outdoor offerings. While here you can test your luck at a racetrack, hike a well-developed network of trails, learn a martial art, or just loaf on a lovely beach.

S **WEAT IN HONG KONG** spills beyond the floors of the stock exchange and dance clubs. If you're in town during the horse-racing season, don't miss the spectacle when gambling-mad punters stake a huge part of their incomes on stallions and mares. Rugby and soccer tournaments draw enthusiastic, if often drunken, fans, and the annual dragon boat races are highly entertaining. Check weekly activity schedules at a Hong Kong Tourist Board (HKTB) information booth for listings of spectator-sport events. Although most activities require a little advance planning, they're well worth the effort.

Updated by
Lara Wozniak

If you want to participate in local activities, you can join the elderly men and women who rise when the roosters crow to perform their ritual morning tai chi in public parks before they head off for a light breakfast of *yum cha* or dim sum. And of course this is the place to study martial arts from karate to tae kwon do. Hong Kongers are also partial to hiking in the mountains, sailing beyond Victoria Harbour into the South China Sea, golfing with coworkers, and playing tennis with friends on weekends.

PARTICIPANT SPORTS

Perhaps because of its British legacy, Hong Kong has long been known as a club-oriented city: whether you're into golf, sailing, squash, or tennis, you'll find that members-only clubs have the best facilities. And several clubs have reciprocal privileges with clubs outside Hong Kong. The Hong Kong Jockey Club offers members of such affiliates free entry to its members' enclosure during racing season (though not use of club recreational facilities). Visitors with reciprocal privileges at the Hong Kong Golf Club are allowed 14 free rounds of golf each year. Other clubs with reciprocal policies are the Hong Kong Yacht Club, Hong Kong Cricket Club, Kowloon Cricket Club, Hong Kong Football Club, Hong Kong Country Club, Kowloon Club, Hong Kong Club, and Ladies' Recreation Club.

Before you leave for Hong Kong, check with your club to see if it has an arrangement with one there. If so, you'll need to bring your membership card, a letter of introduction, and often your passport when you visit the affiliated establishment in Hong Kong. Call when you arrive to book facilities, or ask your hotel concierge to make arrangements.

Golf

Locals generally head up to nearby Shenzhen, China's Special Economic Zone, to enjoy a round or three of golf on the weekends; however, you need a Chinese visa to be able to play in Shenzhen without spending an arm and a leg. Not to worry though: some of Hong Kong's top clubs allow visitors to play their courses.

The **Clearwater Bay Golf and Country Club** permits visitors to play golf on its 18-hole course Monday to Friday with tee-off times between 9:30 and 11:30 AM. ⊠ *139 Tai Aumum Rd., Causeway Bay, New Territories,* ☎ *2719–1595; 2335–3885 for booking office.* ☒ *Green fees are HK$1,400.*

The **Discovery Bay Golf Club,** on Lantau Island, has an 18-hole course open to visitors on Monday, Tuesday, and Friday between 7:30 and 11:45 AM. You must reserve two days in advance. ⊠ *Take Discovery Bay ferry from Star Ferry pier in Central, then catch bus to course (call club for current bus-line info),* ☎ *2987–7273.* ☒ *Greens fees HK$1,400,* *club rental HK$160, golf-cart rental HK$190, shoe rental HK$50; ½-hr lesson HK$400.*

The **Hong Kong Golf Club** allows visitors to play on its three 18-hole courses at Fanling, in the New Territories Monday through Friday from 7:30 AM to 2 PM. ⊠ *Just off Fanling Hwy.,* ☎ *2670–1211 for bookings; 2670–0647 for club rentals.* ▣ *Greens fees HK$1,400 for 18 holes, club rental HK$250; ½-hr lesson HK$300.*

The **Tuen Mun Golf Centre** is a public center with 100 driving bays and a practice green. ⊠ *Lung Mun Rd., Tuen Mun,* ☎ *2466–2600.* ▣ *HK$12 per bay, HK$12 per club, HK$12 per hr per 30 balls.* ☉ *Daily 8 AM–10 PM.*

Health Clubs

Most Hong Kong health clubs require membership; the person behind the desk will look at you blankly if you try to explain that your health club at home might have a reciprocal arrangement. The majority of first-class hotels have health clubs on their premises, and California Fitness Center and Tom Turk Fitness Club will let you enter for a reasonable day rate.

The **California Fitness Center** (⊠ 1 Wellington St., Central, ☎ 2522–5229; ⊠ 99 Percival St., Causeway Bay, ☎ 2577–0004; ⊠ 88 Gloucester Rd., Wanchai, ☎ 2877–7070) has guest passes for HK$300 per day.

Situated alongside the Midlevels outdoor escalator, **New York Fitness** (⊠ 32 Hollywood Rd., Central, ☎ 2543–2280) sells a one-week pass for HK$500.

Tom Turk Fitness Club (⊠ Asia Pacific Finance Tower, 3 Garden Rd., 3rd floor, Central, ☎ 2521–4541; ⊠ HK Scout Centre, 8 Austin Rd., Tsim Sha Tsui, ☎ 2736–7188) charges HK$100 for a weekday visit before 5 PM, HK$150 after 5 and on weekends.

Hiking

Lush lowlands, bamboo and pine forests, rugged mountains with panoramas of the sea, and secluded beaches are the little-known alter ego of Hong Kong. In fact, about 40% of Hong Kong is protected in 23 parks, three marine parks, and one marine reserve. A day's hike (or two days if you're prepared to camp out) takes a bit of planning, but you'll see the best of Hong Kong. You'll seem farther than you really are from the buildings below, which appear almost insignificant from this perspective.

Don't expect to find the wilderness wholly unspoiled, however. Few upland areas escape Hong Kong's relentless plague of hill fires for more than a few years at a time. Some are caused by dried-out vegetation; others erupt from small graveside fires set by locals to clear the land around ancestors' eternal resting spots. Partly because of these fires, most of Hong Kong's forests, except for a few spots in the New Territories, support no obvious wildlife other than birds—and mosquitoes. Bring repellent.

Gear

Basic necessities include sunglasses or hat, bottled water, day pack, and sturdy hiking boots. Wear layered clothing; weather in the hills tends to be very warm during the day and colder toward nightfall. The cliff sides get quite windy. Of course, if you're planning to camp, carry a sleeping bag and tent.

Great Outdoor Clothing Company (⊠ 2/F, Silvercord Bldg., 30 Canton Rd., Tsim Sha Tsui, ☎ 2730–9009) doesn't sell the same range of

SMOOTH MOVES

WHEN YOU ARRIVE in Hong Kong, chances are you'll be suffering from jet lag. If you wake up at 4 AM raring to go, you can wander down to any public park and watch some of the more than 100,000 Hong Kongers who practice tai chi each morning.

Just before dawn it's not unusual to see young businessmen and retired grandparents practicing tai chi: slowly stretching, breathing deeply, and moving in ways most Western teenagers can't manage. There's no better advertising for tai chi than seeing an octogenarian balance on one leg, with the other outstretched and held high for a long moment before gracefully swinging into another pose that requires balance, coordination, and strength.

The art of tai chi consists of slow, steady, flowing movements with moderate postures—suitable for people of all ages, flexibility, and fitness levels to practice. It offers physical and mental benefits and may give you insights into the philosophical path followed by thousands throughout the centuries. While that may be common knowledge, few people know that tai chi is also a subtle, sophisticated, and scientific method of self-defense.

The founder of tai chi was Chang San Feng, a Taoist, who was born in AD 1247. His accomplishments were such that during the Ming Dynasty news of his fame reached the ears of the Emperor. Titles and honors were showered on Chang, and a magnificent mansion was built for him on Wutan Mountain as a special gift from the provincial governor.

One of the greatest tai chi masters was Yang Lu Chan (1799–1872) who, during the Ching Dynasty, served as the chief combat instructor to the Imperial Guard. He practiced tai chi for many years, and his fighting ability earned him the nickname "Invincible Yang."

To follow in their footsteps you need to study under an accomplished master. Only a good master can correctly demonstrate techniques, identify faults, and give proper advice and guidance that will help you progress. You will also experience a more calming feeling when studying under an accomplished master.

If you want to try tai chi while you're in Hong Kong, contact the **Hong Kong Tourist Board (HKTB)** (☎ 2508–1234). Under the guidance of a tai chi master, you can learn simple breathing and relaxation exercises. Free classes are offered at Hong Kong Park every Tuesday, Friday, and Sunday from 8:15 to 9:15 AM.

camping equipment, backpacks, sleeping bags, and clothes you'd find in the United States or in the United Kingdom, but it'll do in a pinch.

Timberland (⊠ Shop 212, Pacific Place, 88 Queensway, Admiralty, ☎ 2868–0845) sells hiking boots, backpacks, and appropriate clothing.

World Sports Co. Ltd. (⊠ 83 Fa Yuen St., 2/F, Mong Kok, ☎ 2396–9357) is probably comparable to your favorite camping store back home, catering to your every outdoor need with a very helpful staff. It stocks everything from pocket knives and woolly socks to gas burners and tents.

Maps

Before you go, pick up trail maps at the **Government Publications Centre** (⊠ Pacific Place, Government Office, ground floor, 66 Queensway, Admiralty, ☎ 2537–1910). Ask for blueprints of the trails and the Countryside Series maps. The HM20C series comprises handsome four-color maps, but it's not very reliable.

Trails

You can hike through any of the territory's country parks and around any of the accessible outlying islands. Here are two short, one-day hikes and two camping treks on the most popular trails.

Dragon's Back. This is a relatively easy, half-day, meandering walk with lots of straightaway sections on southeastern Hong Kong Island. It boasts some surprisingly wild country a world away from the urban bustle. You start out walking through woodland, but this soon gives way to wind-pruned grass and bamboo jungle along the ridge that is the spine of the dragon. The foliage grows over the path, so you are shaded. At about the halfway mark you reach a great place to stop, take a drink of your bottled water, and absorb the scenery. On a clear day the trail affords tremendous views over the south of the island, Shek O, and the South China Sea. If it's windy, you may see daredevils paragliding and children of all ages (usually of the adult variety) flying remote-control airplanes from the cliff-side middle point of the trail. From here you walk down a sandy path that at times looks like it is cutting through the hills of the Highlands in Scotland, although the trail is more rambling than rugged. Follow it to the main road to catch one of the frequent well-marked buses to Shek O, where you can mingle with the villagers and day trippers as you stroll along the soft white beach that has some interesting rocks and the occasional shell or two. You can take a bus or taxi home from Shek O. Distance: 4 km (2½ mi) (3 hours hiking, 60 to 90 minutes traveling). While you could easily do this hike on your own, contact Martin Williams (☎ 2981–3523) for a guided tour.

Lantau Island. Take a ferry ride from Central on Hong Kong Island to Lantau Island, then take a scenic bus ride along Lantau's southern coast and up to Ngong Ping, below the summit of Lantau Peak, Hong Kong's second-highest mountain. Here, you can see Big Buddha, visit Po Lin Monastery, and stroll through the old Tea Gardens to a vantage point with stunning views of Shek Pik reservoir and the South China Sea beyond. Then you can hike a path that drops, levels, and takes you to the road leading toward Kwun Yam Temple. Named after the Goddess of Mercy, this beautiful Taoist temple is set on a wooded hillside from where you can see more temples. Enjoy a break at this temple before heading along a quiet level road. Distance: 7 km (4½ mi) (3½ hours hiking, about 2½ hours traveling). Longer stretches of uphill walking, however, make this trek more strenuous than the Dragon's Back hike. You can hike on your own, or contact Martin Williams (☎ 2981–3523) for a guided tour.

McLehose Trail. Named after an ex-governor of Hong Kong, this trail is the course for the annual McLehose Trailwalker, an international run/walk for charity. This grueling event covers 97 km (60 mi) and must be completed nonstop; teams winning first place have finished the walk in an astonishing 15 hours. The average hiker can tackle sections of the McLehose trail in one day; otherwise, it's a four- or five-day trip from beginning to end. This splendidly isolated path through the New Territories starts at Tsak Yue Wu, beyond Sai Kung, and circles the High Island Reservoir before breaking north. Climb through Sai Kung Country Park to a steep section of the trail, up the mountain called Ma On Shan. Turn south for a high-ridge walk through Ma On Shan Country Park. From here you walk west along the ridges of the eight mountains, also known as the Eight Dragons, that gave Kowloon its name. (The last emperor of the Sung dynasty is thought to have named the peninsula Nine Dragons, for these eight peaks plus himself.) You may see wild monkeys on the trail near Eagles Nest; they are, in fact, very tame. After you cross Tai Po Road, the path follows along ridge tops toward Tai Mo Mountain, 3,161 ft above sea level. This is the tallest mountain in Hong Kong and is sometimes capped with snow. Continuing west, the trail drops gradually to Tai Lam Reservoir and then to Tuen Mun, where you can catch public transportation.

Wilson Trail. This trail is 78 km (48 mi) long, from Stanley Gap on Hong Kong Island to Nam Chung in the northeastern New Territories. You have to cross the harbor by MTR at Quarry Bay to complete the entire walk. The trail is smoothed by steps paved with stone, and footbridges aid with steep sections and streams. Clearly marked with signs and information boards, this popular walk is divided into 10 sections, and you can easily take just one or two; traversing the whole trail takes about 31 hours. It begins at Stanley Gap Road, on the south end of Hong Kong Island, and takes you through rugged peaks that offer a panoramic view of Repulse Bay and the nearby Round and Middle islands. This first part, Section 1, is only for the very fit. Much of the trail requires walking up steep mountain grades. For an easier walk, try Section 7, which begins at Sing Mun reservoir and takes you along a greenery-filled, fairly level path that winds past the eastern shore of the Sing Mun Reservoir in the New Territories and then descends to Tai Po, where there's a sweeping view of Tolo Harbour. Other sections will take you through the monkey forest at the Kowloon Hill Fitness Trail (Section 5), over mountains, and past charming Chinese villages.

Jogging

The best stretch of land for jogging is **Bowen Road.** It's an 8-km (5-mi) run back and forth on a wooded street that's closed to vehicular traffic. **Victoria Park** at Causeway Bay also has an official jogging track.

The **Hong Kong Running Clinic** is open to all levels of ability, including those training for marathons, and meets every Sunday morning at 7 from April through December. There is no charge for visitors. Doctor Dan Neisner, who runs the club, recommends shorter runs in the oppressively hot summer months. ⊠ *Meet at the parking lot in front of Adventist Hospital, 40 Stubbs Rd., Happy Valley,* ☎ *2835–0555 Health Promotions Department.*

Junking

Dining on the water aboard large pleasure craft—which also serve as platforms for swimmers and water-skiers—is a boating style unique to Hong Kong. Junking has become so popular that there is now a fairly large junk-building industry producing highly varnished, plushly appointed, air-conditioned junks up to 80 ft long. After a day out on a junk, sailing by the shimmering lights of Hong Kong Island on the ride back into town is spectacular.

These floating rumpus rooms serve a purpose, especially for denizens of Hong Kong Island who suffer from "rock fever" and need to escape for a day on the water. Also known as "gin junks" because so much alcohol is consumed, these junks are commanded by "weekend admirals." If anyone so much as breathes an invitation for junking, grab it.

You can also rent a junk. The pilot will take you to your choice of the following outer islands: Cheung Chau, Lamma, Lantau, Po Toi, or the islands in Sai Kung Harbour. **Simpson Marine Ltd.** (⊠ Aberdeen Marina Tower, 8 Shun Wan Rd., Aberdeen, ☎ 2555–7349) is an established charter operator whose crewed junks can hold 35–45 people. Prices begin at HK$2,800 for an eight-hour day trip or a four-hour night trip during the week, HK$4,500 on summer weekends. The price goes up on holidays. You need to reserve in advance; half of the fee is required upon receipt of a signed contract, the remaining half at least five days prior to departure. **Jubilee International Tour Centre** (⊠ Far East Consortium Bldg., 121 Des Vouex Rd., Central, ☎ 2530–0530) is another established charter outfit recommended by the HKTB.

Martial Arts

C. S. Tang at the **Hong Kong Chinese Martial Arts Association** (⊠ Sports House, 1 Stadium Patch, Room 1008, So Kon Po, Causeway Bay, ☎ 2394–4803 or 2504–8164) can advise you on where to find short-term martial-arts instruction, with courses that last from 10 days to a few months.

The **Martial Arts School** (⊠ 446 Hennessy Rd., 3/F, Causeway Bay, ☎ 2891–1044) of master Luk Chi Fu uses the white-crane system of internal-strength training. This method is one of the schools of *chi kung* or *noi kung*, the names for internal-strength kung fu, as opposed to the more violent type seen in the movies. This gentler version is said to be the forerunner of yoga. It relies on quick thinking, controlled breathing, and an instant grasp of the situation at hand; at the advanced level, a student can absorb blows and use spears and knives as if they were an extension of his or her body. Now run by the master's son, Luk Chung Mau, the school is open to anyone who will be around Hong Kong long enough to take an ongoing class.

Paragliding

The **Hong Kong Paragliding Association** (⊠ Union Commercial Bldg., 12–16 Lyndhurst Terr., Room 202, Central, ☎ 2543–2901) will recommend an instructor. Weather permitting, you can soar over Hong Kong at an altitude rarely experienced by the populace. Paragliders are usually sighted over the scenic Shek O Peninsula. (If you just want to watch, you can spy takeoffs and landings from the hike along Dragon's Back.)

Sailing

To sail here, you must belong to a yacht club that has reciprocal privileges with one in Hong Kong. Contact the **Hong Kong Yacht Club** (☎ 2832–2817) to make arrangements. Sometimes members need crews for weekend races, so experienced sailors can check the "crew wanted" board in the club's Course Room.

Scuba Diving

Bunn's Divers Institute (⊠ 38–40 Yee Woo St., Causeway Bay, ☎ 2893–7899) runs outings for qualified divers to areas like Sai Kung. The cost of a day trip runs HK$700 and includes two dive sessions, one in the morning and another in the afternoon. You'll need to bring your own lunch.

Mandarin Divers (⊠ Aberdeen Marina Tower, 8 Shun Wan Rd., Aberdeen, ☎ 2554–7110) offers two-week open-water training for a cost of HK$4,250, including boat rental, equipment, and certification (medical certificate required).

Skating

The Glacier is part of Festival Walk, an extensive entertainment complex in Yau Yat Tsuen, next to the Kowloon Tong KCR station. It's the largest ice-skating rink in Hong Kong. You can rent figure skates that fit larger feet (up to a man's 11½). ☎ 2265–8888. ✎ *HK$50 weekdays, HK$60 weekends.* ⊙ *Mon.–Sat. 10–10, Sun. 1–10.*

The **Ice Plaza** in Cityplaza II on Hong Kong Island, has a first-class ice-skating rink. During the week this rink allows you to skate for an unlimited amount of sessions provided you don't leave the rink. ⊠ *1111 Kings Rd., Taikoo Shing,* ☎ *2885–4697.* ✎ *HK$40 morning session, HK$50 afternoon session.* ⊙ *Weekdays 8–noon and 12:30–10 PM; Sat. 7–9 AM, 12:30–2, 3–5, 5:30–7:30, and 8–10; Sun. 7–noon, 12:30–2:30, 3–5, 5:30–7:30, and 8–10.*

Squash

The **Hong Kong Urban Council** runs many public squash courts in the Territory and provides a **central booking service** (☎ 2927–8080 or 2922–8008). You can reserve courts up to 10 days in advance, and should do so as early as possible. Bring a passport for identification. Most courts are open from 7 AM to 10 or 11 PM and cost HK$27 for 30 minutes, HK$54 for an hour. The Urban Council can give directions, or you can contact the court directly.

Harbour Road Indoor Games Hall (⊠ 27 Harbour Rd., Wanchai, ☎ 2827–9684).
Hong Kong Squash Centre (⊠ Cotton Tree Dr., across from Peak Tram Terminal, Central, ☎ 2521–5072).
Laichikok Park (⊠ 1 Lai Wan Rd., Kowloon, ☎ 2745–2796).
Victoria Park (⊠ Hing Fat St., Causeway Bay, ☎ 2570–6186).

Swimming

Public swimming pools close in winter but fill to capacity in summer, late April to late September. With no lane ropes, swimmers must weave past other bodies, and the congestion can sometimes be as bad as in the streets. Most travelers use the clearer and more relaxing pools in their hotels. (☞ *also* Beaches, *below*).

Tennis

Public tennis courts are usually booked far in advance. To reserve one you'll need identification, such as a passport. Most courts open from 7 AM to 10 or 11 PM and cost HK$42 in the daytime and HK$57 in the evening. For further information, contact the Hong Kong Urban Council (☞ Squash, *above*) or the **Hong Kong Tennis Association** (⊠ Sports House, 1 Stadium Path, Room 1021, So Kon Po,

Causeway Bay, ☎ 2504–8266). The following courts are open to the public:

Bowen Road Courts (⊠ 7 Kennedy Rd., Wanchai, ☎ 2528–2983) has four courts.

Hong Kong Tennis Centre (⊠ Wongneichong Gap, Happy Valley, ☎ 2574–9122) has 17 courts.

Kowloon Tsai Park (⊠ 13 Inverness Rd., Kowloon Tong, ☎ 2336–7878) has eight courts.

Victoria Park (⊠ Hing Fat St., Causeway Bay, ☎ 2570–6186) offers 14 courts.

Waterskiing

Patrick's Waterskiing & Windsurfing (⊠ Stanley Main Beach, Stanley, ☎ 2813–2372) is run by the friendly, laid-back man himself. Patrick will take you to the best waters in the Stanley Beach area and give you pointers on your waterskiing or wakeboarding technique. The fee—HK$700 per hour—includes a range of equipment and life jackets. To rent a speedboat, equipment, and the services of a driver, contact the **Waterski Club** (⊠ Pier at Deep Water Bay Beach, ☎ 2812–0391) or ask your hotel for the names and numbers of other outfitters. The cost is usually about HK$580 per hour. Some junk-hiring companies also provide speedboats for waterskiing for an extra charge (☞ Junking, *above*).

Windsurfing

The popularity of this sport was declining until Hong Kong's native daughter Lee Lai-shan sailed off with the gold medal in the 1996 Summer Olympics in Atlanta. Now windsurfing centers at Stanley Beach, on Hong Kong Island, and Tun Wan Beach, on Cheung Chau Island, will gladly start you on the path to glory with some lessons. **Patrick's Waterskiing & Windsurfing** (☞ Waterskiing, *above*) offers a full-day course for HK$880; the more experienced can rent windsurfing boards for HK$70–$120 a day. For windsurfing information, contact the **Government Sports Centre** (⊠ St. Stevens Beach, Water Sports Centre, Wong Ma Kok Path, Stanley, ☎ 2813–5407).

SPECTATOR SPORTS

Horse Racing and Gambling

Horse racing is the nearest thing in Hong Kong to a national sport. It is a multimillion-dollar-a-year business, employing thousands of people and drawing crowds that approach insanity in their eagerness to rid themselves of their hard-earned money. Even if you're not a gambler, it's worth going to one of Hong Kong's two tracks just to experience the phenomenon. If you exclude the stock market, which is by far the territory's largest single gambling event, the only legalized forms of gambling are horse racing and the lottery. Nearby Macau (☞ Chapter 8) is another story—there you can get your fill of casino gambling.

The "sport of kings" is run under a monopoly by the Hong Kong Jockey Club, one of the most politically powerful entities in the territory. Profits go to charity and community organizations. The racing season runs from September through June. Some 65 races are held at one or the other of the two courses, most often on Saturday and Sunday at Shatin and Happy Valley, with an occasional Wednesday-night session at Happy Valley. The **HKTB** (☎ 2508–1234 hot line) organizes tours to the club and track. Costs range from HK$245 to HK$490 and can include transfers, lunch, and tips on picking a winner. Alternatively, you can watch the races from the public stands, where the atmosphere is lively and loud—this is highly recommended for a truly local experience, and the cost is only HK$10. Both courses have huge video screens at the finish line so that gamblers can see what's happening every foot of the way.

The **Happy Valley Race Track** (⊠ Hong Kong Jockey Club, 1 Sports Rd., Happy Valley, ☎ 2966–8111 or 2966–8364), on Hong Kong Island, is one of Hong Kong's most beloved institutions. It holds mostly night races on Saturday or Sunday.

The **Shatin Racecourse** (⊠ Tai Po Rd., Shatin, next to Racecourse KCR station, ☎ 2966–6520), in the New Territories, is newer than Happy Valley—one of the most modern racecourses in the world, in fact. Most of its races are run during the day on Saturday or Sunday. The easiest way to get here is by KCR train; on race days, the KCR detours to the Racecourse stop, between Shatin and University. A walkway from the station takes you directly to the racetrack. By car, take the exit marked RACECOURSE from Tai Po Road, just past central Shatin.

Rugby

One weekend every spring (usually in March), Hong Kong hosts the international tournament of Sevens-a-Side teams, otherwise known as the Rugby Sevens or simply "the Sevens," at the Hong Kong Stadium (use exit F in the Causeway Bay MTR), which, unbelievably in this space-pressed city, exists only to host this tournament. The whole town goes half mad. To avoid camping outside the stadium all night to buy tickets, you can purchase them in advance from an overseas agent; for a list of agents contact the **Hong Kong Rugby Football Union** (⊠ Sports House, 1 Stadium Path, Room 2001, So Kon Po, Causeway Bay, ☎ 2504–8300, ℻ 2576–7237).

BEACHES

Hong Kong is not known for its beaches, but it's surrounded by hundreds of them and has a thriving sunbathing culture. About 40 of the beaches around Hong Kong and its outlying islands are "gazetted"—cleaned and maintained by the government, with services that include lifeguards, floats, and swimming-zone safety markers.

The scenery is often breathtaking, but pollution is a problem in Hong Kong waters, so before you embark on a day out, check the *South China Morning Post* for pollution ratings of the more popular beaches. Moreover, the occasional shark has been spotted in the waters of the New Territories. We restrict our recommendations to the beaches that offer a variety of activities in addition to swimming. Check with the HKTB before taking the plunge, and don't swim if a red flag—indicating either pollution or an approaching storm—is hoisted. The red flag flies often at Big Wave Bay (on the south side of Hong Kong Island) because of the rough surf. Check with the HKTB or listen to announcements on the radio or TV before heading out there.

Swimming is extremely popular with Hong Kongers, which means locals pack most beaches on summer weekends and public holidays. The more popular beaches, such as Repulse Bay, are busy day and night throughout the summer.

Almost all beaches can be reached by public transportation, but knowing which bus to catch and where to get off can be difficult. Pick up bus maps at an HKTB information booth before you start out. You can also take a taxi, but it will cost around HK$150 or more depending on where you're staying. Beaches on outlying islands connect to Central by the Hong Kong Ferry, and are often a short walk from the pier.

Hong Kong Island

Big Wave Bay, Hong Kong's most accessible surfing beach, lives up to its name and is frequently closed for swimming as a result. The beach has kiosks, barbecue pits, a playground, changing rooms, showers, and toilets. ⊠ *From Shau Ki Wan take Bus 9 to the roundabout; walk about 20 mins along the road, which is usually lined with cars on weekends.*

At **Deep Water Bay** the action starts at dawn every morning, all year long, when members of the Polar Bear Club go for a dip. The beach is packed in summer, when there are lifeguards, swimming rafts, and safety-zone markers, plus a police reporting center. Barbecue pits, showers, and rest rooms are open year-round. A taxi from Central will take about 20 minutes. ⊠ *Take Bus 6A from Exchange Sq. Bus Terminus; for a scenic route, take Bus 70 from Exchange Sq. to Aberdeen and change to Bus 73, which passes the beach en route to Stanley.*

Repulse Bay has changing rooms, showers, toilets, swimming rafts, swimming safety-zone markers, and playgrounds. Several Chinese restaurants dot the beach, and kiosks serve light refreshments. The Lifesaving Club is at the east end and resembles a Chinese temple, with large statues of Tin Hau, Goddess of the sea, and Kwun Yum, Goddess of mercy. ⊠ *Take Bus 6, 6A, 64, 260, or 262 from Exchange Sq., or Bus 73 from Aberdeen.*

Shek O, not far from Big Wave Bay, is almost Mediterranean in aspect. A wide beach with shops and restaurants nearby, it has refreshment kiosks, barbecue pits, lifeguards, swimming rafts, playgrounds, changing rooms, showers, and toilets. The views are magnificent as the bus begins its descent toward the heart of the small village. ⊠ *Take the MTR from Central to Shau Ki Wan (there is a bus from Central to Shau Ki Wan, but it takes between 1 and 2 hrs), then Bus 9 to the end of the line.*

Stanley Main, a wide sweep of sand, is popular with the windsurfing crowd and has a refreshment kiosk, swimming rafts, changing rooms, showers, and toilets, plus a nearby market. It also hosts the annual dragon boat races, usually held in June, in which friendly teams paddle out into the sea, turn around, and, at the sound of the gun, race ferociously back to the beach. It's a great day out, but head out early to claim a spot along the beach, as it gets chaotically crowded. Contact the HKTB for more details. ⊠ *Take a taxi from Central, about 45 mins; Bus 6, 6A, 6X or 260 from Exchange Sq.; Bus 73 from Aberdeen.*

Turtle Cove, isolated but scenic, has lifeguards and rafts in summer, barbecue pits, a refreshment kiosk, changing rooms, showers, and toilets. ⊠ *From Central take the MTR to Sai Wan Ho and change to Bus 14; get off at Tai Tam Rd. after passing the dam of Tai Tuk Reservoir.*

The New Territories

Expansive Sai Kung Peninsula has some of Hong Kong's most beautiful beaches, and many of these are easily reached by public transportation. Here are the three most popular:

Pak Sha Chau is a gem of a beach, with brilliant golden sand. Located on a grassy island near Sai Kung Town, it can only be reached by sampan. (Go to one of the small piers at the waterfront in Sai Kung to look for sampans. A driver will probably approach you. You must negotiate a fee, but you can expect to pay about HK$100.) Amenities include barbecue pits and toilets. ⊠ *Take MTR to Choi Hung, then Bus 92 to Sai Kung.*

Sha Ha's waters are sometimes dirty, but because they remain shallow far from shore, this beach is ideal for beginning windsurfers. You can take lessons or rent a board at the **Kent Windsurfing Centre** (☎ 2813–2372). Facilities include refreshment kiosks, a coffee shop, and a Chinese restaurant in the adjacent Surf Hotel. ⊠ *Take MTR to Choi Hung, then Bus 92 to the end of the line at Sai Kung, and walk or take a taxi for about a mile.*

Silverstrand is always crowded on summer weekends. Though a little rocky in spots, it has soft sand and all the facilities, including changing rooms, showers, and toilets. ⊠ *MTR to Choi Hung, then Bus 92 or taxi.*

The Outer Islands

A day trip to one of Hong Kong's islands is a terrific way to spend some time outside the city. If you take a morning ferry to Lamma, Lantau, or Cheung Chau, you can combine a beach trip with a sightseeing tour of the island (☞ The Outer Islands *in* Chapter 2).

Cheung Sha is a popular beach, only a short taxi or bus ride from the Silvermine Bay ferry pier. Its mile-long sandy expanse is excellent for swimming. All the standard facilities are available. ⊠ *Take the ferry from Central to Silvermine Bay. Buses meet the ferry every half hr on weekdays and Sat.; on Sun. and holidays buses leave when full, which is often on a sunny day.*

Hung Shing Ye, on Lamma Island, is popular with young locals. It is known as Power Station Beach because a massive plant is clearly visible from the beach, but that doesn't deter sunbathers, who materialize whenever the rays smile down. There are showers, toilets, changing rooms, barbecue pits, and a kiosk, but no swimming rafts. ⊠ *Take the ferry from Central to Yung Shue Wan and walk through the village, then over a low hill.*

Lo So Shing, also on Lamma Island, is popular with local families. It's an easy hike on a paved path from the fishing village of Sok Kwu Wan. Facilities include a kiosk, barbecue pits, swimming rafts, changing rooms, showers, and toilets. ⊠ *Take the ferry from Central to Sok Kwu Wan, then walk for 20–30 mins.*

Tung Wan is the main beach on Cheung Chau Island. On weekends its wide sweep of golden sand is so crowded with sunbathers that it's barely visible. You'll see it from the ferry as you approach the dock—at one end of the beach is the Warwick Hotel. Plenty of restaurants along the beach offer refreshments, seafood, and shade. Amenities include changing rooms, showers, and toilets. ⊠ *Take the ferry from Central to Cheung Chau ferry pier and walk 5 mins through the village to the beach.*

7 SHOPPING

Hong Kong is not the mercantile paradise it once was, but many practiced shoppers still swear by it, returning year after year for such items as Chinese antiques, Chinese porcelain, pearls, watches, cameras, eyeglasses, silk sheets and kimonos, tailor-made suits, and designer clothes at outlet prices.

Updated by
Lara Wozniak

RENT INCREASES, unstable economies in the rest of the region, and a tendency for manufacturers to open outlets elsewhere in the world have put a damper on the megabargains for which Hong Kong was once known. Although the lack of sales tax helps cut prices, you might still find that clothes, computers, and many electronic items cost about the same as they do in the United States, or even slightly more. But this is not to say you won't find some good values; you just have to know when and where to look.

We've divided this chapter into two handy sections for mastering the art of shopping in Hong Kong: the first is divided into regions, the second into categories. To many Hong Kongers, especially women, shopping is a sport, a pastime. When Hong Kong women shop they don't go out to buy a blouse or a pair of trousers, they go out to *shop*. They scout areas and scour markets, carrying designer shopping bags advertising previous scores. If you ask one of these shopaholics where to buy a specific item, the answer will not be a specific shop, but a whole section of town. If you want to shop as the experts do, you should learn the regions. The Western tendency, however, is to shop for specifics. Given short visits to Hong Kong, sometimes this style of shopping is unavoidable, which is why the second half of the chapter is divided into categories of potential purchases such as carpets or women's clothing.

If you are coming to Hong Kong just to shop, you should plan your visit for the end-of-season sales (January–February and July–August). This is when prices are slashed anywhere from 50% to 90% in major department stores and boutiques. Many major boutiques are in malls or shopping complexes in the basement of office buildings and hotels. It might seem incongruous to mall-crawl in Hong Kong—the land of bargain alleys and outdoor markets—but the advantage is air-conditioning and big-name designers all piled on top of one another. Still, some of the best deals are found in the local boutiques and in the freestanding designer shops.

Although shopping in Hong Kong can be a thrilling adventure, you need to be careful. Electronics shops selling the ever-popular photographic and hi-fi gear in Tsim Sha Tsui have a fearsome—and, regrettably, well-earned—reputation. Watch out for absurd discounts (to get you in the door), the switch (after you've paid, they pack a cheaper model), and the heavy, and sometimes physical, push to get you to buy a more expensive item than you want. It is also not uncommon for jewelers in the midprice range to offer you a discount of 10%–20% if you look at a few items and seem moderately interested. Be wary if a salesperson tries to drop the price much lower, however; you might go home to find you've purchased an inferior or defective item. Know, too, that in spite of the credit-card decals on the door (every card you could possibly imagine and more), most stores will insist on cash or add 3%–5% to the total. Shopping at stores with the Hong Kong Tourist Board (HKTB) decal on the window buys you some protection, since the shop belongs to the organization, but if you have trouble, head for the police, the Consumer Council, or the HKTB itself.

If you're really determined to shop till you drop, **Asian Cajun Ltd.** (⊠ 12 Scenic Villa Dr., 4th floor, Pokfulam, ☎ 2817–3687) leads customized shopping tours for visitors seeking good buys in antiques, art, jewelry, designer clothes, and specialty items. Escorted tours, which include hard-to-find shops and private dealers, are US$100 per hour (not including transportation), with a three-hour minimum, for up to four people.

MAJOR SHOPPING AREAS

Hong Kong Island

Hong Kong Island shopping districts are listed here from west to east. All of them are easily accessible by MTR stations. Visiting them all in one day is conceivable but would likely be exhausting. Try working in two or at most three regions per shopping day.

If you are interested in everything from antiques to clothing to furniture, consider shopping in Western and nearby Central together. Start with the streets behind Western Market for some traditional Chinese atmosphere, where spices, herbs, and aphrodisiacs are sold amid old, walk-up buildings. Mah-jongg shops, tea sellers, and packed dim sum restaurants abound. Then head up the main thoroughfare Des Voeux Road if you want to quickly work your way over to the department stores and boutiques in Central. More interesting, though, is a walk along Hollywood Road, renowned for its plethora of antiques and curio shops. Once you've reached Central, Hollywood turns into Wyndham Street, which also has antiques, statuary and ceramic shops, and carpet shops. Depending on how many of the small antiques shops you wander in and out of, shopping in both Central and Western will most certainly take a full day. If you walk, wear comfortable shoes and remember to buy bottled water along the way.

Western District

The Western District is one of the oldest and most typically Chinese areas in Hong Kong. (Take the MTR to Sheung Wan or the tram to Western Market.) Here you'll find craftsmen making mah-jongg tiles, opera costumes, fans, and chops (seals carved in stone with engraved initials); Chinese-medicine shops selling ginseng, snake musk, shark's fin, and powdered lizards; rice shops and rattan-furniture dealers; and cobblers, tinkers, and tailors. You'll also come across alleyways where merchants have set up stalls filled with knickknacks and curios.

The streets behind Western Market (☞ *below*) are some of the best places to soak up some of Hong Kong's traditional Chinese atmosphere. Wing Lok Street and Bonham Strand West are excellent browsing areas, with shops selling herbs, rice, tea, and Chinese medicines. Visit **She Wong Yuen** (✉ 89–93 Bonham Strand) for a taste of snake's-gall-bladder wine. Heading uphill, don't miss the stalls selling bric-a-brac on Ladder Street, which angles down from Queen's Road in Central to Hollywood and Caine roads. Hollywood Road is lined with Chinese antiques and collectibles; it turns into Wyndham Street in Central.

Shun Tak Centre (✉ 200 Connaught Rd.), attached to the Macau Ferry Terminal, offers a selection of boutiques selling clothing, handbags, toys, and novelties. If you're waiting for the Macau Ferry, have a look around; otherwise, a special trip is not required since most of the stores here are chain stores and can be found all over Hong Kong.

The Victorian redbrick structure of **Western Market** (✉ Des Voeux Rd., Sheung Wan) was built in 1906 as a produce market. The first two floors are filled with shops selling crafts, toys, jewelry, collectibles, and fabrics, but it's certainly not worth a special trip. You can find these goods elsewhere in town.

Two of Hong Kong's largest Western-style department stores, Sincere and **Wing On,** are technically in Central but you will pass them as you are walking from Western to Central.

Central District

Otherwise known as Hong Kong's financial and business district, Central has an extraordinary mixture of designer boutiques, department stores, and narrow lanes full of vendors selling inexpensive clothing and knockoffs of designer goods.

Many exclusive shops are housed in Central's major office buildings and shopping complexes such as the **Landmark,** on Des Voeux Road, **Prince's Building,** on 10 Chater Road, and **The Galleria at Nine Queen's Road,** all of which are connected by elevated walkways. If couture labels are what you're after, don't miss shopping here. While absorbing the piped music, golden hues, and spacious settings of these interconnected shopping arcades, you will find Christian Dior, the internationally renowned fashion designer; Coach, makers of fine leather handbags, purses, and belts; giftware from Lalique; and a whole range of designer boutiques.

In the **Shanghai Tang Department Store** you'll find fine silk Mandarin jackets for men and women, as well as an exciting array of silks and cashmeres in brilliant colors.

If you are visiting from Britain, you'll recognize **Marks & Spencer** (better known as Marks & Sparks); however, you may find the discounts here aren't much better than you will find at home. In the **Jardine House,** at Connaught Place, across from the Central Post Office, check out the **Oxfam Hong Kong** shop in the basement. Even if you are not a secondhand shopper, it's worth a look for all the designer labels selling for a fraction of their original cost.

You can hunt for bargains on clothing, shoes, woolens, handbags, and accessories in the stalls that fill **East and West Li Yuen streets,** between Queen's Road and Des Voeux Road. Watch out for pickpockets in these crowded lanes. On Wyndham Street you'll find art, antiques, and carpets, and nearby Lan Kwai Fong has art galleries and clothing boutiques in its small office buildings.

Admiralty

Bounded by Central on the west and Wanchai on the east, Admiralty is another mall-crawler's dream world. Here you'll find the Admiralty complex that comprises four shopping centers connected by elevated walkways: **Admiralty Centre, Pacific Place, Queensway Plaza,** and **United Centre.**

Wanchai District

More famous for its Suzie Wong–style nightlife than for daytime shopping, Wanchai has some interesting holdings for the curious or adventurous shopper. Tattoos, for example, are available on Lockhart Road, traditional Chinese bamboo birdcages on Johnston Road. Wandering through vegetable and fruit markets in the lanes between Johnston Road and Queen's Road East, you'll see dozens of stalls selling buttons and bows and inexpensive clothes. Queen's Road East (near the junction with Queensway) is known for shops that make blackwood and rosewood furniture and camphor-wood chests. There are more furniture shops on Wanchai Road, off Queen's Road East.

Causeway Bay

Causeway Bay is a major shopping point for Hong Kongers precisely because you can get just about anything here, from electronics to shoes to clothes. It is dominated by two large Japanese department stores: **Mitsukoshi** and **Sogo,** which are directly across the street from one another on Hennessy Road, so it's easy to visit both. Hennessy Road is filled with smaller shops selling jewelry, watches, stereos, cameras, and

Shopping Centers, Department Stores, & Markets

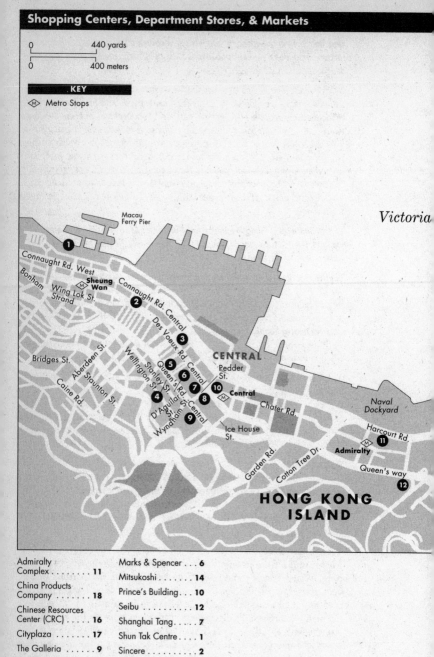

0		440 yards
0		400 meters

KEY

⬦M⬦ Metro Stops

Victoria

Macau Ferry Pier

Connaught Rd. West

Bonham

Wing Lok St.
Strand

Sheung Wan

Connaught Rd. Central

Des Voeux Rd. Central

Bridges St.

Aberdeen St.

Staunton St.

Caine Rd.

Wellington St.

Stanley St.

Queen's Rd. Central

D'Aguilar St.

Wyndham St.

CENTRAL

Pedder St.

Central

Chater Rd.

Ice House St.

Garden Rd.

Cotton Tree Dr.

Naval Dockyard

Harcourt Rd.

Admiralty

Queen's way

HONG KONG ISLAND

Admiralty Complex **11**

China Products Company **18**

Chinese Resources Center (CRC) **16**

Cityplaza **17**

The Galleria **9**

Joyce Boutique . . . **11**

The Landmark **8**

Lane Crawford **4**

Li Yuen Streets East and West **5**

Marks & Spencer . . . **6**

Mitsukoshi **14**

Prince's Building . . . **10**

Seibu **12**

Shanghai Tang **7**

Shun Tak Centre **1**

Sincere **2**

Sogo **15**

Times Square **13**

Wing On **3**

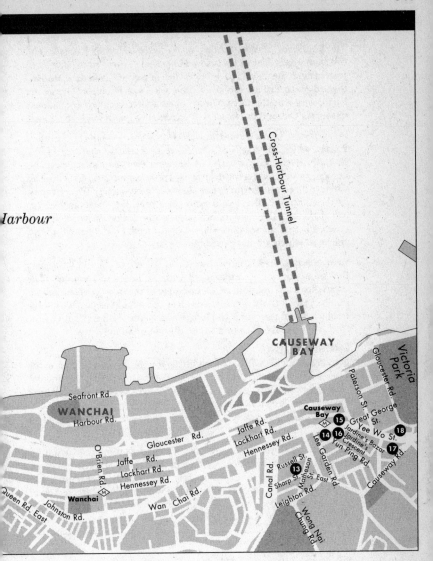

Harbour

Cross-Harbour Tunnel

CAUSEWAY
BAY

Victoria
Park

Seafront Rd.

WANCHAI
Harbour Rd.

Gloucester Rd.

Paterson St.

Gloucester Rd.

Causeway
Bay
Ⓜ ⑮ Great George St.

Jaffe Rd.

Yee Wo St.

⑱

Lockhart Rd.

⑭ ⑯ Jardine's Bazar

Hennessey Rd.

Jardine's Crescent

⑰

O'Brien Rd.

Jaffe   Rd.

Yun Ping Rd.

Lockhart Rd.

Causeway Rd.

Hennessey Rd.

Canal Rd.

Russell St.

Lee Garden Rd.

Wanchai Ⓦ

Sharp St. East

Matheson St. East

Johnston Rd.

Wan Chai Rd.

Leighton Rd.

⑬

Queen Rd. East

Wong Nai Chung Rd.

electronic goods, and parallel Lockhart Road has several good shoe stores featuring brands from Nine West to Rockport.

The boutiques of Vogue Alley, at the intersection of Paterson and Kingston streets, feature the best of Hong Kong's own fashion designers. Just behind the Excelsior hotel is the **In Square (Windsor House)**, toward Victoria Park opposite the Park Lane Hotel on Gloucester Road, with a mall plus two floors of computer supplies. The **Chinese Resources Center (CRC)** has a vast selection of goods made in China.

Behind Sogo (away from the waterfront) are two streets: Jardine's Bazaar, which has stacks of Chinese restaurants, and Jardine's Crescent, which is an alley of bargain-basement clothes and accessories. This market, a traditional favorite for inexpensive clothing, is geared toward Chinese shoppers, so you're not likely to find too many Western sizes. At the end of the alley, you'll experience a bustling "wet market" (so called because the vendors are perpetually hosing down their produce), where Chinese housewives shop for fresh produce and for fresh chickens, which are slaughtered on the spot.

Times Square, on Matheson Street (on the site of the old Causeway Bay tram station), is a megamall with 12 floors of shopping. The streets around Time Square feature some of the most interesting boutiques in Hong Kong. These shops go in and out of business with some frequency, and they cater to Hong Kong women's sizes; if you fit the clothes, you're likely to find some real one-of-a-kind deals.

Eastern District
If you're shopping with or for children, you might want to shop in the Eastern District, which includes North Point, Quarry Bay, and Shauki-wan. The best shopping is in Quarry Bay's huge **Cityplaza,** which houses Hong Kong's largest department store, UNY, as well as more than 400 shops (including toy stores), an ice-skating rink, and a bowling alley.

Stanley
Most people visit with the sole purpose of bargain-hunting at Stanley Market. You should allot at least a half day for this market; and if you dine here, it can be an all-day outing. The area around Main Street has a trendy, artsy ambience. On the way to Stanley Market, stop at Repulse Bay's shopping arcade, in which several stores sell fine reproductions of traditional Chinese furniture.

Kowloon

Kowloon is home to famous Nathan Road, which is a bright-lights, full-on neon experience for visitors. Locals usually don't shop on Nathan Road and tourists usually get ripped off here. But when it comes to outdoor markets, Kowloon draws the locals and the in-the-know tourists who are willing to bargain for their bargains. In addition to good sales at outdoor vending areas such as Temple Street night market and Ladies Market, cultural shopping experiences abound in places such as the Bird Garden or the Jade Market.

Visiting all the outdoor markets in Kowloon in one day may be exhausting. You're better off picking three sites you want to spend some time in rather than rushing through them all.

Tsim Sha Tsui District
Known for its Golden Mile of shopping along Nathan Road, Tsim Sha Tsui is popular with visitors for its hundreds of stereo, camera, jewelry, cosmetics, fashion, and souvenir shops. Branching off Nathan Road are narrow streets lined with shops crowded with every possible type of merchandise. Explore Granville Road, with its embroidery and

Bird Market **9**

Chinese Arts & Crafts . **2**

Chung Kiu Chinese
Products Emporium . . . **3**

Festival Walk **12**

Flower Market **11**

Harbour City **1**

Kansu Street
Jade Market. **8**

Ladies' Market **10**

New World
Shopping Center **4**

Palace Mall **5**

Temple Street
Night Market **7**

Yue Hwa Chinese
Products Emporium . . . **6**

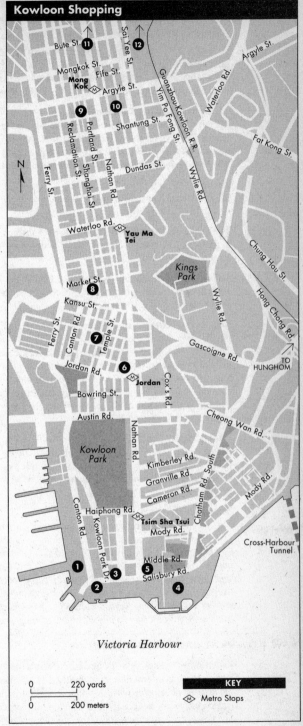

Kowloon Shopping

porcelain shops and clothing factory outlets (not as plentiful as they were a few years ago, but worth a look for serious bargain hunters), and Mody Road, for souvenir shops.

Unfortunately, the shopkeepers on Nathan Road are known to take advantage of unsuspecting shoppers. It's best to be absolutely sure of the quality and price you should be paying before shopping on Nathan Road. Stick to the places we list or those displaying HKTB stickers.

The **China Products Company** has a fairly wide and good-quality selection of household items. At **Chinese Resources Center** you can buy reasonably priced goods made in China. At **Joyce** you can find chic housewares and clothes by such designers as Issey Miyake and Prada. **Yue Hwa Chinese Products Emporium** has a popular medicine counter.

Harbour City, next to the Star Ferry Pier, is the largest shopping complex in Hong Kong, and one of the largest in the world; if you can't find it here, it probably doesn't exist.

The **Peninsula Hotel Shopping Arcade** (⊠ Salisbury Rd., Tsim Sha Tsui), in the landmark hotel, is chock-a-block with upscale designer boutiques—including a branch of Shanghai Tang.

The **Regent Hotel Shopping Arcade** (⊠ Salisbury Rd., Tsim Sha Tsui), with mostly designer boutiques, is adjacent to the New World Shopping Centre.

Tsim Sha Tsui East, an area of hotels, shops, and offices east of Chatham Road, is accessible via minibus from the Kowloon Star Ferry. Fifteen different shopping plazas are clustered here, including Wing On Plaza, Tsim Sha Tsui Centre, Empire Centre, Houston Centre, South Seas Centre, and Energy Plaza. Prices are reasonable, but unless you're the equivalent of an Asian size (about an American size 4) you may have trouble finding clothing here. However, the lively atmosphere makes up for the lack of size diversity.

Hung Hom District

Travel east of Tsim Sha Tsui to Hung Hom, the center of Hong Kong's jewelry and textile industries, for a tremendous selection of bargains in both designer boutiques and factory outlets. Man Yue Street is a good nexus.

Yau Ma Tei and Mong Kok

North of Jordan Road, Tsim Sha Tsui's bright lights and big-city world give way to tenements and overcrowding. You could visit this area in conjunction with Nathan Road. But if you're planning a day of hunting and gathering, skip Nathan Road shops and start here. Here, street signs revert to Chinese, retirees gather to play checkers and mah-jongg in the park, and outdoor markets abound. You can find great deals as well as fakes, pickpockets, and hawking shopkeepers with no-return policies—truly a place to enjoy the bargaining and the chaos of it all.

New Kowloon and New Territories

Kowloon proper ends at Boundary Street, which in the 19th century served as the border with China, marked by bamboo poles. As the New Territories develop, Kowloon, New Kowloon, and the New Territories continue to blend together. The key difference is that the farther out you travel from Kowloon, the less densely populated the area becomes. High-rises still abound in many pockets, but give way to trees, rolling hills, and seaside views. Most of the shopping experience in this region is in malls—the best of which is **Festival Walk** in New Kowloon with its upscale stores and restaurants. In the New Territories you'll find **Maritime Square** mall on Tsing Yi Island and the enormous **New Town Plaza** mall in Sha Tin.

SHOPPING CENTERS AND MALLS

Hong Kong Island

The **Admiralty** complex (✉ Queensway, Central; MTR: Admiralty) comprises four shopping centers connected by elevated walkways: Admiralty Centre, Pacific Place, Queensway Plaza, and United Centre.

Admiralty Centre has reasonably priced optical shops and men's tailors, a chop maker, and an excellent carpet shop.

Perhaps the most popular shopping mall in Hong Kong is glitzy **Pacific Place**, with four floors of upscale shops and restaurants. Its flagship Japanese department store, Seibu, has upmarket products and a vast and varied food department in the basement. Lane Crawford, another upscale emporium, has a branch here. You'll find that in most cases the most expensive stores are on the top floors and the prices go down as you descend. For a break in your shopping, stop by at the multiplex cinema, which screens international releases, or dine at one of the dozens of restaurants. The Marriott, the Island Shangri-La, and the Conrad hotels are all connected to this shopping plaza.

Queensway Plaza is dominated by smaller, lesser-name boutiques, which are worth checking out if you want one-of-a-kind buys without having to scour the street markets.

The **United Centre** houses several furniture shops. It's worth visiting just for Tequila Kola (☞ Furniture and Furnishings, *below*), which sells upscale, handcrafted bedroom sets, couches, fabrics, and gifts.

Cityplaza, one of Hong Kong's busiest shopping centers, is popular with families because of its ice-skating rink, multiplex theater, bowling alley, and weekly cultural shows. Many shops carry children's clothing, with labels such as Les Enfants, Crocodile, Peter Pan, and Crystal. Its selection of more than 400 shops includes plenty of clothing stores for men and women and a number of toy stores. ✉ *1111 Kings Rd., Taikoo Shing, Quarry Bay. MTR: Taikoo Shing.*

The **Landmark** is one of Central's most prestigious shopping sites, housing Celine, Loewe, Gucci, Joyce, Hermès, and other designer boutiques. There are also art galleries and fine jewelry shops. A pedestrian bridge links the Landmark with shopping arcades in Jardine House, Prince's Building, the Mandarin Oriental Hotel, and Nine Queen's Road. ✉ *Des Voeux Rd. and Pedder St., Central. MTR: Central.*

Times Square is a gleaming new complex that packs most of Hong Kong's best-known stores, including Lane Crawford and Marks & Spencer, into 12 frenzied floors. An indoor atrium hosts entertainment ranging from heavy-metal bands to fashion shows to local movie-star appearances; there are also a cinema complex and a dozen or so eateries. At the first basement level are City Super, a popular Japanese supermarket and international food court, and two excellent bookstores. ✉ *1 Matheson St., Causeway Bay. MTR: Causeway Bay, attached.*

Kowloon

Festival Walk is the fanciest mall in Hong Kong and very easy to reach, albeit slightly off the beaten path. Hong Kong's largest Marks & Spencer and a very large Esprit serve as anchors, but the Armani Exchange, Calvin Klein, local Hong Kong designer Vivienne Tam's boutique, and the Italian handbags at Mandarina Duck are what draw the elite crowds. The mall also has the largest ice rink in Hong Kong, perfect if you're shopping with kids who want a respite from the sometimes scorching-hot weather. ⌧ *80 Tat Chee Ave., Kowloon Tong. MTR and KCR: Kowloon Tong.*

Harbour City is the largest shopping complex in Hong Kong, and one of the largest in the world; if you can't find it here, it probably doesn't exist. Harbour City houses **Ocean Terminal, Ocean Centre, Ocean Galleries,** and the Hongkong, Marco Polo, and Prince hotels. At last count there were some 50 restaurants and 600 shops, including 36 shoe stores and 31 jewelry and watch stores. The complex contains a vast Toys "R" Us and a large branch of Marks & Spencer. ⌧ *Canton Rd., Tsim Sha Tsui, next to the Star Ferry Terminal. MTR or Star Ferry to Tsim Sha Tsui.*

New World Shopping Centre is a harbor-front shopping center (next to the New World Hotel) with four floors of fashion and leather boutiques, jewelry stores, restaurants, optical shops, tailors, stereo stores, arts and crafts shops, and the Japanese Tokyu department store. ⌧ *18 Salisbury Rd., Tsim Sha Tsui. MTR: Tsim Sha Tsui.*

The **Palace Mall** is an underground shopping center between the Regent Hotel and the Space Museum (you enter from the promenade between the hotel and the Star Ferry). It's just the place to go when it's pouring rain, but the shopping selection is limited. ⌧ *12 Salisbury Rd., Tsim Sha Tsui. MTR: Tsim Sha Tsui.*

New Territories

Maritime Square, on fast-growing Tsing Yi Island, is full of shops and restaurants. ⌧ *33 Tsing King Rd., Tsing Yi. MTR: Tsing Yi.*

New Town Plaza in Sha Tin is Hong Kong's largest mall, with 350 shops and a huge multiplex theater that draws crowds on rainy days. It's anchored by a Japanese department store called Seiyu. ⌧ *18 Sha Tin Centre St., Sha Tin,* ☎ *2699–5992. KCR: Sha Tin.*

DEPARTMENT STORES

Chinese

Hong Kong's many Chinese-product stores offer some of the most unusual and spectacular buys in the territory—sometimes at better prices than in the rest of China. Whether you're looking for pearls, gold, jade, silk jackets, fur hats, Chinese stationery, or just a pair of chopsticks, you can't go wrong with these stores. Most are open seven days a week but are crowded on sale days and at lunchtime on weekdays. The shopkeepers are expert at packing, shipping, and mailing goods abroad, if not so well schooled in the finer art of pleasant service.

China Products Company has a fairly wide and good-quality selection of Chinese arts and crafts like pottery, statues, and embroidered materials, as well as everyday household items. ⌧ *54 Nathan Rd., Tsim Sha Tsui,* ☎ *2739–3839.*

Chinese Arts & Crafts is a particularly good bet for fabrics, white porcelain, silk-embroidered clothing, jewelry, and carpets. Our favorite specialty item here is the large globe with lapis oceans and land masses inlaid with semiprecious stones, all for a mere HK$70,000. ⌧ *Pacific Place, Admiralty; 26 Harbour Rd., Wanchai; Star House, Silvercord Centre; and 233 Nathan Rd., Tsim Sha Tsui;* ☎ *2827–6667 for information.*

Chinese Resources Center (CRC) has a vast selection of goods made in China including casual clothing, fancy traditional garb, furniture, teapots, and household appliances ranging from rice cookers to televisions. ⊠ *488 Hennessy Rd., Causeway Bay,* ☎ *2577–0222.*

Chung Kiu Chinese Products Emporium specializes in arts and crafts but also has a good selection of traditional Chinese clothing and fine silk lingerie. ⊠ *528–532 Nathan Rd., Yau Ma Tei,* ☎ *2782–1131.*

In addition to the exciting—and expensive—array of silk and cashmere clothing in brilliant colors at **Shanghai Tang Department Store,** you'll find custom-made suits starting at around HK$5,000, including fabric from a large selection of Chinese silks. You can also have a cheongsam (a sexy slit-skirt dress with a Mandarin collar) made for HK$2,500–HK$3,500, including fabric. Ready-to-wear Mandarin suits and unisex kimonos are all in the HK$1,500–HK$2,000 range. Among the Chinese souvenirs are novelty watches with mah-jongg tiles or dim sum instead of numbers. There's a second location inside the Peninsula Hotel. ⊠ *12 Pedder St., Central,* ☎ *2525–7333.*

Yue Hwa Chinese Products Emporium carries a broad selection of Chinese goods such as traditional clothing, statues, tea sets, and embroidered materials. There's also a popular medicine counter. ⊠ *143–161 Nathan Rd., Tsim Sha Tsui,* ☎ *2739–3888;* ⊠ *54–64 Nathan Rd., Tsim Sha Tsui,* ☎ *2368–9165;* ⊠ *301–309 Nathan Rd., Yau Ma Tei,* ☎ *2384–0084.*

Other Department Stores

Joyce Boutique is a local retailer with a concept approach—the hushed interior and beautifully displayed upscale merchandise are meant to reflect the tastes of the owner, local businesswoman and socialite Joyce Ma. In addition to the latest in Western designer fashions for women and men, Joyce sells unique household items. ⊠ *New World Tower, 18 Queen's Rd., Central,* ☎ *2810–1120;* ⊠ *Pacific Place, 88 Queensway, Admiralty,* ☎ *2523–5944.*

Lane Crawford is the most prestigious Western-style department store in Hong Kong, with prices to match. The Central branch is the largest. Special sales here can be exhausting because everyone pushes and shoves to find bargains. There are branches in Pacific Place, Harbour City, and Times Square. ⊠ *70 Queen's Rd., Central,* ☎ *2118–3388.*

Marks & Spencer, the famed British retailer, has good-quality clothing in Western (i.e., large) sizes as well as a popular specialty food market. Many of the large malls have a branch of this popular store. ⊠ *28 Queen's Rd., Central,* ☎ *2921–8321.*

Seibu is the most upscale of the Japanese department stores with branches in Hong Kong. In addition to Japanese products, they carry a wide range of Western brands such as Clarks sandals, Timberlands boots, and Clinique cosmetics. ⊠ *Pacific Place, 88 Queen's Way, Admiralty,* ☎ *2845–4321.*

Sincere sells clothing and household goods made in China as well as imported items ranging from frying pans to jelly beans. You'll also find the full range of makeup counters you'd find in any U.S. department store. Prices tend to be very reasonable. The Sincere Company, which is more than 100 years old, is run by the third generation of the Ma family, grandchildren of the founder Ma Ying-piu. Sincere was the first store to give paid days off to employees, the first to showcase newly arrived imported merchandise in store windows, the first to hire women in sales positions—beginning with the founder's wife and sister-in-law—and the first to establish a fixed-price policy backed up by the regionally novel idea of issuing receipts. ⊠ *173 Des Voeux Rd., Central,* ☎ *2544–2688;* ⊠ *73 Argyle St., Mong Kok, Kowloon,* ☎ *2394–8233.*

MARKETS AND BAZAARS

Each Hong Kong district has an Urban Council–run market selling fresh fruit, vegetables, meat, seafood, and live chickens (chickens are slaughtered out in the open here). Surrounding the markets are small stores selling every imaginable kitchen and bathroom appliance, as well as clothes and even electronics.

Around heavy pedestrian areas you'll find illegal hawkers with a wide variety of cheap goods, but beware—constantly on the lookout for the police, vendors may literally run off with their goods. If so, get out of their way! In summer they often materialize in Tsim Sha Tsui in front of the Hyatt, around Granville and Mody roads, and at the Star Ferry terminal.

Street bazaars and markets embody some of the best things about Hong Kong shopping—bargains, exciting atmosphere, and a fascinating setting. Famous Cat Street—the curio haunt in Upper Lascar Row, running behind Central and Western—is now full of small, high-quality Chinese antiques shops, but in the street outside you'll still see plenty of hawkers selling inexpensive jewelry, opium pipes, Mao buttons, and assorted paraphernalia. Kowloon has the Women's Market, outside the Mong Kok MTR station, with outdoor stalls full of women's clothes. If you rummage around long enough, you might find a designer item at a rock-bottom price.

The Flower Market in Mongkok is a collection of street stalls selling cut flowers and potted plants, with a few outlets specializing in plastic plants and silk flowers. The area takes on an excited hum in the week leading up to the Chinese new year. ⊠ *Flower St., near Prince Edward MTR station.*

Kansu Street Jade Market displays jade in every form, color, shape, and size. The market is full of traders conducting intriguing deals and keen-witted sellers trying to lure tourists. Some trinkets are reasonably priced, but unless you know a lot about jade, don't be tempted to buy something pricey. ⊠ *Kansu St. off Nathan Rd., Yau Ma Tei.* ⊗ *Daily 10–4.*

The Ladies' Market has the same clothing you find in the Temple Street night market, except you can go by daylight. Despite its name, men's and children's clothing are also sold. ⊠ *Tung Choi St., take Nelson St. exit from the Mongkok MTR station, walk 2 blocks east to Tung Choi St.* ⊗ *Daily noon–11.*

Stanley Village Market is not quite the bargain trove it used to be, but you can still find some good buys in sportswear and casual clothing if you comb through the stalls. Dozens and dozens of shops line a main street so narrow that awnings from each side meet in the middle. Stores open early, at about 10, but close between 5 and 6. **China Town** (⊠ 39 Stanley Main St.) has well-priced cashmere sweaters, but remember you get what you pay for as far as quality is concerned. **Sun and Moon Fashion Shop** (⊠ 18A–B Stanley Main St.) sells casual wear, with bargains on such familiar names as L. L. Bean, Yves St. Laurent, and Talbots (keep in mind that some of these are factory seconds). **Allan Janny Ltd.** (⊠ 17 Stanley New St.) has antique furniture and porcelain. Stanley Market is also a good place to buy linens; **Tong's Sheets and Linen Co.** (⊠ 55–57 Stanley St.) has sheets, tablecloths, and brocade pillow covers, as well as silk kimonos and pajamas. The market is most enjoyable on weekdays, when it's less crowded. *Bus 6, 6A, or 260 from Central Bus Terminus, Hong Kong Island, or Bus 260 from the Star Ferry; in Kowloon, Bus 973 from Tsim Sha Tsui.*

Temple Street Night Market is filled with a colorful collection of clothes, handbags, electrical goods, gadgets, and all sorts of household items.

By the light of lamps strung up between stalls, hawkers try to catch the eyes of shoppers by flinging clothes up from their stalls; Cantonese opera competes with pop music; and a constant chatter of vendors' cries and shoppers' haggling fills the air. Adding to the colorful atmosphere here are the fortune tellers, opera singers, and occasionally the odd magician or acrobatic performer who sets up shop here. The market stretches for almost a mile and is one of Hong Kong's liveliest nighttime shopping experiences. You can go as early as 5 PM and leave by 10 PM, although the best time to come is about 8 PM. It's best to hire a local guide to take you; ask at your concierge desk about tours. Some of the surrounding neighborhoods may be unsafe at night. ⊠ *Kowloon. Near Jordan MTR station.*

SPECIALTY SHOPPING

Time is a valuable entity in Hong Kong, and you may be limited to the amount necessary to scour the districts. If you're looking for something specific, below is a list of shopping items and places where you can find them.

Antiques

China has laws against taking items more than 120 years old out of the country, but Hong Kong's antiques dealers can, at least officially, sell whatever they want to. So ancient porcelain, textiles, and specialty furniture are still available. Everyday furniture and pottery are not considered national treasures and are not affected by the export laws.

Auction Houses

Hong Kong auctions are interesting even if you don't go in with a particular goal. Watch for auction announcements in the classified section of the *South China Morning Post*.

Christie's (⊠ 2203 Alexandra House, 22nd floor, 16–20 Chater Rd., Central, ☎ 2521–5396, ℻ 2877–1709), a prestigious international house, carries very fine and expensive pieces.

Lammert Brothers (⊠ Union Commercial Bldg., 12–16 Lyndhurst Terr., mezzanine floor, Central, ☎ 2545–9859) caters to locals with less-expensive goods.

Sotheby's (⊠ 4–4A Des Voeux Rd., Central, ☎ 2822–8100, ℻ 2810–6239), a well-respected international house, caters to a clientele to whom money is no object.

Victoria Auctioneers (⊠ Century Sq., 1–13 D'Aguilar St., 16th floor, Central, ☎ 2524–7611) carries both reasonably priced and high-end art and furniture.

Shops

HOLLYWOOD ROAD AND WYNDHAM STREET

Hollywood Road and Wyndham Street, which is one long lane that runs from Central to Western, is undeniably the best place for poking about in shops and stalls selling antiques from many Asian countries. Treasures are hidden away among a jumble of old family curio shops, sidewalk junk stalls, slick new display windows, and dilapidated warehouses. You will also find great furniture here.

C. L. Ma Antiques (⊠ 43–55 Wyndham St., Central, ☎ 2525–4369) has Ming Dynasty–style reproductions, especially large carved chests and tables made of unlacquered wood.

Dynasty Furniture Co. (⊠ 68A Hollywood Rd., Central, ☎ 2369–6940) has *netsukes* (small statues) skillfully carved out of tagua, a rain-forest nut that looks a lot like ivory.

A SHOPPER'S PARADISE

NO MATTER WHY YOU COME to Hong Kong, and whether or not you're a shopper by nature, it's highly unlikely that you'll leave here without having bought something. Hong Kong does a roaring trade in bargain-priced luggage simply because so many travelers run out of space in their suitcases.

There are good reasons for this: Hong Kong's status as a free port, where everything other than alcohol, tobacco, perfumes, cosmetics, cars, and some petroleum products comes in without import duty; access to a skilled and still relatively inexpensive labor force just across the border in China; and the highly competitive retail business, the result of a local free-trade policy that encourages shopkeepers to try to undercut one another.

What else makes Hong Kong special? Because it's small and heavily populated, Hong Kong has had to grow upward and downward rather than outward. There are shops and small businesses in all sorts of unexpected places—a boutique might be up a back staircase of a scruffy building in the alleyway; in the basement of a lighting shop; on the 13th floor of an office building. Space is limited and precious in Hong Kong, so don't confine yourself to the main roads if you're really bargain-hunting. This is the land of free trade; shopping around is a prerequisite to any successful purchase.

The pressure from salespeople can be exasperating. If you're just browsing, make this very clear; don't be pushed into a purchase. While you're looking around, note ballpark prices and descriptions on the shop's business card. Always ask for discounts—you might get deeper ones for multiple purchases. Expect 10% to 50% off; you'll likely get larger discounts in the outdoor markets. Everywhere, except in Japanese department stores and some of the larger boutiques, discounts abound. Don't be shy. Bargain. This is the accepted and expected way of conducting business all over Asia. Don't take the salesman's word for it when he assures that his price is the "very best": shop around. Once you've looked around at other places and have a good idea how much you should pay, go back to the shop of choice first thing the next morning. Remind the salesperson that you are the first customer; it's a superstition that works in your favor. Local shopkeepers believe if they sell to the first customer who walks into their store, they will have a good business day.

If you plan to shop in the outdoor stalls and alleys, don't dress up; being well dressed will not help your bargaining position. Inspect the goods you buy very carefully; many are seconds. When you buy clothing, inspect the actual item handed to you; if you've chosen it based on a hanging sample, you might end up taking home a different, seriously flawed item. Having made your selection and struck the right price for it, you're ready for the exchange of money. Although credit cards and traveler's checks are widely accepted, surcharges are common, so you may get a better price if you pay cash. Make sure you get the worldwide guarantee that carries the name or logo of the relevant sole agent in Hong Kong, and, for electronics, make sure there's a service center in your home country. Lastly, get a fully itemized receipt for any major purchase.

Whether you're drifting about in the comfort of an air-conditioned shopping mall, exploring the factory outlets of Hung Hom, or poking through alleys and backstreets, you're getting a look at the life and guts of Hong Kong. It's as much a cultural experience as a shopping expedition, and that's the best bargain of all.

Eastern Dreams (✉ 47A Hollywood Rd., Central, ☎ 2544–2804; ✉ 4 Shelley St., Central, ☎ 2524–4787) has antique and reproduction furniture, screens, and curios.

Honeychurch Antiques (✉ 29 Hollywood Rd., Central, ☎ 2543–2433) is known especially for antique silver jewelry from Southeast Asia, China, and England.

Schoeni Fine Arts (✉ 27 Hollywood Rd., Central, ☎ 2542–3143) sells Japanese, Chinese, and Thai antiques, Chinese silverware, such as opium boxes, and rare Chinese pottery.

Teresa Coleman (✉ 79 Wyndham St., Central, ☎ 2526–2450) carries antique embroidered pieces, including magnificent must-see kimonos.

The Tibetan Gallery (✉ 55 Wyndham St., Central, ☎ 2530–4863) sells antique *Thangkas,* or meditation paintings, incense holders, and prayer rugs from Tibet.

True Arts & Curios (✉ 89 Hollywood Rd., ☎ 2559–1485) is a cluttered shop with good buys in embroidered items (including minute slippers for bound feet), silver, porcelain, and snuff bottles.

Yue Po Chai Antique Co. (✉ 132–136 Hollywood Rd., Central, ☎ 2540–4374) is one of Hollywood Road's oldest shops, and it has a vast and varied stock.

Zitan Oriental Antiques (✉ 43–55 Wyndham St., ground floor, Central, ☎ 2523–7584) sells antique furnishings only from mainland China. Look for traditional wood wedding beds or intricately carved armoires.

CAT STREET

Cat Street (or Upper Lascar Row), once famous for its thieves' market of secondhand stolen goods, now has almost as many small antiques shops as Hollywood Road itself. They're lined up behind the outdoor stalls selling old—or at least old-looking—jewelry, curios, and assorted bits of junk.

Cat Street Galleries (✉ 38 Lok Ku Rd., Sheung Wan, Western, ☎ 2541–8908) is a ground-floor cluster of shops selling porcelain and furniture.

China Art (✉ 15 Upper Lascar Row, Western, ☎ 2542–0982) has fine furnishings, mostly from the Suzhou area of China, and leads tours roughly once a month to its warehouse in southern China.

OTHER AREAS

Altfield Gallery (✉ 248–249 Prince's Bldg., 10 Chater Rd., Central, ☎ 2537–6370) carries furniture, fabrics, and collectibles from all over Asia.

Charlotte Horstmann and Gerald Godfrey (✉ Ocean Terminal, Tsim Sha Tsui, ☎ 2735–7167) is good for wood carvings, bronzeware, and furniture.

Eileen Kershaw (✉ Peninsula Hotel, Tsim Sha Tsui, ☎ 2366–4083) sells fine Chinese porcelain and jade carvings.

Art

Like other major cosmopolitan cities around the world where the monied class is looking for aesthetic investment, Hong Kong has a lively contemporary gallery scene, much of it concentrating on the best work coming out of China and Southeast Asia.

Galleries

Asian Art News, a bimonthly magazine, sold at bigger newsstands for HK$50, is a good guide to what's happening in galleries around the region. If you want a firsthand look at the latest trends in Asian art, plan to spend a day gallery-hopping in Central and in Lan Kwai Fong.

Alisan Fine Arts Ltd. (⊠ Prince's Bldg., Central, ☎ 2526–1091) was one of the first galleries in Hong Kong to promote Chinese artists living abroad. It shows a wide range of contemporary art with an East-meets-West flavor.

Fringe Gallery (⊠ 2 Lower Albert Rd., Central, ☎ 2521–7251), part of the Fringe Club, is a showcase for young, not-yet-famous Hong Kong artists, both Chinese and expat.

Galeriasia (⊠ 1 Lan Kwai Fong, 6th floor, Central, ☎ 2529–2598) promotes artists from Asia, with exhibits from Burmese and Vietnamese artists.

Galerie La Vong (⊠ 1 Lan Kwai Fong, 13th floor, Central, ☎ 2869–6863) highlights the works of today's leading Vietnamese artists, many of whose creations reveal an intriguing combination of French impressionist and traditional Chinese influences.

Hanart TZ Gallery (⊠ Room 202, Henley Bldg., 2nd floor, 5 Queen's Rd., Central, ☎ 2526–9019) shows contemporary Chinese artists from the mainland, Taiwan, Hong Kong, and abroad.

Plum Blossoms Gallery (⊠ Coda Plaza, 51 Garden Rd., 17th floor, Central, across from Botanical Gardens, ☎ 2521–2189) shows Chinese and Western art, along with antique textiles and Tibetan carpets.

Sandra Walters (⊠ 501 Hoseinee House, 69 Wyndham St., Central, ☎ 2522–1137) runs a public showroom with a wide range of late-19th-century to contemporary Western and Chinese art; call for an appointment.

Schoeni Art Gallery (⊠ U.G. floor, 21–31 Old Bailey St., Central, ☎ 2525–5225) exhibits a dramatic mix of abstract, realist, and political paintings by contemporary mainland-Chinese artists. Once a year Schoeni mounts a show of European masters.

Wagner Art Gallery (⊠ Lusitano Bldg., 4 Duddell St., 7th floor, Central, ☎ 2521–7882) is owned by an Australian couple who make it their mission to introduce Hong Kong to the best Australian artists. From time to time there are shows of major contemporary names.

Wattis Fine Art (⊠ 20 Hollywood Rd., 2nd floor, Central, ☎ 2524–5302) specializes in 18th- to 20th-century European paintings and the work of contemporary artists living in Hong Kong, both Chinese and expat.

Zee Stone Gallery (⊠ Yu Yuet Bldg., 43–55 Wyndham St., Central, ☎ 2810–5895) displays a combination of contemporary Chinese paintings and antique Tibetan silver and carpets. It sells Chinese furniture as well.

Framers

It may be worth having your artwork framed in Hong Kong, as prices are much lower than in Europe and the United States. The following framers are reputable and centrally located:

Man Fong (⊠ 1 Lyndhurst Tower, Lyndhurst Terr., Central, ☎ 2522–6923).

Po Shu Frame & Glass Co. (⊠ 255 Queen's Rd. E, ground floor, Wanchai, ☎ 2891–4039).

Wah Cheong (⊠ 174 Wai Yip St., ☎ 2523–1900).

Beauty and Cosmetics

Aveda Environmental Lifestyle Store (⊠ Shop 003, Ocean Centre, Harbour City, Tsim Sha Tsui, ☎ 2110–0881) sells animal- and environment-friendly, makeup and bath and beauty products.

Clarins (⊠ Peninsula Hotel, Salisbury Rd., 7th floor, Tsim Sha Tsui, ☎ 2315–3271) is the place to go when you're ready for a little relaxation. The amazing staff here excels in facials, massages, and other body treatments. The full range of gentle Clarins products are available for sale, too.

Mannings (⊠ Entertainment Bldg., 30 Queen's Rd., Central, ☎ 2868–4388; ⊠ Haiphong Mansion, 101 Nathan Rd., Tsim Sha Tsui, ☎ 2369–2011) is a chain you'll find throughout the city. It sells everything from shampoo and lotions to emery boards and cough medicine.

Sa-Sa Cosmetics (⊠ G/F 14 Kai Chiu Rd., Causeway Bay, ☎ 2895–3302; ⊠ 200 Nathan Rd., Jordan, Kowloon, ☎ 2317–1820) can be found throughout town. They sell discounted cosmetics, from cheap glittery styles to designer lines. You can find some great perfume sales for the likes of Calvin Klein One or Ralph Lauren perfume; the prices are nearly always lower than those offered at international airport duty free shops.

Cameras, Lenses, and Binoculars

Many of Hong Kong's thousands of camera shops are clustered in the Lock Road–lower Nathan Road area of Tsim Sha Tsui, in the backstreets of Central, and on Hennessy Road in Causeway Bay. If in doubt about where to shop for such items, stick to HKTB shops. (Pick up the HKTB shopping guide at any of the board's visitor centers.) All reputable dealers should give you a one-year worldwide guarantee. If you want to buy a number of different items in one camera shop (most also stock binoculars, calculators, radios, and other electronic gadgets), you should be able to bargain for a good discount. You may find good bargains at unauthorized (but legal) dealers, but these shops will most likely not provide a guarantee.

Always be on the lookout for con jobs, as tourists are frequent targets. Quite often merchandise is physically switched so that you select one type of camera only to discover back in your hotel room that you've been given another. Another ploy is to lure you in with word of a great deal, tell you that particular model is out of stock, and begin an aggressive campaign to sell you a more expensive model. **Don't be rushed; compare prices in several shops.** If a shop will not give you a written quote, you don't want to do business with them. Be advised that paying by credit card may increase the final bill by 3%–5%, regardless of what the card companies say.

Photo Scientific Appliances (⊠ 6 Stanley St., Central, ☎ 2522–1903) is where local photographers shop for equipment. Expect good prices on both new and used cameras, lenses, video cameras, and accessories.
Williams Photo Supply (⊠ 341 Prince's Bldg., 10 Chater Rd., Central, ☎ 2522–8437) stocks an array of photography needs.

Carpets and Rugs

Regular imports from elsewhere in China and from Iran, India, Pakistan, Afghanistan, and Kashmir make carpets and rugs a very good buy in Hong Kong. Plenty of carpets are also made locally. Though prices have increased in recent years, carpets are still cheaper in Hong Kong than in Europe and the United States. China Products Company and Chinese Arts & Crafts provide some of the best selections and price ranges.

Chinese Carpets
Carpet World Ltd. (⊠ Shop 271 Ocean Terminal, Harbour City, 3 Canton Rd., Tsim Sha Tsui, ☎ 2730–4000) has a wide selection.
Tai Ping Carpets Ltd. (⊠ 816 Times Square, 1 Matheson St., Causeway Bay, ☎ 2522–7138; ⊠ Wing On Plaza, 62 Mody Rd., Tsim Sha

Tsui East, ☎ 2369–4061) is highly regarded for locally made carpets, especially custom-made rugs and wall-to-wall carpets. The store takes 2½–3 months to make specially ordered carpets; you can specify color, thickness, and even the direction of the weave. Tai Ping's occasional sales are well worth attending; check the classified section of the *South China Morning Post* for dates.

Other Asian Carpets

On Upper Wyndham Street, in Central, several shops sell Central Asian, Persian (Iranian), Turkish, Indian, Pakistani, Tibetan, and Afghan rugs—just don't expect miraculously low prices. Note: American citizens are now allowed to import Persian rugs into the United States.

Chine Gallery (✉ 42A Hollywood Rd., Central, ☎ 2543–0023) specializes in Mongolian rugs and carpets.

Mir Oriental Carpets (✉ 52 Wyndham St., Central, ☎ 2521–5641) is one of the most appealing of the Wyndham shops for its service and large stock. New selections arrive frequently.

Oriental Carpet (✉ 41 Wyndham St., Central, ☎ 2523–9502) has a large stock of carpets from Iran, Pakistan, Afghanistan, and China (Persian designs only). The staff is extremely helpful and friendly.

Oriental Carpets Gallery (✉ 44 Wyndham St., ground floor, Central, ☎ 2521–6677) specializes in hand-knotted carpets and rugs from Iran, Afghanistan, Pakistan, and Russia.

Tribal Rugs Ltd. (✉ Admiralty Centre, 18 Harcourt Rd., 2nd floor, ☎ 2529–0576), a bit out of the way in a run-of-the-mill shopping mall, sells a variety of rugs from many countries.

Ceramics

For a full range of ceramic Chinese tableware, visit the various China Department stores, which also have fantastic bargains on attractively designed vases, bowls, and table lamps. Inexpensive buys can also be had in the streets of Tsim Sha Tsui, the shopping centers of Tsim Sha Tsui East and Harbour City, the Kowloon City Market, and the shops along Queen's Road East in Wanchai.

Antiques and Reproductions

Sheung Yu Ceramic Arts (✉ Vita Tower, 29 Wong Chuk Hang Rd., Aberdeen, ☎ 2845–2598) carries good reproductions.

Yue Po Chai Antique Co. (✉ 132–136 Hollywood Rd., ground floor, Central, next to Man Mo Temple, ☎ 2540–4374) is the best place for antique ceramic items.

Factory Outlets

Ah Chow Factory (✉ Hong Kong Industrial Centre, 489–491 Castle Peak Rd., Block B, 7th floor, Laichikok, ☎ 2745–1511) is a popular place to score deals. Take the MTR to the Laichikok station and follow exit signs to Leighton Textile Building/Tung Chau West.

Overjoy Porcelain (✉ 10–18 Chun Pin St., 1st floor, Kwai Chung, New Territories, ☎ 2487–0615) has good bargains. Take the MTR to the Kwai Hing station, then grab a taxi.

Chinese Gifts

If you're stuck for a gift idea, think Chinese. How about an embroidered silk kimono or a pair of finely painted black-lacquer chopsticks? Or a Chinese chop, engraved with your friend's name in Chinese? These are available throughout Hong Kong. For chop ideas, take a walk down Man Wa Lane, in Central near the Wing On department store.

For those who live in cold climates, wonderful *mien laps* (padded silk jackets) are sold in the alleys of Central or in the various shops featuring Chinese products. Another unusual item for rainy weather—or even as a decorative display—is a hand-painted Chinese umbrella, available very inexpensively at Chinese Arts & Crafts and China Products Company. Chinese tea, packed in colorful traditional tins, is sold in the teahouses in Bonham Strand and Wing Lok Street in Western. A bit more expensive, but novel ideas, are padded tea baskets with teapot and teacups, and tiered bamboo food baskets, which also make good sewing baskets.

Clothing

Children's
Plenty of stores in Hong Kong sell Western-style ready-to-wear children's clothing. You can also shop for adorable traditional Chinese-style clothing for tots in two Central clothing alleys—Li Yuen Street East and West.

Crocodile Garments Ltd. (⊠ Ocean Terminal, Tsim Sha Tsui, ☎ 2735–5136; and other locations all over town) sells Western-style children's clothes.

Mothercare (⊠ Windsor House, 311 Gloucester.Rd., Causeway Bay, ☎ 2882–3468; ⊠ Prince's Bldg., Central, ☎ 2523–5704; ⊠ Ocean Terminal, Tsim Sha Tsui, ☎ 2735–5738), a British firm, carries baby clothing and maternity wear.

Designers
Burberry (⊠ The Landmark, Pedder St. and Des Voeux Rd., Central, ☎ 2862–3511; ⊠ Sheraton Hotel Towers, 20 Nathan Rd., Tsim Sha Tsui, ☎ 2368–6303) sells their distinctive plaid design on everything from trench coats to mini-skirts.

Chanel (⊠ Prince's Bldg., 10 Chater Rd., Central, ☎ 2810–0978; ⊠ The Peninsula, Tsim Sha Tsui, ☎ 2368–6879) carries break-the-bank pieces that some women can't live without.

Christian Dior (⊠ The Landmark, Pedder St. and Des Voeux Rd., Central, ☎ 2869–8333) offers high-end fashion for design-conscious shoppers.

Escada (⊠ Pacific Place, 88 Queen's Way, Admiralty, ☎ 2845–4321) is the perfect place to find versatile day-to-evening wear.

Fendi (⊠ The Landmark, Pedder St. and Des Voeux Rd., Central, ☎ 2524–5668; ⊠ Pacific Place, 88 Queensway, Admiralty, ☎ 2918–0771; ⊠ Sheraton Hotel Towers, 20 Nathan Rd., Tsim Sha Tsui, ☎ 2367–0781), the chic handbag purveyor, also carries shoes and other accessories.

Giorgio Armani (⊠ Shop 07–12 Times Square, Russell St., Causeway Bay, ☎ 2506–2018) carries the Italian designer's glamorous evening wear along with casual wear.

Hermès (⊠ The Galleria, 9 Queen's Rd., Central, ☎ 2525–5900; ⊠ The Peninsula, Tsim Sha Tsui, ☎ 2368–6739) sells chic, classic silk and leather accessories.

Louis Vuitton (⊠ The Landmark, Pedder St., Central, ☎ 2366–3731; ⊠ The Peninsula, Tsim Sha Tsui, ☎ 2366–3731) is the place to go for handbags and trunks, but also unisex clothing in modern fabrics.

Versace Collections (⊠ Pacific Place, 88 Queen's Way, Admiralty, ☎ 2525–8329; ⊠ Shop 106–113 Times Square, Russell St., Causeway Bay, ☎ 2506–2281) sells the sexy and colorful Italian high-end clothing line.

Tailor-Made
Along with Hong Kong's multitude of ready-to-wear-clothing stores, you can still find Chinese tailors to make suits, dresses, and evening gowns. Unfortunately, many of the next generation in tailors' families

are leaving the business, so don't wait too long to visit their shops. All tailors keep records of clients' measurements so that satisfied customers can make repeat orders by mail or telephone. Keep a copy of the original measurements in case you need to change them. Here are some other do's and don'ts:

For a suit, overcoat, or jacket, give the tailor plenty of time—at least three–five days—and allow for a minimum of two proper fittings plus a final one for finishing touches. Shirts can be made in a day, but you'll get better quality if you allow more time.

Tailors in hotels or other major shopping centers may be more expensive, but they're conveniently located and will be more accustomed to Western styles and fittings.

Have a good idea of what you want before you go to the tailor. Often the best plan is to take a suit you want copied. Go through the details carefully, and make sure they're listed on the order form, together with a swatch of the material ordered (the swatch is essential).

When you pay a deposit (which should not be more than 50% of the final cost), make sure the receipt includes all relevant details: the date of delivery, the description of the material, and any special requirements.

FOR MEN

A-Man Hing Cheong Co., Ltd. (⊠ Mandarin Oriental Hotel, Central, ☎ 2522–3336) is known for European-cut suits and custom shirts and has a list of distinguished clients.

Ascot Chang Co. Ltd. (⊠ Shop 130, Prince's Bldg., 10 Chater Rd., Central, ☎ 2523–3663; ⊠ Peninsula Hotel, Salisbury Rd., Tsim Sha Tsui, ☎ 2366–2398; ⊠ Regent Hotel Arcade, 18 Salisbury Rd., Tsim Sha Tsui, ☎ 2367–8319) has specialized in custom-made shirts for men since 1949. Clients have included George Bush and Andy Williams.

David's (⊠ Mandarin Oriental Hotel, 5 Connaught Rd., Central, ☎ 2524–2979; ⊠ Wing Lee Bldg., 33 Kimberley Rd., Tsim Sha Tsui, ☎ 2367–9556) is an excellent shirtmaker.

Jimmy Chen Co. Ltd. (⊠ Peninsula Hotel, Tsim Sha Tsui, ☎ 2536–6333) can make suits, shirts, and whatever else you need.

Sam's Tailor (⊠ Shop K, Burlington Arcade, 94 Nathan Rd., Tsim Sha Tsui, ☎ 2721–8375) is one of the most famous of all Hong Kong's custom tailors, having outfitted everyone from European royal families to American and British politicians and, of course, your average tourist looking for a bargain.

W. W. Chan & Sons (⊠ Burlington House, 92–94 Nathan Rd., Tsim Sha Tsui, ☎ 2366–9738) is known for top-quality classic cuts and has bolts and bolts of fine European fabrics. Chan will make alterations for the lifetime of the suit, which should be about 20 years. Tailors also travel to the United States several times a year to fill orders for their customers; if you have a suit made here and leave your address, they'll let you know when they plan to be visiting.

FOR WOMEN

Hong Kong tailors do their best work on tailored suits, coats, and dresses, performing less well with more fluid styles or knit fabrics. Tailors are the place to order a traditional Chinese cheongsam. As for patterns, you can bring in an item to be copied or choose a style from one of the tailor's catalogs; you can also bring in a photo from a magazine or, if you're skilled with pencil and paper and sure of what you want, bring in a sketch.

A good tailor has a wide selection of fabrics, but you can also bring in your own. Visit Chinese Arts & Crafts for beautiful Chinese bro-